P...
TOREY HAYDEN

"Torey Hayden deserves the kind of respect
I can't give many people.
She isn't just valuable, she's incredible."
—*Boston Globe*

"[Hayden] persuades us that even the most
withdrawn and troubled child can be reached
if someone takes the time, pays attention,
and sincerely, deeply cares."
—*O, The Oprah Magazine*

"She's awfully, awfully good. . . .
She never fails to convey all the tearful and chilling
moments this involvement of hers brings."
—*Chicago Tribune*

"This remarkable teacher . . .
reminds us that love takes many forms."
—*New York Times*

"[Her] characters will haunt you."
—*Indianapolis News*

"A fine storyteller. . . . Hayden has a gift."
—*Washington Post Book W...*

Lost Child

Books by Torey Hayden

One Child
Somebody Else's Kids
Murphy's Boy
Just Another Kid
Ghost Girl
The Tiger's Child
Beautiful Child
Twilight Children
Lost Child

Lost Child

The True Story of a Girl Who Couldn't Ask for Help

TOREY HAYDEN

_wm_

WILLIAM MORROW
An Imprint of HarperCollins_Publishers_

HarperCollins books may be purchased for educational, business, or sales promotional use. For information, please email the Special Markets Department at SPsales@harpercollins.com.

Originally published in the United Kingdom in 2019 by Bluebird, an imprint of Pan Macmillan.

FIRST U.S. EDITION

Library of Congress Cataloging-in-Publication Data has been applied for.

ISBN 978-0-06-283606-9

19 20 21 22 23 PC/BRR 10 9 8 7 6 5 4 3 2 1

Lost Child

PART I

chapter one

In March I saw the first skylark. Not the bird, of course. On our high, windswept moors, it was much too early in the year for skylarks. This one had been drawn on a sheet of A4 paper, the ordinary kind you put in printers, and at first glance I missed the bird altogether. Meleri reached across to point to the very bottom right-hand corner. Putting on my reading glasses, I held the paper up to the car window to see a drawing that was not much bigger than my thumbnail. The weather was being typically Welsh that day, heavily overcast and 'mizzling' – too heavy to be mist, too light to be drizzle – making the back seat of the car as dim as a disused chapel. On the page, the tiny bird crouched midst blades of prickly looking grass, its eyes bright, its expression shrewd, as if it knew something I didn't. Its plumage was highly coloured, more that of a macaw than a skylark. Minuscule musical notes rose up along the right-hand edge of the paper to indicate its song.

'Don't you think that shows talent?' Meleri asked. 'She's only nine.'

'What's her name again?'

'Jessie. Jessie Williams.'

The tiny details of the drawing, so precise and intricate, mesmerized me.

Meleri opened the elasticated portfolio file resting on her knee and took out three more drawings and handed them to me. Two were done in felt-tip pen like the one I already held. The other was in pencil, the lines so pale and spidery that I could hardly make them out in the dim light. The same small bird locked eyes with me in each of them.

'I like that she does them,' Meleri said. 'They seem cheerful to me. As if Jessie still has hope.'

I had met Meleri Thomas the first time a number of years earlier. It was in Cardiff, in the green room of a TV studio for the Welsh-speaking channel S4C, where we were both appearing on the morning breakfast show. I was there to promote one of my books, and she was taking part in a panel discussion about children's rights. Meleri caught my attention immediately, because chances are she would have caught anyone's attention. Her features were bold, attractive, almost Italianate – large dark eyes and long, dark hair – and she was dressed in a figure-hugging knit dress in a startling shade of emerald green. These aspects would have been striking enough on their own, had there not also been the fact that Meleri looked remarkably similar to popular TV chef Nigella Lawson. For just a moment I thought that's who it was and was curious why she would appear on a Welsh-speaking panel about children's rights.

Green rooms always have an edgy atmosphere. Almost everyone waiting to go before the television cameras feels anxious for one reason or another, and as a consequence, even if you don't know each other, it's common for people sitting together in a green room to make small talk as a distraction from nerves. This was challenging for me on this particular occasion, because everyone was speaking Welsh. I had only newly learned the language and was not quite fluent. More to the point, my American tongue still did not always take kindly to Welsh pronunciations. Subsequently, my only real memory of that occasion was the clanger I dropped. The weather always being a good topic for small talk, I'd thought to remark on how much I was enjoying the crisp frosty days we were having. In the unanticipated hilarity that followed, I discovered the Welsh word for 'frost' is pronounced remarkably similarly to the Welsh word for 'sex'.

When Meleri and I met again, it was at a small conference for social workers and other youth support workers, once again in Cardiff. I recognized her flowing black hair and glamorous clothes immediately. We laughed at the memory of my embarrassing blooper, and I was forced to admit that my Welsh was even worse these days than it had been then, as I'd moved to a new area where the dialect was much different. While I still read the language reasonably well, I'd pretty much stopped speaking it.

'That's *my* area,' Meleri said, as I was explaining this. 'That's where I live!' And then, 'Oh, if you're so close, please,

5

you must come out to Glan Morfa. I have so many children I'd love you to see.'

It took two more years before I found myself being driven along a largely urbanized beachfront that segued from one coastal town to the next on the way to the children's group home, Glan Morfa.

The whole area was run down, from the derelict industrial port built to serve now-disused quarries to the dreary pleasure beach with its broken roller coaster and shuttered kiosks. Then came the endless miles of holiday parks, row after row of faded caravans tinged with rust, all empty in the off season.

The car turned down a long single lane between two of these caravan parks. The road was badly potholed, so we slowed to a crawl. Indeed, it was such a bumpy ride we couldn't help but laugh in the back seat because we were so jostled, but then through a small grove of scraggy trees deformed by the sea wind, a long, low building appeared. Its stripped back, brutalist architecture hinted at a 1960s construction date. The white paint around the windows was peeling. The pebbledash walls were the colour of porridge. Meleri sensed my dismay at such bleak surroundings and said, 'We're hoping the council can afford to paint this year, although I think they are going to spend the money on repairing the road.'

Inside, however, was a different world. The entrance area was well lit and painted in white and bright gradations of turquoise. There were posters up and photographs on a bulletin board of group activities and days out. At the far end was a glassed-in office with a calendar, individual schedules and numerous photos of the children on the walls. I was introduced to Joseph and Enir, the staff in charge.

As I entered the office area, Enir flipped on the electric kettle, took out four mugs and measured instant coffee into them. 'You take it white?' she asked, and added milk before I answered. Joseph opened a round purple tin to reveal an assortment of biscuits. 'You're in luck,' he said cheerfully. 'There are still some Penguin bars left.' He handed one to me.

We spent a very pleasant fifteen minutes getting acquainted. Enir was twenty-eight. She'd been working at the group home for four years, liked the shift work because it fitted in well with her young daughter's schedule at school and was looking forward to her holiday in Majorca in the summer. Joseph looked to be in his early forties. He had been working at Glan Morfa for almost ten years, longer than anyone else, and was now the day manager. He liked the work, he said. He realized for most people it was not a career, but for him it was. He enjoyed 'being on the front line', as he put it, where he could help the children coming to Glan Morfa grow and change while they were there. He tried to give them a sense of belonging, a sense of being cared for, and this seemed to have happened, as several of the 'graduates' – the children who had reached eighteen and moved out of the Social Services system – still returned regularly to visit Joseph.

After we'd shared coffee, Meleri and Joseph took me down a hallway adjacent to the office and into a small room crammed with furniture. Two brown armchairs and two small filing cabinets were against one wall, and a well-worn beige sofa was against the opposite one. In the middle, with just barely enough room to get around it, was a sturdy wooden table with a white-patterned Formica top and four orange plastic chairs pushed up to it.

'It isn't grand,' Joseph said. His tone wasn't apologetic, just matter of fact. 'But this is our therapy room. Or should I say "therapy room" in quotes, because it's also the conference room, the interview room, the I-need-to-get-this-kid-out-of-the-chaos-and-talk-to-him room and, as you can see, the store room.'

Meleri had gone to get Jessie, so I chose a chair on the right-hand side of the table and sat down.

A few minutes later, the door opened and Meleri entered with a young girl. 'Here is Jessie,' she said. 'And Jessie, this is Torey.'

The child gave me a warm, friendly smile.

She was a pretty girl in a faintly old-fashioned way, although that sense may have come solely from her clothes. Instead of the leggings and colourful jumpers most girls her age wore, Jessie was dressed in a well-washed cotton dress and beige cardigan that wouldn't have looked out of place in the 1970s. Her hair was straight and not quite shoulder length, a soft red, parted on the side and held out of her face with a clip. Her eyes were true green. She was small, looking younger than nine.

'Hello,' I said. 'Would you like to sit down?' I indicated the chair directly across the table from me, as it was the nearest to where she was standing.

Jessie didn't take it. Instead, she came around the table and pulled out the chair next to mine, but she didn't sit down. Instead, she paused, giving me a long, appraising stare.

'I donated my hair,' she stated. 'That's why it's not very long. It was down here before.' She indicated about halfway along her upper arm. 'But then I cut it and now they're going to make it into a wig for a little girl who doesn't have any hair because she has cancer.'

'That was very kind of you,' I said to this unexpected onslaught of information.

'My hair grows very fast.'

'You did a thoughtful thing. Now, if you'd like to sit down . . . Perhaps Mrs Thomas can sit there on the sofa, if she wants, and you can sit in that chair. I've brought some things with me that we can do together,' I said.

Jessie made no effort to move. 'You have nice hair,' she said. 'Can I touch it?'

Before I could answer, she did. 'It's very nice hair.'

'Thank you.'

'It's curly. Like movie star hair. Are you a movie star? Because that's the kind of hair movie stars have.'

My hair is *not* movie star hair. What I had regarded as 'body' when I was living in Montana's dry climate had transmuted into wild and unmanageable corkscrews in the humidity of Wales. Most days I looked like a sheep.

Jessie pulled one curl out to its full length and held it with just enough tension to be not quite appropriate. Her gaze was unwavering. 'You could donate this hair. It's long enough. Have you thought about it?'

'I think it's a little too curly.'

'It's kind to do, donating your hair. You should.'

'Thank you, I'll consider it,' I said, beginning to feel a bit wrong-footed in this conversation.

'I think you're a movie star,' Jessie said, 'and that's why you won't donate your hair.'

'Thank you for the compliment, but would you let go, please, because you're holding it just a little bit too hard.'

Jessie continued to maintain eye contact and a slight, very faintly challenging smile crept across her lips. She had control of the situation and she knew it. She also knew that I knew it.

'Would you sit down, please?' I asked again.

'You've a funny voice.'

'I do, don't I? That's my accent. It's American. Would you sit down, please?'

'What's this?' She let go of my hair and leaned across the table to take hold of the leather case I'd brought with me. I would refer to this as my 'box of tricks', because in the old days it had been a literal cardboard box, containing pens, paper, puppets, playing cards and other things children find amusing. These days it was more practically housed in a satchel.

Jessie undid the buckle and looked in. Her eyes lit up. 'Look! You've got Staedtler pens. And they've not ever been opened before! They've still got the sticker fastening them shut. I'm going to use them. I'm going to draw something. You have some paper in here?'

I put my hand across the open case. 'Let's talk just a little bit first. Let's get to know each other.'

'Why?' she replied.

'Because I think that's helpful. Don't you?'

'No.' She took one of the pens out of the packet and began to draw on her forearm.

'Let's not do that,' I said, and lifted the pen out of her fingers.

Meleri, who had sat behind us on the sofa, leaned forward and said, 'There will be plenty of other times you can draw. Torey is planning to come and see you each week.'

'Why?' Jessie asked.

'We're thinking it would be nice for you to have someone here just for you. To help you with some of the things that are troubling you,' Meleri replied.

'Nothing's troubling me,' she said. Her tone was not defiant. If anything, it was slightly apologetic, as if she felt sorry for me, having come all this way for no reason.

'Let's spend a couple of moments getting to know each other,' I said. 'Tell me what kinds of things you find interesting.'

'These.' She pointed to the pens.

'Yes, you like to draw, don't you? What other things do you enjoy?'

Jessie brought her shoulders up in an exaggerated shrug. 'I don't know.'

'Let's start with . . . ice cream. What's your favourite kind of ice cream?'

'I'm lactose intolerant,' she replied.

'*Jessie*,' Meleri interjected. 'No, you're not.'

'Yes, I am. It gives me the squirts. And you just don't know it.'

'Never mind,' I asked. 'What about TV? What's your favourite programme?'

Jessie exhaled dramatically. 'Can I use these pens now?'

On the table directly in front of me was the folder containing Jessie's skylark drawings, so I opened it and took out the picture on top. 'Mrs Thomas showed me your wonderful drawings. I love the colours you've used for the skylark.'

Another frustrated sigh and Jessie fell forward to put her forehead on the table. 'Jeee-sus,' she muttered under her breath.

'I can also tell you'd like to start using the pens right away.'

'Well, *yes,*' Jessie said into the table top. Still keeping her forehead on the Formica, she swivelled slightly and lifted her left arm to peer back at Meleri. 'Is she always like this?' she asked in deadpan. We both burst out laughing, which I suspect was what Jessie intended.

Finally Jessie sat up, grabbed the drawing of the skylark and held it up in front of her face. 'I drew this for Idris,' she said. 'Give me a pen and I'll write his name on it. Then everyone will know it is for him.'

'Who's Idris?' I asked.

'My brother. He's eighteen. He lives in Switzerland, but he's coming next week to take me out. We'll go to Rhyl. To the leisure centre. So let me have a pen. I'll put his name on it. It's really meant for him. You shouldn't have it. That's the problem with this place. They keep taking my drawings away and I want to keep them for my family.'

'Jessie, none of that's true,' Meleri interjected.

'It *is*. Look, you've got all my stuff in this folder. These are *my* pictures. I didn't draw them for you.'

'No, Jessie, what's not true is your brother. You don't have a brother. He doesn't live in Switzerland. You're not going to Rhyl.'

'Yes, I do have a brother,' she said sharply.

'No, you do not. Please. We've talked about this before. Many times before. Remember our Progress Plan? The telling stories bit?' Meleri asked.

'I've got a brother. You just don't know about him. He got killed. When I was a baby.'

'Jessie . . .' Meleri said, a warning note in her voice.

'He was at a night club and he went outside to have a smoke and bad men came. They shot him in the head and put his body in a skip.'

'*Jessie. Please,*' Meleri warned. 'You know the rules. You'll be in time out.'

Jessie looked sideways at me, a smirk on her lips, and shrugged good-naturedly, as if this were all a game.

Not sure how to pick up the conversation from here, I handed her the pens.

Jessie's eyes lit up. Snapping the packet open again, she counted aloud to ensure there were twenty. Taking out a dark green pen, she pulled the drawing of the skylark over in front of her. Turning it over to reveal the back, which was blank, she tested the pen by drawing a couple of small lines. One by one she removed each of the other colours and tried them in the same way.

'I want to get it just right,' she said, 'so that Idris will be proud of me.' Picking the paper up, she appraised the coloured marks closely, tipping the paper one way and another in the wan fluorescent light, as if they were of great importance. Then setting the paper down, she turned it back to the side with the skylark on it and held up the set of pens. She gave them a long, hard look. My sense was that she was deliberating what to do. I could almost feel her thinking, but I had no sense of what was coming next. Her actions seemed oddly disjointed to me, as if everything were being done in a context I didn't know. The ordinary steps involved in writing or drawing on a piece of paper just weren't there.

Picking out the dark green pen again, the one she'd chosen originally, Jessie considered it once more, then abruptly she began to scribble over the paper in stark, violent movements.

My first instinct was to stop her, because she was completely destroying the lovely skylark drawing, but I refrained and let her carry on. Back and forth, back and forth she went in broad agitated strokes. Soon she began to pant, as if she were undertaking hard physical exercise.

I looked over Jessie's head at Meleri. She widened her eyes to indicate how bizarre Jessie's behaviour was, but there was a cognizance to her expression that told me this wasn't the first time she'd seen it.

For three or four minutes Jessie continued to scribble until she had covered the entire page. The skylark, the grass it had been standing in, the musical notes up the side all disappeared under dark green ink. Finally Jessie leaned back, gasping, and dropped her hands to her sides. 'I hope you have another piece of paper,' she said to me.

I nodded uncertainly.

'I had to scribble on that one.'

'I wonder if you were feeling angry because we said the story of Idris wasn't true, so you tried to take the picture away from us?' I said.

'Nah,' she replied nonchalantly. 'I just wanted to get the devil out of me.'

'How do you mean?' I asked.

'Didn't Mrs Thomas tell you?' Jessie said, nodding back over her shoulder to Meleri.

'Tell me what?'

'I'm possessed. I'm waiting for the exorcist.'

'No, she didn't tell me that. Because I'm quite sure Mrs Thomas doesn't believe that. And I don't either.'

'It's okay,' Jessie said cheerfully. 'You don't have to believe things for them to be true.'

'I don't accept such things are true,' I replied. 'I've worked with many, many children over the years but not a single one of them has been possessed. Not for real. Sometimes they have done naughty things. Sometimes really bad naughty things. But that's because they're scared. Or they're confused. Or they really, really need people to help them.'

'That's those kids, not me. Because I do have the devil in me,' Jessie replied, 'and it's for real.'

'I don't believe that.'

She smiled sweetly. 'You will.'

chapter two

When I first started teaching in the US in the early 1970s, we were still finding our way forward with childhood mental illness. Socializing autistic children with the use of cattle prods was considered extreme but still acceptable. Both domestic violence and physical child abuse were only just beginning to be recognized as inappropriate. People agreed all along that, no, it was never a good thing to discipline a child to the point of injury, but obedience was held in higher regard, and methods used to ensure children behaved well were considered a matter for the family, not the courts. Most people did not believe child sexual abuse existed, except in the most depraved of circumstances.

It's hard now to imagine what those times were like, how the experts could have thought what they did, how we blamed parents for so many issues that we now know are present at birth, and, worse, how we did not see nor hear so many of the things children were telling us. I am saddened to think of the anguish we professionals must have caused families with our ignorance.

Nonetheless, there was also a magic that sprang from the innocence of that era. Drug intervention was largely unknown. Insurance companies were rarely involved. Problems were seldom reduced to chemical imbalances or the predetermination of genes. We relied instead on spending time with the child to understand him or her, and because we didn't yet have answers to most of the problems we faced, the possibility for change was always present.

Capitalism, however, was never far behind each forward step we took. If something looked like it might work, in no time at all someone wrote a book about it, someone made a programme of it, someone started charging money. Pharmaceuticals increasingly became a part of this chain. Ritalin was first to appear on the scene in the 1980s; from that point, the game changed.

The relationship between psychiatry and the pharmaceutical companies quickly grew incestuous. As new drugs were developed, our diagnosis bible, the DSM, mushroomed in size. This was not because new mental illnesses were being discovered, but because differences in human behaviour were being reclassified as mental illness in order that insurance companies could cover the skyrocketing prescription prices.

When I arrived in the UK in the early eighties, I was surprised to find an entirely different approach. Indeed, not just a different approach, an entirely different mindset. There were no contracts, no IEPs (Individual Education Plans), no drugs, no insurance companies. Much of the structure I was accustomed to in American schools and therapeutic settings was missing, including a clear-cut order of referral between education, the medical community and Social Services.

In the beginning, the British system for handling children with special needs looked ragtag to me. Buildings were often old to the point of ancient and crumbling. Literally. Learning materials were frequently in short supply, meaning children shared textbooks and other necessities. Specialists such as school psychologists were few and far between. What seemed oddest of all, however, was the presence of charities. Rather than people being charged for services as I was accustomed to in the US, charities, both big and small, came in to take up the slack when the government could not afford to provide the services themselves. I discovered charities providing inner city preschool programmes, breakfast programmes, learning support, counselling rooms and provision for numerous specific special needs. Indeed, some charities were so well integrated with government services that it wasn't always obvious to me who was providing which service.

We had our charities in the US, but they tended to be either affiliated with religious groups or large, corporate bodies involved mainly in research. They weren't up close and personal, providing everyday services to ordinary local programmes. I had never seen government and non-governmental bodies work in such a cohesive fashion before. It didn't take long for me to realize that, different as it was to what we did in the US, the system worked. More than that, it was often a lifeline to poor communities and to very rural communities, which did not have the population or local income to support specialist programmes.

Once I'd become acclimatized to this different approach, I grew to like it. It was freer and more flexible than what I'd left in America, and it proved an ideal outlet for my own skills, currently restricted by motherhood and visa regulations that didn't allow me to take employment as anything other than a writer. I was free, however, to volunteer my services, so I soon became part of the very system that had surprised me so much on arrival, taking on a position with local children's services through one of the major charities.

Meleri and I returned to the staff room after seeing Jessie. While she went to make us both a cup of tea, I sat down at the table, pulled a thick folder over and opened it.

All too commonly, the background of boys and girls in care is a litany of dysfunction: broken families, violence, drug and alcohol abuse. The notes on Jessie's family, however, didn't paint this sort of picture. Her father, Gwyl, was an artist, and her mother, Diane, worked at the local supermarket. They had taken advantage of Margaret Thatcher's right-to-buy scheme to purchase their council house in the 1980s and were proud of being homeowners. Gwyl was an avid gardener and had won prizes locally for his colourful hanging baskets. The family included three older daughters as well as Jessie, plus a Jack Russell dog.

Jessie was an unplanned baby. Her parents were forty-six and fifty at the time of her conception, and as a consequence her mother had initially thought she was going through the menopause when her periods stopped. After a few months of 'persistent bloating', Diane was seen by a consultant gynaecologist. A hysterectomy was planned, but the investigative ultrasound turned up a different explanation for her problems. Diane was five months pregnant.

This was not welcome news. The two eldest girls, Nesta and Kate, were eighteen and twenty and already away from home. Their third child, Gemma, was eight. She too had been a 'surprise baby', coming along when the older daughters were already teenagers. The parents admitted they'd been disappointed when they found out Diane was pregnant with Gemma. They were enjoying the freedom afforded by older children, and had just bought a small caravan with the intention of spending the summer touring Ireland. This wasn't possible with a new baby. The caravan was sold and the money put towards the costs of raising a third child. Diane, in particular, struggled to come to terms with the new family configuration. She suffered post-natal depression severe enough to require three weeks of hospitalization after Gemma's birth.

Then came Jessie. Diane was reported to say she would have had an abortion had she known soon enough, and even as it was she investigated the possibility of a late-term abortion. Gwyl told the social worker that it might have gone more easily if Jessie had been a boy, that perhaps they would have got used to the idea of another child. That she was a fourth girl, that they'd had yet another 'accident' after Gemma, however, felt gratuitously unfair. The money Gwyl made from his artwork wasn't really enough for three children, much less four. The family was deeply in debt at the time of Jessie's arrival, forcing Gwyl to give up his creative career and take a job at the local car factory.

To complicate matters further, Jessie was born prematurely. She spent her first three weeks of life in the special baby unit, and once home she didn't settle. Jessie cried incessantly and refused to feed, often vomiting what she did take. Diane struggled to cope. Fretting that Jessie wasn't getting enough milk from the breast, she switched her to a bottle. This made things worse. Jessie was diagnosed with a cows' milk allergy, and then shortly after with a soya allergy, and ended up on a special formula. At three months, weighing only eight pounds, she was admitted to hospital with 'failure to thrive'. She was readmitted four months later, again with failure to thrive, still significantly underweight, still fretful and difficult to settle. It was at this point that Jessie was identified as an 'at risk' child and placed on the Social Services register for monitoring.

I was curious about this, because it told me that something had concerned someone, something had raised enough red flags that they had contacted Social Services. Being put on the at-risk register usually only happens if abuse or neglect is suspected, or if the parents show a serious deficit in their ability to care for the child, and from what I was reading Jessie presented only health problems. Why the referral?

Diane again developed post-natal depression. There were no notes on how this expressed itself, but the record showed that Diane was also hospitalized twice during Jessie's first year. The notes likewise did not say who cared for Jessie during this time, but I assumed it was her father or elder sisters.

As had happened with Gemma, things appeared to settle down for the family after the first year. Despite her difficult start, Jessie met all the expected milestones at her eighteen-month check-up and appeared healthy, albeit small for her age. Diane was reported as being pleasant and cooperative during the check-up, giving the interviewer the sense that she had overcome her mental health issues. Jessie was described as bright and engaging.

Then came the missing years. Although I could find no official mention of it, Jessie appeared to have been removed from the at-risk register, as there were no social work reports. Indeed, there was only one written record in Jessie's file for the entire period of time between the ages of eighteen months and seven years, and this pertained not to Jessie but to her older sister Gemma. It was from Gemma's form teacher, who described Gemma as a very able student intellectually, but undisciplined and 'a bit feral'. The teacher blamed this on the parents' lax attitude towards raising their children, citing the girls' father Gwyl's belief in 'free ranging' – letting children grow up as free of adult interference as possible, encouraging them to determine their own pace, to find their own entertainment and solve their own problems – as he felt this would keep their originality intact and lead to their being freer, more creative adults. The teacher wrote that all it had done in Gemma's case was result in a boisterous child, totally disinterested in adult authority and skilled at orchestrating mayhem. To the teacher's dismay, Gwyl had seemed pleased to hear this, perceiving this behaviour as a mark of Gemma's free spirit.

Jessie next came to the attention of the authorities the year she was seven, and this time with a bang. Literally. She had set fire to weeds in a vacant lot that had quickly spread to a nearby shed. A gas canister inside exploded, resulting in a dramatic, albeit fairly small, inferno and several thousand pounds of damage.

Investigators quickly determined Jessie was responsible for the blaze. They discovered she had previously set several other small fires in the neighbourhood. Delinquent fire setting is unusual in girls, and Jessie, at seven, was young to be engaged in arson, so despite the spectacular nature of the shed fire it was deemed the result of childish curiosity, rather than pathology.

That assessment changed the next year, when she was eight. After an argument with her mother, Jessie had gone into the kitchen, turned on a hob on the cooker and pulled the curtain from a nearby window over it. The whole kitchen was set alight. Fortunately, everyone escaped safely, but the house was badly damaged.

This incident did bring the family once again to the attention of Social Services and, on investigation, a bleak picture of family chaos soon emerged. Jessie was an extremely difficult child. Prone to explosive temper tantrums when thwarted, she would gouge holes in furniture, throw breakables against the walls, tear her clothes and attempt to hit, cut, bite and otherwise hurt her parents and sisters. She would urinate on her parents' or Gemma's bed when angry, and they were so worried about her fire-setting problem that Jessie was literally locked in her bedroom at night to ensure she couldn't get hold of matches or lighters while the family slept. Her worst behaviour, however, had been reserved for the family dog, whom she tormented mercilessly, running at it and screaming in its face, pinching it and hitting it. On two occasions she had thrown it into hot bath water and once tried to cut off its tail. After this attack the poor animal was rehomed.

Social Services defended their lack of involvement, saying Jessie's behaviour elsewhere had not drawn attention to the home situation. Indeed, at school Jessie was one of the brightest children in the class, always completing her work on time, responding well to praise and ever eager to learn new things. Her teacher acknowledged that Jessie had a short fuse and could lash out inappropriately, and she said that there had been few times when Jessie was nastily vindictive; however, for the most part, Jessie responded well to clear boundaries, and consequently her behaviour in class was always considered to be within normal limits.

In the teacher's opinion, her only significant problems were social. Lying was her biggest issue. Unbearably competitive, Jessie was so desperate to be best at everything she did that she often lied to give herself an advantage. And sometimes she just lied for lying's sake, from what the teacher could tell. This quickly got on the nerves of the other children. Jessie was anxious to have friends, but she didn't seem to understand the irritation or betrayal the other children felt when they fell victim to her lies. Distraught at having no one, Jessie tried to buy the other children's friendship with candy and even money, which, the teacher said, had resulted in a few sad instances of her having been exploited by some of the more entrepreneurial children.

Despite Jessie's relative success at school, the litany of destructive behaviours at home made frightening reading, and I was astonished she had gone undetected as long as she had. However, I was more astonished by her parents' response, when the home fire once again brought the family to the attention of Social Services, because they categorically did not want any of the help that was offered. Instead, they wanted their daughter removed from their home and they didn't want her back. Full stop.

Jessie was eight. I instantly felt sorry for her, reading this, because how frightening and confusing it must be to have your parents so openly want to give you away. Saying that, I did also feel for her family. Her behaviour sounded nightmarish, to say the least, and how difficult it must have been for them to bring them to the point of wanting to give up on their own child. But give up they did. Jessie's parents were adamant that she had to go.

Meleri hoped that the situation could be rehabilitated, that with the appropriate therapeutic help for Jessie and support for her parents, she could eventually return home, but it was clear that, for the time being, Jessie did need to be removed.

A chaotic period followed. Jessie went through three foster homes in very short succession, because of her difficult behaviour. It was at this point Jessie was given the diagnosis of reactive attachment disorder or RAD. This is a mental health condition where a child finds it difficult to form attachments to others, and is normally the result of not having consistent, loving care in early childhood. This may be due to being separated from the primary caregiver through death, illness or unforeseen circumstance, to having too many different caregivers in infancy to form a close bond, as can happen in situations such as orphanages, or to abuse and neglect. Typically, children with this disorder find it difficult to form appropriate social relationships, and they are often hostile, demanding and manipulative, with poor impulse control and other emotional and behavioural difficulties.

Children who have RAD can recover, but it is often a long, slow road, and sadly love alone is not enough. Such children require structure, security and consistency often over an extended period of time to help them relinquish old, inappropriate patterns of behaviour and learn more helpful ones.

Unfortunately, foster children are particularly vulnerable to this problem because the unstable nature of their lives tends to reinforce the idea that attachments do not last. Most come into the system because of early experiences of abuse and neglect and are often already suffering some degree of attachment disorder. They then go forward, moving from home to home, caretaker to caretaker, having little experience of the structure and consistency they need.

This was very much the case with Jessie. Her first placement ended within hours of her arrival, when she threatened
to squeeze the foster family's two pet hamsters to death. Her
second lasted eighteen days, terminating after a disastrous
visit to church when Jessie urinated on the newly dedicated
pew cushion. The third resulted in Jessie being returned at
11 p.m., her belongings chucked into a black bin bag. As an
emergency measure she was placed in the Glan Morfa children's home, and that was where she remained.

Meleri took over Jessie's case when she arrived at Glan
Morfa, and she felt both concern and frustration. Glan Morfa
was a medium secure unit, designed to handle children with
severe behavioural problems. The staff were more highly
trained and the programme more structured than in most
group homes. It was, however, constructed with adolescents
in mind, not children, and while there was another girl there
who was eleven, Jessie was still the youngest. Meleri badly
wanted a foster placement for her, a proper home where
Jessie could have the one-to-one attention she craved, but it
would need to be a therapeutic home with experienced foster
parents, and these were few and far between.

As I closed the folder, I looked over at Meleri. She was nursing her cup of tea. The room was cool, so she held it with both
hands to warm them. Looking up, she met my eyes. 'So what
do you think?' she asked.

I pulled my own cup of tea over. It had been too hot at first;

now it was lukewarm. I reached for the spoon and stirred it before picking it up.

Interpreting my pause for dismay, Meleri said, 'This is so different from what you had in America, isn't it? You're not used to this cowboy set-up, where everything is patched together and we can never afford the help we need. You had so much over there, didn't you? Psychologists in the schools and therapists of every kind and lots of special programmes . . .'

I shrugged. 'I'm not sure we had so much. The kids here get lost because the state can't afford the help they need. The kids there get lost because their parents can't afford the help they need. Or the insurers won't pay for it. The result is much the same. Kids get lost in every system.'

'But that's what I don't want,' she said. 'I look at Jessie and think: all you should have on your mind is unicorns and boy bands. You don't deserve this life.'

I smiled and paused to stir my tea again. 'Well, let's see what we can do.'

chapter three

When Jessie came into the small room to meet me on my next visit, she was wearing yellow trousers and a pink top with a glittery design on the front.

'Do you like this outfit?' she asked me, pausing at the end of the table.

They were quite ordinary clothes and didn't appear to be new, so in the normal course of things I wouldn't have thought to comment. As I was asked, however, I said, 'Yes, I like it. They are lovely springlike colours and they suit you.'

'Mummy bought me these clothes. They're my favourites. I wore them specially, because I thought you would like to see them.'

'That's kind of you to think of me,' I said, and opened my satchel. Jessie came around the table and sat in the chair next to me.

'I like you,' she said.

'Yes, I like you too,' I replied. 'I'm glad we'll get to spend some time together.'

'I really like your hair.' She reached up and touched alongside my ear.

There was an intimacy to the touch I hadn't expected. It was more of a caress than a touch of curiosity, and as a consequence I stiffened slightly. Jessie smiled at me in a confident manner, almost a knowing way, as if she were aware she had rattled me.

'Do you want me to draw pictures for you today?' she asked, and then she touched my hair again, pushing it back slightly. Lowering her hand, she let it rest on my shoulder. The gesture was affectionate, almost indulgent, as if I were to be gently humoured. I wanted to tell her to take her hand away, but I didn't because it seemed churlish. She wasn't doing anything wrong beyond being in my personal space.

'Here in my case, I have lots of different things to do,' I replied, hoping to distract her. 'Would you like to take a look?' I opened the satchel wide.

'Are you going to come see me all the time?' Again she caressed me but then this time put her arm around my shoulder.

'I'll be coming once a week. On Tuesdays, like today.'

'I want to sit on your lap,' and before I could reply, she did, slithering in-between the table and me. She put her arms around me in a hug and lay her head on my shoulder.

'Are you coming just for me?' she asked beguilingly.

'You might be more comfortable sitting here in the chair,' I replied, and pulled the adjacent orange plastic chair up beside me.

Jessie patted my face and physically turned it to look at her. 'Are you coming just for me?'

'Yes, just for you. We'll play some games and do some drawings and sometimes we'll talk. Sometimes maybe we will go out. Would you like to do that?'

'Just me? Not any of the other children?' Jessie asked. 'Just me?'

'Yes, just you.'

'You wouldn't let dogs in here, would you?' Jessie asked.

This abrupt turn in the conversation caught me off guard, but I went with it.

'No. No dogs,' I said. 'Why? Are you afraid of dogs?'

'No. I'm not afraid of anything.'

'I see.'

'I'm just checking. You wouldn't let cats in here, would you?'

The way she was asking sounded mischievous to me, so I replied, 'Nope. No cats. No dogs. No other children. No cows. No horses.' I paused, and then added playfully, 'But what about goats? Shall we allow goats?'

Jessie looked at me like I'd lost my mind.

I laughed. 'I'm being silly, aren't I?'

Her eyes narrowed. Slipping off my lap, she stood up. 'Why did you say that? About goats?'

'I was making a joke.'

'Don't. Okay? I don't like jokes. I don't think there is anything to laugh at.'

'All right.'

'Are you sorry?'

31

'I'm sorry you feel upset.'

'Well, you should be,' she replied flatly, and sat down.

Within a few moments, Jessie reached over and took the coloured pens out of my satchel and opened the packet. I was curious if we'd have a repeat of the scribbling episode, but it didn't happen this time. Instead, she selected a clean sheet of paper, smoothed it out, picked up a pink pen and began to draw.

I also took a piece of paper.

'What are you doing?' she asked.

'I thought I would draw too. You draw your picture and I will draw mine. Then we can show each other.'

'No. I don't want you to draw.' Jessie moved the packet of pens out of my reach. 'No, wait. I've changed my mind. You can draw, but I'm going to choose what colour you get.' She took out a brown pen and held it towards me. 'Now draw what I tell you. Draw a goat.'

'A goat?'

'Yes. There.' She tapped the middle of the paper.

My goat-drawing skills did not meet Jessie's exacting standards. 'Oh, bad picture!' she cried. She reached across me and scribbled it out with the pink pen. 'Do a better one. Do it bigger. Right here.' She pointed to the right-hand corner of the paper.

I made another attempt, starting this time with the goat's forehead and drawing down around the nose.

'No! No, no, no!' she said. She reached across to scribble it out again. 'Do a *better* job. Draw a proper goat.'

'Perhaps you should draw it?' I suggested.

'No, *you* draw it.'

'How do you think I could make it better?'

'Give it horns. Like this.' She drew a curlicue on the paper.

I drew a third goat, but instead of drawing it from the side as I had the other two, I drew this one face onwards, so that it stared out of the paper at us. I added large, curly horns that would have looked more appropriate on a ram.

'Yes!' Jessie said approvingly. She snatched the paper up to examine it more carefully.

'You like the big horns,' I said.

'Yes. To butt you with.' She pushed the paper at me.

'You feel like butting me with those horns.'

Two or three times, Jessie hit my arm with the piece of paper. Then she paused to look at it again. 'You drew the devil,' she said. 'I made you draw the devil. Ha, ha, ha!' Laying the paper on the table, she traced her finger around the head and horns of the goat.

Abruptly she snatched the paper up again and hit it against my face. 'The devil is going to get you.' She laughed gleefully.

I pushed the paper down. 'This is too rough a game. I don't like being hit.'

'The devil doesn't care. And you can't stop the devil.'

'The devil has no power here. This is a safe space. And I am a safe adult. I am stronger than the devil. So when I say that it is time to stop, it is time to stop. Hand me the paper, please.'

'Nooo. I haven't had a go yet. I want to use the pens.'

'Jessie, hand me that piece of paper, please.'

'That's not fair. You got to draw, but I didn't.'

'You can draw on the other piece there. Hand me that one, please.'

'You're not fair. You said I could draw and now you say I can't. That's *inconsistent*.'

'I do not want to be hit with paper. Hand it to me, please.'

Jessie slammed it down against the table top.

I took the paper and placed it on the other side of me. 'What happened that made me say we were playing too roughly?' I asked.

'It's not fair I can't draw.'

'Yes, I hear that. And you can draw in a minute. But tell me first why I said it was too rough a game? What happened that was too rough?'

'I don't know. You just got angry, that's all.'

'You were hitting me in the face with the paper. That was too rough. So I asked you to stop. I'm not angry, but I did not like being hit in the face.'

Jessie was watching me. Indeed, throughout the whole time I was talking, she had maintained eye contact and gave no indication that she felt embarrassed or guilty about her behaviour. Now, instead of responding to my words, she reached a hand out and caressed the side of my head again.

'I just *love* your hair,' she said.

*

There were three people on duty in the group home that afternoon – Joseph, Enir and Helen. Enir was out, having taken two of the children to visit the dentist, and Helen was in the TV room with the other children. Only Joseph was in the staff room when I came in, after my time with Jessie was finished. He was at the small table, writing in a notebook, and looked up when I entered. *'Paned?'* he asked and rose to his feet. This was short-hand Welsh for what Brits elsewhere called a 'cuppa' in English – a cup of tea – and it had taken my American soul more than a little while to get used to this ritual of immediately being offered tea in virtually every setting. I'd not been a tea drinker when I'd first moved to the UK. We didn't even have this kind of tea in rural Montana, when I'd grown up. I acquired the habit quickly, however, realizing 'social pariah' status lay down the non-tea-drinking path.

Sitting down at the small table, I watched Joseph deftly making our drinks. He was chatting amiably as he did so, telling me that he preferred loose-leaf tea to teabags and that his wife, when she got a chance, bought their tea at a special shop in Chester. I studied him as he worked. He was of average height and build and appeared to be of Mediterranean extraction, with dark hair and dark eyes. Joseph was utterly ordinary except for one thing: his personality. He had about him a charming joie de vivre that made you feel as if there were nothing in the whole world he would rather do than be there with you. He made me feel special by doing nothing more than sharing a cup of boring office tea with me. I found this fascinating. I hardly knew Joseph and yet I immediately felt comfortable with him. As I watched him making the tea, I wondered what subliminal cues I was perceiving to make me react as I did.

Settled with our tea, we chatted light-heartedly. Joseph was curious how I had come to be in this obscure part of Wales, and he wanted to know about America and why I'd left. That got us on to politics, and from there it was a short jump to talking about how hard it was to provide the necessary services to children in care when there was so little money to go around. Joseph voiced his gratitude to the various charities that subsidized everything from spectacles to holidays for the kids, and for skilled people like myself who gave of their time. Eventually the conversation came around to Jessie. I was curious how Joseph saw her in day-to-day life in the children's home.

'The truth?' he asked. 'She's a nine-year-old confidence trickster.' His tone was affectionate, but I could also hear the exasperation.

'How do you mean?'

'Jessie does a line in lying like I've never seen. I kid you not. The older children have nothing over on her. Lying to keep yourself out of trouble or avoid having to do something you don't want to do, that I understand. Or lying to big yourself up. Everyone lies about stuff like that. But Jessie lies in all sorts of random situations where you wouldn't expect it. For instance, I asked her the other day if she had had any of the apple crumble at dinner. Several children had told me how good it was, so I asked, just to make conversation. Jessie says no. So I ask why. I ask if she doesn't like apple crumble.

Again, just being conversational. There was no pressure on her to give a specific answer. It didn't matter to me one way or the other if she did or didn't eat crumble, if she did or didn't like it. She says no, she can't eat it because she's allergic to apples. I knew immediately this was a lie, because she drinks apple juice at break all the time, but then Damien pipes up with, "Jessie had two portions at dinner." So, in fact, she *had* eaten the apple crumble.'

Joseph smiled good-naturedly. 'That's our Jessie. All smoke and mirrors.'

'Wow,' I said.

'Other times, it's not quite so benign. Jessie very intentionally sets out to mess with people's minds. We had an example of that yesterday. One of our boys, Robin, is a bit vulnerable, a big boy who still does a lot of little kid things. We're all a bit careful with him because he gets hurt easily. Even the other kids can be quite tender towards Robin. Except Jessie . . .

'Robin's got this little dog on a keychain that his mother gave him. It's his good luck charm, and he carries this thing with him everywhere. Yesterday, he was on dining room duty and had to wash down the tables after lunch; so, he set the keychain down on the back counter while he worked, and then he forgot to pick it up again. Later, when he was in the day room, he realized it was missing, and, of course, panic stations.

'Jessie was in the day room as well and she says, "I saw Martin sweep it into his water bucket when he was wiping down the back counter." This alarms Robin and he immediately runs to the big sink in the back kitchen where the water is emptied to see if it is in the drain. It isn't. Robin's crying by this point. He thinks it's gone down the drain, and Helen was trying to reassure him that it was too big to go down the drain. It wouldn't fit through the holes. Jessie pipes up, "Martin ran his water through the strainer first to get all the bits out and he threw them into the compost bin." We keep this huge plastic dustbin by the back sink where all food waste from the meals go, and eventually it goes out to be emptied into the garden. You can imagine what a nasty bin this is, all full of kitchen scraps, the stuff kids haven't eaten, and slop water. Poor Robin is beside himself, thinking that his keychain has got lost in this mess. So he's out rummaging through all this muck, and pretty soon half the staff are helping him, at which point Jessie says, "I saw them empty the bin after lunch out in the garden compost." So Robin then wants to go out into the rain, out into the mud in the back garden to sift through the compost for his keychain.

'I wasn't in on all this. I was working in the office at the time, but Robin has to ask my permission to go out in that part of the garden, so he came into the office, sobbing, panicking, and a complete mess from going through the waste bin. He tells me this sorry tale and I say, hold on, none of that's true, because your keychain is right here. I explain that when I'd gone into the dining room after the kids were finished, I'd seen it on the back worktop and knew Robin must have forgotten it; so picked it up expressly to keep it safe from one of the other kids mucking around with it. I'd had it the whole time and was just waiting to run into him.'

Joseph shook his head. 'Which means Jessie was just winding him up the whole time. There was absolutely no benefit to her whatsoever in telling him she had seen his keychain thrown away. She hadn't even been in the dining room after the meal, because it hadn't been her turn to clean up. So she knew nothing about it. Everything she said was made up specifically to hurt the boy for the sake of it, and no other reason.'

'Did you talk to her about it?' I asked.

'Yes, of course I did. And that generated a whole new set of lies. I said, "Robin said that you told him you saw Martin wiping down the back worktops and he swept the keychain into his water. That's untrue. You weren't in the dining room then." And she says, "Robin misunderstood what I said. I was only suggesting that maybe Martin accidentally got it in his water. I was just trying to be helpful." I said, "No, Robin didn't misunderstand. You gave him specific details." And she says, "Well, I never said I was in the room." And so the conversation went. Every time I would say something, Jessie would have a counterargument. She couldn't just say, "Okay. I lied; I got caught; I'm sorry." Jessie can never say that.'

chapter four

Home for me those days was a small hill farm high up on the Welsh moors not far from Snowdonia, where I lived with my husband and daughter. Getting there meant a twenty-mile drive inland from the coast, leaving behind the main roads to drive through a network of small lanes that climbed steadily upward almost a thousand feet from the sea plain before opening onto moorland, then across the moor on a single track road until it dipped over the brow of a hill and back onto developed farmland. There was our eighteenth-century stone farmhouse and cluster of barns, where we raised pedigreed Black Welsh Mountain sheep and a few cattle, plus hens and ducks and a very gobbly pair of turkeys, who took unnatural pleasure in playing on our young daughter's swing set.

To go from the urbanized coast up onto the moors was to traverse worlds. The last part of the drive was nothing but heather, sphagnum moss and sheep. Even in the worst of weather, when rain was so heavy the wipers couldn't keep it off the windscreen or wind whipped mist across the open land like tattered ghosts, I loved this place. Today, however, it was sunny and pleasantly warm – spring was well underway – so I drove with the window of the car down to better smell the luscious moorland air and hear the birds as they startled up.

A skylark rose, its distinctive liquid trill filling the air. Bringing the car to a stop on the tiny lane, I watched as it flew way up into the sky to perform a complicated ballet. A second skylark rose from the heather in the distance and began to sing too, and then a third and a fourth, all whirling, dipping and warbling across the heath.

I immediately thought of Jessie. Skylarks are, in fact, dull little birds to look at, no more brightly coloured than a house sparrow, and only a little larger. All their beauty is in their song. There was something, however, in the colourful way Jessie portrayed them that captured this, transposing brilliant feathers and brilliant song. As I sat in my car, arm on the window, warm spring sunshine coming through the windscreen, and listened to the skylarks, I thought how lovely it would be to bring Jessie here.

My mind went practical then. The first thoughts had been warm and fuzzy, about what a great experience it would be to come together to this place of skylarks. Then suddenly I was thinking about the realities. Did they let children go out with support staff? What would be involved releasing her? Could I do it on a Saturday or would I be restricted to the time slot I was due to work with Jessie on Tuesday afternoons? And then I grew even more practical. Could I build this into my sessions with her? Create a reward system to encourage appropriate behaviour? The skylarks rising and falling beyond the car window were largely forgotten.

The next Tuesday, I came prepared with a plan of action. I hadn't gone quite so far as to build in the skylark idea yet, but I knew that along with building a rapport with Jessie, I simultaneously needed to establish boundaries to keep her inappropriate touching and her craving to control in check. One of the best methods I'd found for structuring therapeutic sessions was to play board games or card games with the child. Most children enjoyed this format, and the rules inherent in playing the game would give us a template for setting boundaries. Most children would accept the third-person neutrality of a game, so this avoided the inevitable power struggles that came about if I started off by setting the boundaries myself. In this instance, I decided on the strategy game we call checkers in America, known as draughts in the UK, where one player attempts to capture all the other player's pieces to become the winner.

I liked checkers for several reasons. First, it required only a basic board and pieces, which were cheap to buy or straightforward to make. Second, the rules were simple to understand and the game itself was satisfying to play. Also important was the fact that it was a fairly easy game to throw in the opponent's favour, if I found this necessary. What I liked best, however, was that it required just enough concentration to keep the players focused, but not so much that we could not make conversation at the same time. This made it an ideal therapeutic activity.

Jessie's need for control was likely to be a reaction to her unsettled life and feeling out of control herself. Her worry about the devil being inside her, making her do things, also reflected this need. For a child like this, games were a good way of building trust between us. They provide a safe, predictable structure that allows the child to know what is coming next. The format ensures the focus isn't acutely on the child, so that if conversation becomes too difficult or scary, we have an easy means of shifting our attention and allowing the game to ground us again.

I had one further reason for choosing checkers with Jessie: she would need to sit opposite me. I had not been comfortable with the way in which she had invaded my personal space in the previous sessions. While not overtly sexual, her behaviour had been too intimate. I wanted more time to observe what was going on before addressing the behaviour directly, but it needed to stop. The game provided a legitimate reason to put the table between us without making Jessie feel she'd been doing anything wrong.

This was my well-laid plan anyway. Jessie, however, was all about anarchy. When she entered the room, she came immediately to my side of the table and sat down next to me.

'Look what I have,' I said, and opened out the black-and-red checkerboard. 'A game for us to play. Would you please sit on that side, and I'll show you how it's played.'

'I don't want to do that,' Jessie replied flatly.

'Have you ever played this game?' I asked.

'Yes, millions of times, which is why I said I don't want to do it. It's boring.'

'How about just one game, okay? Humour me.'

'What's that mean? Are you trying to be funny?'

'It is an expression that means "Be nice to me". Be nice and play one game with me.'

'Why didn't you say that? Is it because you're American and can't talk English?'

I grinned. 'No. It's just the way I talk.'

'Besides, you said I could draw.'

'One game,' I said. 'Then we can draw. Sit on that side, please.'

Jessie frowned.

I grinned at her with a twinkle in my eye. 'I bet I can beat you.' I opened the cloth bag containing the checkers. Spilling them out onto the table, I started to sort them into blacks and reds.

She remained unmoving.

'I'll show you how it's played.'

'I don't need you to show me. I know how it's played. I said that. I've played it a bazillion times before. And I don't like it. Besides, there's no horse pieces. Those aren't the right pieces at all.'

'You're thinking of chess. This is a different game. You go sit in that chair, so you are closer to your side of the board.' I indicated the chair on the opposite side of the table. 'I'll explain how it's played.'

For several moments more Jessie remained beside me, making eye contact, willing me to give in. I smiled slightly and didn't blink.

She sighed heavily. '*One* game then. Since you're going to make me do it anyway.' She got up and moved around to the other side and sat down.

'It's called checkers,' I said, as I set up the board. 'Here people call it draughts, but if you don't mind I'm going to call it checkers because that's the name I'm used to.'

'See, you don't speak English.'

'Yes, I do speak English,' I said. 'Checkers is the American English word.'

'We're not in America,' Jessie replied, 'so you shouldn't be using American words.'

'You would prefer I call it draughts?' I asked.

'Actually, you should call it *ddrafftiau*, because we're in Wales.' She looked up, a glint of mischief in her eye. 'Actually we should be speaking Welsh. *Dwy ddim yn hoffi chwarae ddrafftiau.*'

The temptation was to speak back to her in Welsh to prove that I understood perfectly well that she'd just told me she didn't want to play checkers, because my sense was that Jessie hoped I hadn't, but I realized it was just that: temptation. Jessie was trying to lure me into a weaker position, because that one Welsh phrase would inevitably lead to another. I knew her command of the language was better than mine, so eventually I wouldn't be able to respond. As the session was meant to be about playing checkers, not who could speak the best Welsh, by shifting the focus, she would be taking control.

Instead I asked, 'Do you want to have the black pieces or the red pieces?'

Jessie sat.

'I'm going to choose black,' I said when she didn't respond, and began to set the pieces out on the matching squares.

'No, I want black,' she said.

'All right.' I turned the board around so that the black pieces were on her side. 'So, here is how we play . . .' and I began to explain the rules, because I was quite certain Jessie hadn't played the game a bazillion times before, and possibly not even once. She sat motionless, her hands in her lap. Jessie was quite a pretty girl. Her eyes in particular were attractive because they were a very clear, true green. I was thinking this as I was talking to her, because she never once took her eyes off me.

'Shall we decide who makes the first move?' I asked.

'I've decided I want the red after all.'

'All right,' I said and turned the board again. Reaching in my bag, I took out a ten pence piece. 'In checkers, we traditionally flip a coin to see who gets to start. Heads or tails?'

'That's an American thing,' Jessie said.

'Yes, it probably is.'

'We don't do that here.'

'But today we will,' I replied. 'Heads or tails?'

'It hasn't got any tail on it. It's got a lion.'

'A lion's got a tail,' I replied. 'And I'm going to choose heads. So when I flip the coin, if Queen Elizabeth comes up on top, I get to start first.'

'I've decided I don't want the red. It's too red. I want the black.'

Thus went the entire hour, Jessie attempting to divert my efforts at every turn. We managed to play the game for only about fifteen minutes before time ran out and we had to stop. I tried to make the game as enjoyable as possible, including ensuring that there were plenty of opportunities for Jessie to capture my pieces and progress easily across the board. None-theless, it remained a thoroughly unsatisfying activity. Jessie just could not stop struggling for control of the session. She was not interested in winning the game. Indeed, I suspect she saw even that as giving me a victory.

While driving home, I could think of nothing but the relentless power struggle that had just taken place. Jessie's beautifully drawn skylark pictures were what had pulled me onto this case, and she had been so delighted with the packet of new pens the first day. Should I have stayed with that activity and not tried to change so soon to the game of checkers? I had to admit that the conversation with Joseph had influenced me and that, as a consequence, I had been anticipating problems more than I should have. I was now thinking it would have been better to go more slowly and follow what Jessie wanted to do for a while longer as a means of establishing trust.

That was my traditional approach, the one I was accustomed

to. Client-led play therapy or talk therapy was what I had been taught in the 1970s. The therapist sat back, largely passive, and observed, while the child took the lead. Time did not matter.

So much had changed, however, in the ensuing decades. One of the biggest of these changes was the philosophical shift away from the relationship-based milieu and towards a quasi-scientific, efficacy-based approach. Client-led therapy required time and highly trained professionals, and both were expensive. Moreover, what was happening in the therapy sessions was often 'fuzzy' and immeasurable, making it impossible in the short term to see if progress was being made. In the late 1970s, treatment began to focus on more time-efficient remedies, such as drugs, cognitive therapies and behavioural 'economies', featuring contracts, rewards and built-in assessments of accountability that were not dependent on a relationship with the therapist. These interventions could be administered by anyone trained in the skills, which made behaviourism a popular choice for special classes and group-living settings where there was a regular change of staff.

The other big transformation over the forty years I had been working was our greatly increased understanding of mental health disorders and allied issues. When I had started out, health care professionals did not believe young children could suffer depression. At a conference presentation, I remember showing a series of slides I'd made of notes a nine-year-old in one of my classes had written, which detailed her wish to kill herself. The presentation was greeted with shocked horror. At that time, childhood was still regarded as a happy, innocent period which gifted the child with resilience. The belief that depression did not happen before adolescence was deeply ingrained. Similarly, we know now that autism is a neurological difference that is present from birth. In the 1960s and 1970s, however, the overarching belief was that autism was a psychological disorder, the result of cold or distant parents who did not sufficiently nurture their children. So the parents of autistic children in that era not only had the challenge of coping with a disabled child, but also with the fear and guilt that their bad parenting had caused it.

Looking back now at some of the children who were in my early classrooms, I see many of their problems in a very different light today to how I saw them then, and I would address them differently were I with these children now. This was particularly true of sexual abuse. In the early days of my career, we professionals had precious little understanding of this kind of abuse and even less ability to recognize when it was happening. Once again, that overarching belief that childhood was a sacred time of innocence and resilience coloured our perceptions of what was really happening. It is difficult nowadays to remember exactly how uninformed we were, how culturally influenced, and subsequently, how genuinely inconceivable these issues were. Client-led therapy was popular in that era, I suspect, because we understood so little that there wasn't much else we could do except sit and listen.

These days, our approach is very different. Recognizing

many disorders as having a physical component, pharmaceuticals now play a big part in treatment plans. The changing culture means children spend much more time indoors, in supervised activities, and in front of screens. Financial constraints, due to lack of funding, either privately through insurance or publicly through government, mean most people can no longer afford the months, or even years, of client-led intervention. Treatment programmes tend to be limited to six or twelve weeks and documentable results are expected within that time.

Because my earliest role had been as a teacher and not a therapist, I'd never operated on a solely client-led basis when working with children. Classrooms, by definition, have inherent goals that are expected to be met within the school-year frame. So I'd always been used to working to a schedule. Over the years, I'd skated among the many popular theories, taking from each of them what had seemed believable and sustainable, and what had worked for me. The heavy emphasis on behaviourism when I was starting out in the 1970s had taught me the value of objectivity and consistency, and to look not only at the problem behaviour itself, but at the 'chain' – what happened before to make the behaviour occur and what happened after as a consequence of that behaviour. The lingering remnants of both Freudian and humanistic psychology had taught me to be open to the influence of the past and to the unique internal world of each individual. However, neither behaviourism nor the talk therapies felt like the answer to me. I'd always been a very process-oriented person, my focus inevitably on what was happening right here and now. So I tended to watch a lot, to observe as objectively as possible, and use what I observed like puzzle pieces to build up a picture of the child and his or her issues. It was like playing Jenga, going behaviour by behaviour until I found the ones holding everything together.

I was, however, well aware that while this was my method of operation, it needed to fit within the greater framework of councils, Social Services and schools. In Jessie's case, there were very specific goals. Social Services wanted to see her out of the system, preferably returned to her family, or, if this wasn't possible, then to an appropriate long-term foster home. My task was to do what I could to facilitate this.

chapter five

When Jessie appeared in the doorway, she paused, surveyed the room, then entered. She came to my side of the table. 'Are you going to make me play that game today?'

'You know what?' I said. 'I've had a big think about what we do together. You didn't want to play checkers last time, and that made me think, Maybe Jessie has a reason for that. So today you can decide for yourself. Here are the choices: we can play checkers or we can draw. Which would you rather do?'

'You talk weird,' she replied.

'Yes, I have an accent. I was born in America.'

'No, I mean you talk weird. You say, "Maybe Jessie has a reason for that", like Jessie isn't in the room. I'm right here. And you're always saying, "This makes me think this. That makes me think that." It's weird.'

I smiled. 'It's just how I learned to say things.'

'It's like if someone drew a cartoon of you, that would be in the bubble over your head. It's weird.'

'Yes, might be.'

Jessie reached forward and touched my hair. 'But I still like you,' she said. Before I could respond, she had her arm around my neck and she sat down on my lap.

'Yes, I like you too. But you know what? I'm not comfortable when people touch me without asking.'

'Why not?'

'Sitting on laps and touching faces are intimate things to do to another person, so we do them only when we know the other person wants to be touched that way too.'

'See? There you go again, talking weird. Why do you say "we"? Are you the Queen?'

'No, I am most definitely not the Queen.'

'She talks like that. Says "we" instead of "I". Because she's royal. Are you royal?'

'What do you think?' I replied, grinning.

Jessie locked both her arms around my neck and put her face very near mine. 'I think I want to be your baby, that's what I think. I want you to be my mummy. You can adopt me. Then you could say "we" all you wanted.'

'That would be nice, wouldn't it? Just now, however, you and I are going to be friends instead, and we're going to work together on some various things, so that you will be ready to have a mum and a dad of your own when the time comes. That's my job here. Helping you get ready for a family.'

'I've already got a family.'

'Yes, I know.'

'So I don't need to get ready for another family.'

'Get ready for going home to your own family.'

'I don't need to get ready. I was born to them.'

I grinned at her. 'Which means I can't adopt you, can I? Because you already have a mummy.'

'Yes, but I want to be your baby now,' Jessie said, and snuggled against me. 'I want you to hold me like I'm yours.'

'I'm thinking it would be better if you sat here beside me,' I said, and extricated her. 'Sit here and tell me about your family. I'd like to hear, because I don't know very much about them.'

Jessie smiled broadly at this suggestion. 'Okay, I'm going to tell you everything. I've got two sisters. One is named Nesta and one is named Kate. Nesta is twenty-seven and she's a hairdresser. She's really beautiful, and when I go home she's going to make me beautiful too. She's going to show me how to do make-up. Kate is twenty-nine and she's really beautiful too. She has long red hair down to here.' Jessie measured on her upper arm. 'Her hair is all wavy and she looks like a warrior princess. Like Boudicca. She's learning catering at college so that she can work in a hotel. A posh hotel. The kind that gives everyone chocolates on their bed at night. And she's going to bring me some.'

'That sounds interesting,' I said, trying to keep scepticism out of my voice.

'My dad works at a garage. And my mum works at Poundland. And guess what? At night when she comes home, she brings boxes of Jaffa Cakes. Whenever there's any broken boxes where the biscuits got ruined or something, my mum can bring them home for us.'

'That would be nice. But you know, that not quite what I heard about your family.'

'I thought you said you didn't know very much. So I'm telling you stuff you didn't know.'

'I think you might be telling me stuff *they* don't know either,' I said, and grinned.

Jessie broke into silly laughter.

'So why don't you tell me about your real family?'

'I am.'

'*I* think you're telling me porkies.'

Jessie started to laugh so uproariously that I thought she'd fall off her chair.

'Mrs Thomas told me your dad was named Gwyl and he worked at the car factory.'

'No, he's not my dad. He's my mum's second husband. My real dad is called Selwyn and he works at the garage. The big one, near the roundabout. He does important stuff there, like fix the wheels on lorries going to Ireland. They break down and my dad drives this big truck out to them and fixes them and it's *dangerous*, because he has to do it right on the road. And my mum works at Poundland and brings me as many Jaffa Cakes as I can eat, when I'm at home.'

'And I'm going to go home next month,' Jessie added.

I was quite certain almost none of what Jessie had told me was true, but I was beginning to feel a bit lost – there were so many quick twists and turns in her tales. All I could think to do was get her back onto ground I knew.

'Is Gemma still at home?' I asked.

'Gemma?' Jessie replied. 'Who's Gemma?'

'Your sister. I thought you had three sisters. I understood that Gemma was still in school.'

'Where did you get that idea?' Jessie asked in an incredulous tone.

'That's what's in your notes, Jessie.'

'Then why are you asking me?'

My shoulders dropped in frustration.

'Ohhh,' she said with a sudden tone of recognition. 'Oh, I know what you mean now. *That* Gemma. She's not my sister. She's my stepsister. She's Gwyl's daughter.'

'But your mum is her mum? Yes?'

'No. Gemma's my stepsister. My ugly stepsister. She has a mole right here,' Jessie said, and pointed to her chin, 'just like the stepsister in Cinderella. You've got a mole. Right there on your neck.' She pointed to my neck. 'You ought to get it removed.'

'Thank you, but I'm okay with it.'

'You shouldn't be. It makes you look like an ugly stepsister. I could drill it out for you. I could take a pencil like this and just poke it out.' And before I was able to respond, Jessie had snatched up a pencil that had been lying on the table and pressed the point into the mole on my neck. She did it very gently, such that it did not hurt, but this didn't distract me from the fact I had a sharp, pointed object just over my jugular vein.

'Would you take that down, please?' I said quietly. 'We don't stick people with pencils.'

'Ah-ah, the Queen speaks again. *We* don't do that, dear. Besides, I'm not sticking you. It's just there, on your mole.'

'Please take it down.'

Lowering the pencil, Jessie smiled beguilingly at me. She was unusually good with eye contact and didn't seem the least bit phased by a direct gaze. Inclining her head in a chummy manner, she said, 'I love you.'

Jessie had taken control of this session just as successfully as she had the previous ones. My best-laid plans were to give her the limited choice of the game or drawing, and getting her to sit opposite me, and here we were, Jessie sitting beside me as I tried to talk her out of doing surgery on my neck. What struck me was how creepily charismatic she was. Her eye contact, her delightful smiles, even her tendency to touch or be physically close created a chemistry that was simultaneously charming and unsettling, and made interrupting her to re-orientate the session challenging.

Once Jessie had lowered the pencil from my neck, I quietly removed it from her fingers and lay it again on the table. 'Okay, what would you like to do today? Play checkers? Or draw?'

Jessie reached a hand up to caress the side of my face. Gently, I took her hand down.

'I do love you,' she said.

'Which would you like to do?'

'I'm glad you're coming to work with me. You're just the person to get the devil out of me.'

As considerately as I could, I lifted her off my lap and stood up. 'Which would you like to do?' I opened my satchel up.

'Draw,' Jessie said with a tone of boredom, and reached in to take out the felt-tip pens.

I walked around to the opposite side of the table and pulled out the chair to sit down. Jessie picked up the pens and came around to the same side.

'No, I prefer to sit across from you,' I said.

'And I prefer to sit there,' she replied, and plopped into the chair next to me.

Thus it went. Every single thing I did was questioned and countered. Jessie remained agreeable throughout, never getting cross or awkward, but she wasn't going to give an inch. Neither was I. What I found intriguing was Jessie's ability to perceive this. She pushed me right up to the point where my next move would be to impose my will, and then she'd switch to something else. She read my behaviour correctly every time. Which basically meant she stayed in control, even when acquiescing.

Eventually we did get settled and she began to draw. This time there was no scribbling or 'devilish' drawing. Instead, Jessie began one of her intricate skylarks down in the bottom right-hand corner of the paper.

Several minutes passed with no conversation whatsoever. I was glad for this interlude, as it gave me time to collect my thoughts after what had been a tiring session. It also gave me time to observe Jessie.

Elbow on the table, she rested her head on her left forearm as she drew the minute bird. She had chosen pink and green for the bird's feathers and created them with short, delicate strokes.

'What can you tell me about your picture?' I asked as she worked.

'I don't know.'

'Why a skylark?' I asked.

Jessie didn't answer. However, she stopped drawing. She had been colouring in one of the wings with a fuchsia-pink pen and she lifted it up off the paper.

I wasn't sure she would answer. Our conversations had thus far been as much a minefield of control as the rest of our activities. She mostly replied 'I don't know' or other nondescript answers such as 'Maybe' or 'Could be' to any efforts I'd made to draw her out.

This time, however, she said, 'Because it's happy.'

I attempted to reflect the sentence back, saying, 'Skylarks make you feel happy?'

'No, I didn't say that. *It's* happy. The skylark's happy.'

She was still in the same pose, her head resting on her left forearm. The fingers of her left hand twined through her hair. For the first time she did not make eye contact with me. She kept her gaze on the picture.

'You're drawing it because the skylark is a happy bird?'

'No, you're not listening. Because *it's* happy.'

I was confused. Trying to make a better effort at

understanding what she was trying to say, I replied, 'This skylark's happy?'

'*No.*' She sat upright and I saw the tears then. 'No, you don't *get it*!'

'Jessie . . . Jessie, it's not a big deal. It's okay.'

'It's *not* okay. That's what you don't understand. Nobody understands that.' She grabbed up the drawing and crumpled it into a ball. Fiercely, she threw it across the table at me. 'I don't want to be here. I don't want to ever be in here. *I hate you!*'

With that, Jessie leaped to her feet and ran out of the room.

The drawing had hit my shoulder and fallen to the floor, so I bent down and picked it up. Smoothing it out, I lay it on the table and looked at it.

The bird was so delicate. The drawing itself could only have been an inch high and yet all the details were there – the little beak, the beady eyes, individual feathering on the wings. Jessie had been filling in the colours, so it looked a bit lopsided with one wing bright pink and the other still white.

I sat, not quite sure what had happened, not quite sure what to do next. There was almost half an hour left of our allotted time together. Because we were working here in the group home, where Jessie also lived, walking out of sessions unsupervised wouldn't endanger her, so there was no need to go after her. I considered whether or not I should. She might do better cooling down on her own, where she was in control of her time and space, but then again she might use it to get up to mischief. I was also concerned that my not going to find her might be interpreted as not caring what happened to her, but then again she might regard making me go after her as a victory.

Before I could decide the door opened, and there stood Joseph with a tearful Jessie just in front of him. 'I think this young lady is supposed to be in here now,' he said.

Jessie looked ready to sob.

'Do you want to be in here now?' I asked. 'It's okay if you say no. You may choose to go in the TV room, if you prefer, and I will leave. But it's also okay if you want to come back in.'

Jessie regarded me for a long moment, her lips pressed tightly together.

Joseph nudged her. 'But it isn't okay just to stand here in the doorway, not making a decision,' he said. 'Decide right now or I will decide for you.'

'I'll come back in,' Jessie said. Without prompting, she crossed over to sit down on the opposite side of the table from me.

Joseph left, closing the door behind him.

Jessie seemed entirely deflated. Sighing, she leaned forward almost to the point where her face was on the table.

We sat several moments in silence.

'I can see you have strong feelings just now. I want to understand what happened. Can you describe how you are feeling?'

'Like I want to kill myself.'

'That's a very strong feeling. Can you tell me more about it?'

She shook her head. 'I don't know.'

'Would you like me to try and help you feel better?' I asked. She nodded. 'Yes.'

'Let's start by sitting up like this.' I straightened up. 'Then do what I do: take in a deep breath. In, like this . . .' I demonstrated, drawing in a long, slow breath. 'Hold it and count to five . . . and then let it out in one big puff, like you are saying the word "Hah".' I did it again to demonstrate.

Jessie sat up straight. The third time I did it, she joined me.

'Again. In, hold, and, Hah!'

The noise almost made her smile.

'That feels good, doesn't it? One more time, but this time imagine when you take the deep breath that you are drawing in nice clean air, and when you say Hah you are shooting all the bad air out of your body.'

Jessie repeated the deep breath.

'Now let your head relax. Let it flop a little bit forward as you relax the muscles in your neck.'

Jessie took me literally and flopped way forward until her head was on the table again. I didn't say anything about it, but instead just carried on. 'See if you can focus your attention on the top of your head. Try to bring your mind right there at the tippy-top of your head, to your hair. Can you feel your hair lying on the top of your head?'

'I can,' Jessie said.

'Good job. And now I'm going to ask you some questions. Just think the answers to yourself. Ready?'

Jessie nodded.

'So you are right at the top of your head. How does it feel

there? Can you feel your hair? Can you feel the skin there on the top of your head? Don't say. Just see if you can notice. Can you tell if your skin is hot or cold?'

'I can. It's hot and prickly like it's on fire,' Jessie said.

I didn't correct her for talking out loud again, because it wasn't really important.

'Now, see if you can feel your forehead. Can you focus on the skin there? Just notice it. Don't use words. Just notice if you can be aware the skin on your forehead.'

Part by part, I went down over her body, going from her forehead to her eyes, to temples, to jaw and on down, asking her to notice the sensations she was feeling. When we got all the way through to her feet, I said, 'Now see if you can feel your whole body. Everything together from top to toe.'

'It feels like my skin's crawling,' she said. 'Like I'm inside and crawling under my skin and I can't get out. Like I can't think of any way to stop this feeling unless I peel my skin off.'

'That sounds unpleasant,' I said.

'It is,' she replied. 'When I get too crawly, I take a knife and scrape my skin. I scrape and scrape until it bleeds. Then I cut. I keep cutting until it bleeds.'

I didn't respond immediately and this caused Jessie to lift her head for the first time since I'd started the relaxation exercise. She looked across the table at me. Her expression was unreadable.

'Can you show me where you are cutting?' I asked.

I meant for her just to point, but she immediately got up from her chair and came around to where I was seated. 'I have to take my trousers down,' Jessie said, and she began to unbutton her trousers. 'Nobody knows I do it. Because I do it on my pussy.'

'You're cutting yourself on your pussy?'

She nodded.

I put my hand out over hers to stop her undressing. 'I'm glad you've told me about this, because it's important for grownups to know. But if you need to show me your pussy, I think we ought to have another staff person come in first. Is that okay?'

Jessie stopped. 'No.'

'Enir? Would it be all right if Enir came in?'

'No. I don't want Enir to know.'

'This isn't a good secret to keep, Jessie. If you are cutting yourself, it's important to share it with adults you trust. That way we can help when you have such strong feelings.'

'I don't want Enir to look at my pussy.'

'Okay. That's fine. But I'm not comfortable having you take your trousers down when it's just me here. So, for the moment, let's just talk about the feelings you have when you want to cut yourself, and we'll leave looking at it for another time.'

Dropping her hands away from her waistband, Jessie looked at me. That devilish spark was gone from her expression. Her eyes were sad. 'Can I sit on your lap?' she asked meekly.

'Why don't you sit on the chair here beside me and I'll put my arm around your shoulder. How's that?'

She shrugged. 'I guess. Whatever.'

*

As soon as I got home, I phoned Meleri to discuss the session. I was unaware of anything in Jessie's notes about self-harm, but I was increasingly concerned about sexual abuse. There was a solicitous undercurrent to Jessie's touchy-feely behaviour that implied knowledge beyond her years. I hadn't said anything previously to Meleri about it because I didn't want to over-interpret. It was possible Jessie's stroking and touching were part of an elaborate manipulative routine and there was nothing sexual intended, so I had hoped to spend more time observing before saying anything. However, the session that afternoon had forced my hand.

I told Meleri how Jessie's physical contact felt to me as if it had a sexual overtone, and she acknowledged that, yes, other staff had also felt uncomfortable with this behaviour. There had been three incidents where Jessie had touched Joseph's genital area. The first time Joseph said it may have been accidental. Several of the kids were fooling around, running back and forth in the games room, and Jessie had run into him, so she may not have meant her hand to go there. However, the other two times happened when she had been sitting next to him on the sofa in the TV room, and on both occasions she had knowingly put her hand on his trousers.

I asked about Jessie's behaviour with other children. Had there been any sexualized incidents? I was concerned that, as Jessie was the youngest child in the group home, she was more vulnerable to sexual predation by the older kids. If she was being flirtatious with them, this would compound the risk.

To Meleri's knowledge, there had been no sexually inappropriate behaviour among the children. Jessie had a difficult relationship with the girl who was closest in age to her, an eleven-year-old named Melanie, but it had all involved what Meleri called 'pre-teen girl stuff' – who was friends with whom and who was giving whom the silent treatment. The only other problem Meleri was aware of was some persistent name calling. In her early days at the home, Jessie had been fierce and stand-offish. Some of the older children nicknamed her '*Gath puss*', which was hybridized Welsh-English for 'Kitty', because they found her 'scratchy'. Meleri said that was the kids' official explanation, but it was probably more because 'puss' easily became 'pussy' and, given a Welsh pronunciation, it sounded like 'piss'. Needless to say, the staff discouraged this nickname, but Meleri said it persisted, in spite of their efforts.

I asked about self-harm. Meleri was not aware of Jessie cutting herself, but several of the children at the group home did self-harm. It was a serious problem that they had to deal with on a regular basis, but so far there had been no reports of Jessie doing it.

Then Meleri added, 'It wouldn't surprise me. Jessie will be well aware of other children doing it. She will have seen the attention it brings. Heard kids saying stuff. With all her pent-up anger, I've almost been expecting it.'

That wasn't the reply I'd hoped for, although I knew myself this was both a contagious behaviour and an all-too-typical form of release for youngsters who felt a high level of emotional pressure that they couldn't articulate. However, it seemed unusual that Jessie was choosing her vulva as a place to cut. In my previous experience with the behaviour, kids chose arms or legs, places that were easy to access. One didn't need to be Freud to suspect an association between cutting one's genitals, destructive sexual feelings and abuse.

I asked if there were any notes in Jessie's medical records about damage to her vulva. Had doctors or nurses noted anything unusual? No, was Meleri's answer, but then Jessie hadn't been for a physical exam since she had come to them.

This left me with one question: was she making it up? It was hard to consider that such a young child could be this manipulative, but it wasn't out of the question. Saying she was mutilating her genitals would have the kind of shock value that was important to Jessie, and it wasn't something we'd be likely to check out right on the spot. On the other hand, this wasn't a comment I could ignore, especially as Jessie had seemed genuinely serious when telling me. So there I was, wondering whether or not I'd been played. Had the devil won this round? Or had a vulnerable little girl shared an important secret with me?

chapter six

I wasn't able to visit Jessie the following week because my young daughter contracted pneumonia and was hospitalized. However, I was able to attend a review meeting, as it was held in the same town as the hospital. Others at the meeting included Meleri, Joseph, Enir and one of the night staff from the children's home, a medical doctor and the Social Services child psychologist, Ben Stone.

One of the first topics was Jessie's self-harming behaviour. She had had a medical examination since I'd seen her, but the doctor found no evidence of cutting around her genital area. The general consensus was that Jessie had lied to me about self-harming there. However, old, well-healed scars on both her legs above the knees indicated that she may have engaged in self-harm at some point. The doctor asked Jessie about this, as had Ben Stone at a later point, but on both occasions she had denied self-harm and said the scars were old injuries she had acquired at home because she often climbed through a barbed wire fence to reach a place she liked to play. Both professionals believed this explanation to be untrue, but they were not surprised by the denial. The examination and questions had left Jessie feeling vulnerable, and this increased her need for control, and by default her lying and manipulation increased. So nothing was conclusive. However, because the scars were old, the professionals felt this was not a particular threat to her stability at the moment.

I asked about sexual abuse, saying that Jessie's telling me she wanted to hurt her genitals when she was angry and upset struck me as a coded message, and even more so now that it had turned out that she wasn't actually cutting herself there.

One of the other social workers disagreed, saying that this was the nature of Jessie's mental health issues. Manipulation expert that she was, Jessie homed in on whatever she believed would be most shocking to you and thus get the biggest rise. He said she had shown this pattern again and again, and it was quite typical that she'd choose something like this with me, because I was new. 'Don't be fooled by her age; this kid is as streetwise as they come,' he warned. 'And never, ever assume Jessie is telling the truth.'

I was annoyed by his analysis. While I was new to Jessie, I was not new to children with Jessie's kinds of behavioural problems. I quite probably had as much first-hand experience as the social worker. More to the point, I suspected his comments were less about Jessie and more about territorial marking. In my capacity as a volunteer from the charity sector, I was well down the hierarchy of the people there, regardless of my experience. His comments were made to ensure I knew my place in the meeting.

I was also annoyed on Jessie's behalf. Whether or not she was trying to manipulate me, that was a grim thing for a nine-year-old to say. Even if it were entirely false, the internal distress and confusion that would prompt her to say such shocking things deserved to be taken seriously.

The conversation moved on from that point and never returned to the topic of sexual abuse. Instead, they talked first about Jessie's parents and the likelihood of getting Jessie home. Everyone agreed that this was still a long way off, for a variety of reasons, and so the conversation turned to foster placement. We all wanted this, but, unfortunately, because of Jessie's difficult behaviours she would require a therapeutic foster home, where the parents had special training in dealing with children with her issues, and there were no places available. A person whose role I did not know raised the possibility of placing her in an ordinary foster home and providing weekly therapy. Meleri reminded her that an ordinary foster home hadn't worked out previously, and the woman emphasized that she meant with therapy. That led to the inevitable discussion of lack of resources, of whether or not the local authority would be able to afford counselling for Jessie, of whether or not there were NHS services nearby and how much of a waiting list there would be. The meeting ended with the acknowledgement that we were probably doing the best we could in the circumstances, but, as in all these cases, our best was not enough.

*

When I next returned to the group home, Jessie didn't want to see me. Joseph coerced her, telling her that he would not let her join the others on a trip to the ice-skating rink later in the day unless she saw me. She stomped past him while he was explaining this situation to me and went into our room.

'You're looking angry,' I said to her, once Joseph had left.

'He didn't have to say that to you. I was going to come. He didn't have to tell you I wasn't.'

'No, you weren't going to come,' I said, 'so he was explaining that. It's usual to tell people if you are not going someplace you're supposed to, and that's what Joseph was doing.'

'You didn't tell me.'

'Didn't tell you what?' I asked.

'That you weren't going to come last week. You didn't tell me. And you didn't come at all,' she said peevishly.

'My little girl was ill. Did the staff not tell you? They were supposed to. I'm sorry, if that didn't happen.'

'No. They didn't tell me.'

I regarded her. My guess was that they had, because I had no reason to think this message wouldn't have been passed on. Whether Jessie was lying or whether she had just forgot, I didn't know. Whichever way, she was aggrieved and stared back at me with that characteristic unflinching glare, green eyes practically aglow.

'Well, I *am* sorry,' I said. 'I know it's disappointing if something doesn't happen when you are counting on it.'

'I wasn't disappointed,' she muttered, 'and I wasn't counting on it. Why do you say that? I don't want to be here anyway.

I never want to be here. I'd rather be in the day room any time. I *liked* not having to come here last week.'

I smiled. 'Yes, well, I'm still sorry.'

She shrugged. 'Whatever.'

Jessie took a seat and I sat down opposite. I set my satchel between us and opened it.

'What's this for?' Jessie asked, and reached into the case. She lifted out a strip of plastic with the numbers zero to ten written on it in permanent marker. 'What do you do with this?'

'That's my measuring stick.'

'It's not a stick. It's a piece of plastic. And it can't measure anything, because it's home-made. You made this. The numbers aren't even evenly spaced. And they aren't centimetres. They're just numbers. So you can't measure anything.'

'It measures happiness.'

'That's stupid,' she said and dropped the plastic strip abruptly, as if it were contaminated.

'I'll show you how it works.' I opened the small tin that held the draught pieces and took out one black and one red one. I shoved the red one across to her.

'I don't want to know how it works. It's stupid. Let's do something else.'

Smoothing out the strip on the table top, I said, 'Okay, so, see the zero? It means "not at all", "zilch", "horrible, horrible, horrible". Zero is the bad end. Ten is the good end. Ten means "yes, a lot", "wonderful, wonderful, wonderful". So, I'll show you how it works. I'm going to measure how much happiness there is in chocolate. Do you like chocolate?'

'I'm not going to play. I told you that. Why don't you ever listen to me?'

'That's all right. The good thing about this game is that I can play by myself. "How much do *I* like chocolate?"' Taking up the black draught piece, I set it on the number eight. 'I like chocolate, but it's not my favourite thing, so I'm going to give it an eight.'

'That's stupid,' Jessie said. 'Chocolate should be ten. Everybody knows that.'

'So you would put your marker on the ten,' I replied and pulled over the red draught piece and set it on the ten. 'What about Brussels sprouts? I'm going to give Brussels sprouts a six, because I quite like Brussels sprouts, but not as much as I like some other vegetables.' I moved my piece to the six.

'*Six?*' Jessie cried in outrage. 'How can you say Brussels sprouts are a six? They are a zero. Definitely a zero. They shouldn't even exist.'

I moved the red piece down to zero, then I pushed the black piece down too. 'You know what I think shouldn't exist? Traffic jams. I hate being stuck in traffic. That's zero happiness for me.'

Sucked into the game, Jessie began evaluating various kinds of food – chips, ice cream, steak pie, mushy peas, lasagne – and she insisted on moving my piece for me, trying to guess what I would rate them. I have broad tastes and genuinely like most food. This seemed to annoy Jessie.

'You can't give mushy peas a seven. Mushy peas are, like, the worst food in the world. *Mushy* peas. That says it all.' She made a gagging sound.

'You think they are horrible, but I don't. Foods taste differently to different people, so on my tongue, they taste nice.'

'But you've given them a *seven*. That's one below chocolate. That can't be.'

'See if you can put yourself in my shoes. See if you can imagine what it must be like to enjoy mushy peas with fish and chips.'

'I *can't*. Nobody can like something mushy yucky like poo. Poo tasting.'

'Just let go of *you* for a minute. Here, sit down,' I said, because in her enthusiasm she had risen up out of her chair to lean across the table. 'I'm going to do something. I want you to close your eyes. We're going to have a little adventure.'

For once, Jessie actually did as I asked, so I reached across the table and took both her hands, like a palm reader. 'First, you've got to relax your mind, because you're going to do something special.'

I could feel Jessie's hands quivering beneath my fingers.

'I want you to feel yourself going down to your hands. Can you do that? Put your attention on your hands. Imagine yourself running down out of your head and into your fingers.'

Jessie kept her eyes closed tight.

'Now, imagine letting yourself run into my hands. Your attention is down in your fingertips. Now run across to my fingertips, to my hands where we're touching. Run your attention up through my arms into my head. You are going to imagine you are me. Okay? Can you do that? Can you let yourself run up into my head so that now you are looking out of my eyes? You're sat across the table from Jessie. Can you see her?'

She nodded slightly.

'You're Torey and you're sat across from Jessie and, suddenly, here comes a nice tray of fish and chips from the chip shop. It's all steamy-hot and smells wonderful, because you're really hungry. There's fish and chips for both of you. Jessie gets hers. Can you see it? A nice piece of fish and lots of chips sitting in one of those nice little cardboard trays from Jones-the-Fish's chippy. That's Jessie's fish and chips. Can you make that image in your mind? But you're still sitting across from Jessie. Can you see Jessie looking down at her fish and chips? Can you see her happy face as she thinks about eating that nice food?'

Eyes still closed, she nodded.

'You're Torey. Seeing things from Torey's point of view, and here comes your fish and chips. A nice piece of fish and plenty of chips in the nice cardboard tray and there in the corner is a little white pot of mushy peas to put over the chips. Mmm! You like that! It looks really good to you. You have a happy face too, because you can't wait to eat your nice fish, chips and mushy peas. Jessie doesn't have any, because she's getting her fish and chips just the way she likes them. But you have some, because you're getting fish and chips just the way you like them. Both of you are feeling happy. Both of you are feeling happiness way up at ten, because of your lunch.'

Jessie's eyes popped open. 'Now you've made me hungry!'

'Yes, I've made me hungry too.'

'Can we go get fish and chips together?' she asked.

'Wouldn't that be nice?'

'*Could* we? Maybe sometime?' Jessie suggested. 'Could maybe you take me out and we could go to Jones-the-Fish's and get them for real?'

'That *would* be nice, wouldn't it? Maybe we can sometime.'

She smiled sweetly at me.

'Were you able to feel what I was talking about?' I asked. 'Were you able to get inside my point of view so that the mushy peas looked a little bit good to you?'

Jessie paused thoughtfully. For several moments, she considered. Then she nodded faintly. 'Sort of. I think it was maybe because I knew *I* wasn't going to have to eat them. I think when it was just about being you and nobody was going to make *me* do it, I could sort of believe maybe they were nice. To you, at least.'

'Good. That's exactly what we were trying to do. See how it feels to be someone else.'

Jessie fell silent. She looked at the table a moment, then lifted her eyes slightly to regard the plastic strip with its numbers. She moved her draught piece along to the ten. Then she moved mine up there as well. The silence continued, as she regarded them.

'That's sort of what I'm doing with the skylark,' she said quietly. 'You asked me that the other time and I couldn't explain. But it's sort of this. Sort of like the skylark's a ten, and I'm trying to see what it's like to be happy. Because the skylark's happy. And when I draw it, it's sort of like I can understand how it feels.'

'I see,' I said.

Silence followed. Then Jessie looked up at me. She put her hand on her chest a moment and said, 'My heart's beating really fast. Like I've been running.'

I nodded. 'Sometimes when we think about certain things, it gives us lots of feelings and that revs our body up and makes our heart go fast.'

She nodded. There was a pause, and she looked down at the plastic strip again. 'My mum couldn't play this game.'

'Why's that?'

'Because nothing is a ten for her. Nothing is even a five.'

'Mrs Thomas told me that your mum has depression.'

Jessie nodded. 'Sometimes she locked herself in her bedroom. When she was having days like that and I was little, I had to stay in my bedroom all the time my sister was at school. Mummy locked the door. I couldn't even come out to go to the toilet. Mummy gave me my potty and I had to use that, because she didn't want me around. Then she would go in her bedroom and lie down and look at the wall.'

'That must have been hard for you.'

'That's how I learned to draw, because there wasn't anything else to do. I was too little to read. I only had two books anyway and I knew what they said without even looking at the pictures. So I drew my own pictures. On paper I took out of the rubbish. I drew so I could be the skylark.'

chapter seven

Meleri and I entered that zone halfway between being colleagues and being friends. I didn't know that much about her
personal life. I'd never met her husband and she had never
met mine; we'd never been to each other's homes. However,
sharing the intensity that inevitably came from working with
difficult situations and challenging people brought us a sense
of closeness and comradeship.

Meleri was a 'Marmite' character. You either loved her or
you hated her. There was no in-between. Everything she said
was in a loud, cheerful, emphatic voice as if she were speaking
to a slightly deaf three-year-old. She flung her hands exuber-
antly around while talking and gave a crazed kookaburra
cackle whenever something amused her. And the clothes she
wore . . . bold, figure hugging and unfeasibly glamorous, she
dressed as if she expected television cameras to turn up at any
moment. The kids adored her for these eccentricities, because
life was just a little more vivid when Meleri was around, but
adults, not so much. She was a bit too Tigger-ish for many. You
expected her to bounce at any moment.

I did love her, however, not only for being the genuine character she was, but also for her passion for her field. Social work is a hard calling, chronically underfunded, understaffed and underpaid, and yet every day social workers must deal with life-changing decisions and situations. Meleri adored what she did, every difficult minute of it, and she was committed to it. I admired that.

Nonetheless, I was increasingly sensing a tiredness. The problem for enthusiastic people is that it's easy for others to keep passing more and more their way because it is clear they enjoy what they do, and they don't say no. This certainly seemed to be the case with Meleri. I knew from other conversations that she often spent weekends chasing up clients she couldn't otherwise reach or trying to arrange case meetings at far-flung corners of our very rural county. Evenings passed writing up notes.

So I invited Meleri out for lunch, not as a case meeting, but just for a break. I chose a little cafe down on the seafront that had tables outside where you could sit and enjoy the breeze coming in off the water.

Meleri was bursting with contagious energy when she arrived. She'd passed a little gift shop on the way to the cafe, and seeing a bowl in the window that she thought would be perfect for her nephew's wedding, she had bought it. Taking it from the bag, she showed it to me. The bowl was huge – at least twenty-four inches in diameter – with a gaudy green-and-yellow South American style design. It was made from a lightweight material, possibly paper mache rather than ceramic, so was only meant to be decorative. It wasn't at all to my taste, but it was very Meleri. She was absolutely delighted with it, thinking it such a beautiful piece of work and wondering if she should go back and get one for herself.

We ordered. Meleri said how nice the cafe was, how pleasant the weather, how wonderful to get away from work for an hour. She expressed pleasure in the bowl again and had to pause and take it out of the bag once more to admire it. With this, she said how special her nephew was to her because she and her husband didn't have children of their own. I recalled her mentioning infertility issues once in passing, but we'd never gone into it. Meleri remarked again on how nice the cafe was. Finally, she took a breath.

I looked out to the sea. On rare days you could see the Isle of Man. Or rather, you couldn't. It was distant enough from our shoreline that the curvature of the earth put it below the horizon; however, complex atmospheric conditions occasionally caused a mirage of it to be visible from our shore. This type of mirage is called a 'Fata Morgana' after the fairy Morgana in Arthurian legend, and it occurs quite commonly on this particular horizon.

I'm not sure quite why this came to my mind just then, in the quiet interlude in our conversation, but thinking on this mirage of the Isle of Man caused me to remember the old fairy tales of mysterious islands that appeared out of the mist and then disappeared, the islands no sailor could find. I could imagine them setting sail to explore a distant shore, only to have it disappear as they approached. Except, in this case, there actually was a real island, just not where they expected it to be.

These meandering thoughts brought Jessie to mind, because her lies were rather like this, mirages of real things, true but not true. Not true, but true. I hadn't meant this lunch to be about work, but suddenly it was.

I said to Meleri, 'Jessie told me that her mother was depressed and stayed in bed all day long. She said her mother often locked her in her bedroom for long periods of time. Is that true? Or is it one of Jessie's stories?'

'I don't know,' Meleri replied. 'Her parents say that she was only locked in as a precaution because of the fire setting. Jessie went off the at-risk register at eighteen months, and so we weren't following the family. She'd only been on it because of the hospitalizations when she was a baby.'

'Yes, about that . . .' I said. 'Why was she put on the register to start with? It seems a bit of an over-the-top reaction, to be honest. Why was that done?'

'The Prozac.'

Perplexed, I lifted a questioning eyebrow.

'Diane felt Jessie was too fussy and reactive and should have been calmer. So Diane gave her Prozac. The pills had been prescribed for Diane herself, but it turns out she was crushing them up and putting them into Jessie's milk.'

I went wide-eyed. *'Prozac?'*

'She honestly thought she was doing the right thing,' Meleri replied, 'that she was doing what a doctor would suggest, if Jessie were brought in.'

'Oh, *come on*. No one would think it was appropriate to give a baby antidepressants. Geez, it's amazing she didn't kill her. *Antidepressants?*'

Meleri gave a slight weary movement of her shoulders. 'The baby was crying. Mum wanted peace and quiet. Who knows? I mean, a crying baby, if it's crying long enough . . . if she couldn't cope . . . Better than knocking the child about, I suppose.'

'I disagree. That's just a different kind of abuse,' I replied.

'I'm not condoning it. I'm just saying. And it may have been ignorance more than anything else. She never tried to hide the fact she was doing it. She told the nurse in the hospital, when Jessie was taken in.

'Of course, the minute they found out, the doctors explained in no uncertain terms that this prescription was meant only for her, and it was dangerous to give to a baby. Jessie improved quickly after that.'

I paused to eat my sandwich.

'Which is a long way round to saying Jessie may not have been making up what she told you,' Meleri said. 'Her mother may have been staying in bed all day. There seem to be broader mental health issues with Diane. This is one of the reasons given for why they want to keep Jessie in care. Gwyl says Diane doesn't have the energy to follow through on the kind of therapeutic programme Jessie would need, and he has enough on his hands coping with Diane. Apparently she doesn't go out very often. He does the shopping and errands and things.'

'Isn't the older daughter still at home? Does she help with the mother?'

'You mean Gemma?' Meleri asked. 'She's been living at her boyfriend's house. She was taking a catering course at the college, but got kicked off it not long ago because she wasn't attending. Gemma's got issues of her own.'

I looked down at the remains of my lunch. The sandwich had come with what was euphemistically referred to as a salad – a single limp lettuce leaf, a slice of tomato and two slices of cucumber. I picked up the lettuce and ate it.

Silence came over us, the sort that comes at the end of a conversation to signal that more than the topic is finished. Lunchtime was almost over. Meleri started rooting through her handbag for money and car keys.

I looked out to sea again, out to where I'd once seen the Isle of Man, and thought not of islands but of happy families and how they too were often no more than Fata Morganas.

chapter eight

From our conversation over lunch, I found out that Jessie's parents almost never visited, and as a consequence they seldom took her on days out from the children's home, so I thought I would. I wanted to tie it in with what we were doing together. During our previous session, Jessie had shown me that while it was hard for her to see things from another point of view, she was actually capable of this important skill and willing to try it; so I thought a lovely way to reinforce that lesson would be to take her out for fish and chips. We decided to go on Saturday lunchtime, and my plan was to go to a little chippy on the main road that ran along the coast. It was only a few miles from Glan Morfa, and nearby there was access to a large beach that was never very busy because it was pebbly instead of sandy. We could eat our fish and chips on the nearby picnic tables and then play in the surf a while afterwards.

When I arrived at Glan Morfa that Saturday, Joseph met me at the front desk to say Jessie could not come. She had been found with matches and, when asked where the matches had come from, Jessie had lied, saying one of the older children had stolen them from the local shop and then planted them in her room to get her into trouble. This, Joseph explained, had been easy to prove untrue, because the child Jessie had accused did not have shop privileges. Joseph said that while they still didn't have the full story, most likely Jessie had stolen the matches when the children had been at the bowling alley the previous evening.

I was disappointed by this turn of events, and I was aware that Jessie would be absolutely gutted. Knowing how excited she had been about the outing, I wondered if this were self-sabotage, that anxiety had caused her to respond to the anticipated treat by getting into trouble, so I didn't want to leave without seeing her. I wanted her to know that while I was sorry things hadn't turned out, it didn't damage anything. I was okay and our relationship was okay, and one day it would happen.

In the playroom, in a far corner by herself, Jessie was sitting scrunched down in one of the big grey chairs. When she saw me approach she didn't bother to straighten up. Only her eyes moved towards me.

I sat down on the arm of an adjacent chair. 'I understand things went wrong and we can't go out today.'

'It is *so* unfair,' Jessie replied crossly. 'I got blamed for something I didn't do. I didn't do it. *Honest*. Cross my heart. But no one ever believes me. Joseph, worst of all. I *hate* him. I hate Joseph so much. I'm going to kill him someday.'

'I can tell you are feeling very angry.'

'No kidding. I'm not joking. I'm going to get a knife and slash his face. And I *will*.' She made a half-hearted slice through the air with one hand.

'You're feeling really furious towards Joseph.'

'He said I took the matches and I *didn't*. I didn't. Really, honestly, Torey, I *didn't*. I didn't even know they were there until he lifted up my stuff. But Joseph blames me for everything. I hate him so much. He never listens to me. Not even one little bit. He just blames me for everything straightaway.'

'You do understand, don't you, that you aren't supposed to have matches at any time,' I said quietly.

'I *didn't* have matches. I *didn't* take them. I *didn't* put them there.' Angry tears filled her eyes. '*You* don't believe me either! Nobody does. I wish I could kill you all. Because I would. I really would. I wish I had a gun. A machine gun with a million bullets in it. I'd go ba-a-a-mmm.' She gunned around the room with her index finger, ending at me.

'Come here,' I said, and reached out my arm.

'I hate you.'

'Yeah, I know. Come here anyway.'

Reluctantly, she rose from the chair and came to where I was perched. I put my arm around her and Jessie fell heavily against me.

'Nobody believes me,' she said tearfully, 'but it *wasn't* me. One of the other kids did it to get me into trouble. And now I can't go out with you. And I wanted to so much.'

'That's very sad. I'm sorry too that we can't go out today. I was looking forward to it, just like you. It feels very disappointing, doesn't it?'

She nodded and began to sob.

'But there will be another time. We will get to go have fish and chips together.'

Abruptly, I jerked back. 'Jessie . . . ?'

My surprise came because she had, without any warning, slid her hand between my legs. I was still on the arm of the chair, my legs together, and had been holding her against my right side. As I was comforting her, she had first put her hand on my right leg, and I hadn't thought anything of it, but then she unexpectedly slid it down. She wasn't touching my genital area, but her hand was very near.

'That's not the right place to be touching,' I said, and gently lifted her hand away.

This made Jessie start to cry again. 'See? You hate me too.'

Being touched so inappropriately had knocked my concentration from our conversation. I didn't know what to think about what had just happened nor what the best response was. And now, I didn't know if she was crying about the stolen matches or about my reaction to her hand. How aware had she been of her hand slipping between my legs? Could it have been simply an accident? That's what I hoped, what I wanted, but it was not at all what I suspected. This made me reluctant to hug her more closely now, because I worried it would send a mixed message, that I had said no, but really didn't mind it. But I didn't want to appear rejecting either. The truth was, in that moment, I didn't know what to do.

'I'm sorry you feel you aren't listened to,' I said at last. 'I care very much about how you feel.'

'Then why won't you believe me when I tell you I didn't take the matches? Because I *didn't*. I'm trying hard to be good. I just want to get out of this ratty place.'

On my way out I stopped to talk to Joseph again. I didn't mention the incident with Jessie's hand going the wrong place, because I still wasn't quite sure what to make of it. A part of me continued to hope it was accidental, that the way she was standing beside me meant that natural movement could have got her hand inadvertently between my legs. Another part of me thought, no, that wasn't possible, nor was it the only time I'd had an icky feeling about where Jessie was touching me. I needed more time with this before mentioning it to staff, because it was a serious allegation, if true. I was more interested in talking to Joseph about the matches incident, because Jessie did seem so genuinely aggrieved.

Joseph had no sympathy for Jessie's position whatsoever. 'This is how this girl operates. She will play you like a violin, and the more sympathetic and understanding you try to be, the more intently she will play you. Every word is a lie. She took those matches.'

'Can you be certain of that?' I asked.

'Yes, I can. There were smokers using the lane right next to us last night and they repeatedly laid down their fags and matches on the scoring desk. I asked them twice not to.'

'But you didn't see Jessie take them?' I asked.

'No, I didn't see her, but she took them. Nicking matches off bystanders when we're out is Jessie's speciality.'

I paused, and Joseph accurately read the doubt in my hesitation. He said, 'Not to accuse you of being naive, Torey, but I'm not exaggerating. This is how Jessie operates. She's without conscience when it comes to lying, and because of it she's more convincing than you'd ever imagine. She's so little, she's so pretty, she's so sweet, and she's so able to look you straight in the eye and tell you whatever shit she thinks you want to hear. And *that's* her real skill. She's absolutely ace at homing in on your weaknesses, on what you are most likely to fall for, and that will be her story. Jessie knows exactly how to play people, and she does it continually. She will play you off against me. She will play you off against Meleri. She will simply play you. It's crucial that you don't get lulled into thinking you'll be able to spot it so it won't happen to you.'

'But what if she *didn't* take the matches, Joseph? By your own admission, you didn't see her take them, so you can't say absolutely that she did. What if she's right? What if this one time one of the other kids *did* plant them? They were there too. I'm sure any number of them are just as capable of taking the matches as she is, probably the cigarettes as well. Those would be good currency here. So who's to say one of them didn't plant them, maybe to get back at Jessie, maybe just to get rid of the evidence? What defence would Jessie have against that?'

'None, probably,' Joseph admitted. 'But it *was* Jessie. I may not have seen it happen, but I'm absolutely certain it did.'

I left feeling frustrated and unsettled. Over the years I had had plenty of experience with children like Jessie, for whom the truth was always fluid. Children who lied to stay out of trouble, children who lied to manipulate, children who lied simply for the sake of it in situations where it seemed to have no purpose. I was willing to accept the likelihood Jessie was lying to me about many things, because this was characteristic of her issues. On the other hand, as with the boy who cried wolf, how do we then tell when a liar is telling the truth? Given the inevitable struggle for hierarchy among the children at the group home, who was to say that another child, knowing Jessie's background, didn't think this would be the perfect way to bully her or get back at her for some previous slight? How would she convey her situation to the staff, to the people who were supposed to protect her, if they automatically assumed that everything she said was untrue?

The whole way home I pondered how to deal with this catch-22 situation.

chapter nine

'You know what I want to do today?' Jessie said, as she came into the room. 'I want to play your game.'

'Which game is that?' I asked.

She already had my satchel pulled over and was undoing the buckle. 'This one.' She lifted out the plastic strip with the numbers on it. Then she grabbed the tin holding the cloth bag with the draught pieces.

Laying the strip on the table she hovered over it. 'I'm going to put how I feel about everyone.' She opened up the bag holding the small round draught pieces. Taking a handful out, she started quickly distributing them along the strip. 'Enir. She's a three. Mrs Thomas. She's a three too. Mrs Caldwell who does the cooking, she's a six, because she's nice. Melanie, who has the room across from me, she's a seven, because she's my best friend. Joseph. He's a one. I hate Joseph. If there was a zero, he'd be a zero. Ffion, the new girl, gets a two because she keeps talking about her stupid cat. I'm fed up hearing about that cat.'

'You've got definite feelings about everyone today.'

'Yes, and you. You're maybe a five, because mostly you're not here. You're not too bad, but sometimes you piss me off.'

'What about your family?' I asked. 'Where would you put your family members on the scale? Where would your mum be?'

This question caught Jessie off guard. She looked at me blankly, then looked at the plastic strip, now mostly covered with draught pieces.

She took another handful of draught pieces from the bag and said in a cautious-sounding voice, 'My family are up there.' She indicated the higher numbers on the strip. 'Maybe, like, they're eights. Maybe, like, my mum's a nine.'

'You sound uncertain.'

She didn't respond immediately. There was only a heart-beat of a pause, but it was detectable. Jessie looked up. 'You've wrecked this game.'

'How so?'

'I wanted to play it my way, so that I could put the pieces on the people I was thinking about. I don't know about my mum and dad. I haven't seen them in a long time. I wasn't thinking about how I feel about them.'

'That's okay, isn't it?' I said. 'It's okay not to know how we feel about someone. It's also okay to feel like someone is a nine one day and a one on another day, because our feelings change. Perhaps something has happened to make us not like that person, maybe they have said or done something to hurt our feelings, and so they are only a low number in our mind. Another day, perhaps we have done something nice together, and so they feel like a high number to us. This makes it hard to place a draught piece on just one number, because feelings change. We feel differently at different times.'

Jessie's hand was still hovering over the upper end of the strip, but she had closed it around the red draught piece she'd been holding. 'Mums and dads should always be a nine. Or a ten. They're your parents, so they should always love you. And you should always love them.'

'You think parents and children should always love each other, no matter what?'

She nodded.

A long pause followed.

Jessie tipped her head and then slowly set the draught piece down on the table, watching her hand as she did so. 'My mum and dad don't want me back. They said that to Mrs Thomas. She has to find a foster home for me.' Reaching out, she slid all the pieces off the plastic strip and put them back in the bag. 'You've ruined this game for me.'

'I'm sorry about that, because I can see you were enjoying it. But let's talk about this a little bit.'

Jessie shook her head. 'No.'

Sitting down in the chair opposite me, she took a piece of paper out of the case and then the felt-tip pens. Selecting the pink pen, she began the now-familiar outline of a little bird.

'What do you remember about living at home?' I asked.

Jessie concentrated on her drawing, letting a long silence follow my words. It was so long, in fact, that I thought she wasn't going to answer.

'My sister used to make me cinnamon toast when she came home from school. She would make toast and butter it and put cinnamon and sugar on it and then put it under the grill until it was bubbling. Then she would cut it into little squares and put it on a plate and give it to me. It was so hot it would burn my mouth.'

'That sounds like a good memory.'

Jessie nodded. 'She did it when our mummy got the screamies. Gemma said we had to be very quiet. She made me cinnamon toast and I could go in her room with her. She cuddled me, if I got scared.'

'How did you feel about that?'

Jessie shrugged. The skylark had taken shape. Jessie took a turquoise pen and gave it wings. The beak was yellow and open.

'What happened when your mother had the "screamies"?'

'Well, like, she screams a lot. She's unhappy because she has the devil in her.'

'How do you mean?'

'Well, like me. Like I've got the devil in me too.'

'How so?'

A song came out of the bird's mouth, signified by tiny black musical notes. They went up the paper, up the edge to the very top. Jessie never answered my question.

The next time I visited, I brought in a group of puppets left from my teaching days. They were a disparate collection: two brown bears, an adorably lifelike sheepdog puppy, a black-

and-white lamb, a wild-eyed hare, a brilliantly hued toucan, a green dragon with leathery wings and gold claws, a monster with a frazzled expression, a unicorn wearing a princess crown, and what I can only describe as a hairy purple ostrich. They were exquisitely detailed puppets, hand-made by a young local artist whom I'd befriended when I lived in Montana, and whose work I tried to support. Most children found the puppets irresistible, because they were so lifelike. They were also quite large, most of them fitting down over the hand so that fingers could power the mouth and, in some cases, ears or other features. All had bodies complete with limbs, and the hairy purple ostrich had flappy wings and legs so long that he stood almost a metre high.

Several people had asked me why I chose to use this motley assortment of unrelated animal puppets in my work instead of human puppets, especially as there were now several good sets of puppets on the market that were specifically designed for therapeutic use, but I found these worked well for me. Children were enchanted by the beauty and detail of these unusual puppets, and by how they slipped onto the hand and right down over the arm to the elbow, which allowed them to be animated in quite realistic ways. The fact that they were not people was, in my experience, a helpful quality. Children seemed more willing to address issues when it didn't feel so close to home. The only real problem I had with them was that if I wanted to bring the whole group they were too big to fit in my satchel, and I had to carry them around inelegantly in a black bin bag.

Black bin bags, however, are not necessarily a bad thing because they stimulate curiosity. Jessie noticed it immediately when she arrived in the therapy room. Her brow furrowed, and in a display of unexpectedly adult-like sarcasm, she said, 'You brought your rubbish with you?'

I grinned. 'No, I have something here I thought would be fun for us.'

'Your rubbish?' The joke was already growing old but I took her persistence with it to indicate Jessie's desire to keep control of the situation when she didn't know what I had in the bag. If it was something good, she could just laugh her comments off as a joke. If it was something horrible, she could confirm disdain, showing me she hadn't been taken in.

I opened the bag and took out the sheepdog puppy. It was the most charming of them all, so realistic that you could position it in your arms in a way that made it very hard at first glance to discern it wasn't a real puppy.

'Ooooh!' Jessie cried in undisguised delight. 'That is *so* cute!'

I had my hand inside the puppy and made its mouth move. 'Arf! Arf!'

'Ooh,' she said again and stroked its face. 'Can I hold it?'

I handed it to her and she put it on her own hand, stroking it with the other hand and making it bark. Leaning forward, I started to pull the other puppets out. Jessie quickly joined me to see what everything was in the bag.

'These are so good,' she said, pulling the toucan onto her

hand and making its beak clack up and down. The toucan bit her on the nose and she laughed.

The unicorn wasn't a hit. 'Look at this stupid one. I expect it poos glitter,' she said dismissively, and lifted its tail. 'It doesn't look nearly as realistic as the others. Probably it's for five-year-olds or something.'

The ostrich, on the other hand, was fascinating to her. '*Look* at this thing!' She put her hand into its head but had to hold her arm up to get the feet to clear the floor. Carefully she lifted its wings up and put them on her shoulders. She stood like that a moment, staring the ostrich in the face. Then, suddenly, she began to pirouette around the small amount of space surrounding the table, clasping the ostrich to her chest. 'Shall we daaaance, la, la, la,' she started to sing as she moved, 'on a bright cloud of music, shall we dance?'

That was a magical moment. Here we were in a small, grim, cramped room, when suddenly everything stopped. The ordinary world dropped away, and a little red-haired girl, singing a song from *The King and I*, swooped across the floor in the arms of a hairy ostrich.

I watched her silently. This was not at all what I'd planned for us to do, and if I ever needed an example of Jessie taking complete control of a session, this was it. Times like these, however, you just don't interfere, because the whole is greater than the sum of its parts. The right thing to do is just sit back and savour the moment.

Jessie knew all the words to the song. She had quite a good voice and sang uninhibitedly as she and the ostrich swirled around the table three or four times. At last, slightly out of breath, she collapsed into the chair beside me. She grinned and said, 'This is just brilliant. This is the best stuff you've ever brought.'

Returning to the bin bag, Jessie peered in and then took out one of the bear puppets. She fitted it on her right hand and made it face her. 'I don't think this one is quite as good as the others,' she said pensively. 'All the others are almost as big as real life, but this one is just ordinary puppet size.' She paused and then added, 'But I suppose you wouldn't want a life-size bear puppet.' That made her laugh. 'You'd have to crawl up its poo hole to make it work!'

She looked into the bag again. 'But look, there's another one just the same.' She put it on her left hand and made the bears face each other.

'Do you think they're cubs?' she asked me. 'Maybe that's why they are small. They are cubs and they lost their mummy bear and they are all alone . . .'

She contemplated this a moment. 'No, I think not. I think they are grown-up bears. A mummy and daddy bear, but you can't tell which is which.'

Jessie made one puppet nod at the other. 'What did you do at work today, dear?'

'Nothing,' the other bear said. 'I went down to the pub instead. I spent all our money in the pub and now you don't get any.'

'You bad bear. Now I'm going to divorce you. I'm going

to run off with the man on TV and do sex with him six times a day.'

'Where are the cubs?' the other bear asked.

'I shut them up in the cupboard. In the *cub*-board. That's where they go. I can't be bothered with cubs. Why? Do you want the cubs?'

'No,' the other bear said. 'No, I never wanted cubs. I just want to work in my garden and go to the pub.'

'I just want to sleep all day,' the mummy bear said. 'Hibernate. I want to hibernate and not do anything, because I'm very, very lazy.'

'Don't do that,' the other bear replied. 'That's how you get cubs. They slip out your vagina. Didn't you know that? When bears are asleep, hibernating, their babies come out their vagina and there they are when the mama bear wakes up in the spring. She's got a bunch of cubs.'

Jessie paused and looked over at me. 'That's true. I saw it on TV once.'

I smiled. 'Kind of true. Bears do give birth in the late winter when they are still in their dens.'

'It happens when you sleep,' Jessie said to the mummy bear puppet. 'You get babies put in your vagina.'

'That bit's not quite true,' I said. 'Bears mate in the summer, so the mama bear is already pregnant when she goes to hibernate. It doesn't happen when they are asleep.'

'It *could*,' Jessie insisted.

'No. The males and the females sleep in separate dens. The female bears are safe when they sleep.'

Jessie regarded me. Very faintly, she shook her head. 'Not everyone is safe. It does sometimes happen when you're asleep. You can get poked in your vagina.'

'Has that happened to you, that someone poked your vagina when you were asleep?'

She shrugged and looked away. 'No, I'm just saying.'

chapter ten

Jessie became obsessed with the puppets. The moment she arrived in the therapy room, she would take each one from the bin bag and lay them side by side on the table.

She particularly liked the puppy, not so much as a puppet but because it looked so lifelike. Several times Jessie told me how she loved dogs, how much she wished the puppy were real, and this intrigued me, because her file showed that tormenting the family dog had been a major problem when she was living at home. This puppet puppy she did appear to adore, and she often brought it special things – a red ribbon to serve as a collar, a little scarf, some bones she had made out of paper. She would set the puppet up in special poses, pet it, cradle it, feed it the pretend bones and then arrange it in a way that looked particularly realistic so that it could watch over us the rest of the session.

I had expected her to take more of an interest in the toucan, because, to my mind at least, it looked very similar to Jessie's skylarks; however, this was not the case. She set it out nicely with the others when removing them all from the bin bag, but otherwise paid it no attention.

Her favourites were the two bears. Despite commenting on several different occasions that they were inferior to the other puppets because they were small, plain and you couldn't tell them apart, these were the ones she kept returning to. She didn't fuss over them as she did the puppy. There was no petting or hair-combing or tying ribbons around their necks, but they were the puppets that always ended up on her hands.

The bears acquired names: Magnus and Eleanor, and most of the time they bickered with each other. Magnus was grumpy and wasteful and liked going to the pub. Eleanor was whiny and lazy. No doubt they represented Jessie's parents to some degree, but I tried not to over-interpret because some of the bears' conversation clearly reflected what was happening in the group home.

Often Jessie held long conversations between the bears that started out silly or trivial and then would take an unexpectedly serious turn.

'Would you just settle down?' Eleanor said. 'You are talk, talk, talking all the time. Every little thing distracts you. You hear a noise and you stop listening to me. You have to go and see what is happening. Go and stick your big nose in business that isn't about you. Would you just settle down?'

'Shut up,' Magnus replied.

'You're going to go in time-out till you get your act together. You're going to have to sit still until you *can* sit still.'

'I'm going to run away,' Magnus replied, and Jessie quickly pulled the puppet out of sight behind her back.

'Come back here,' Eleanor demanded in an exasperated tone. 'You have not "run away". You're just hiding and I know it. Tell the truth. You never tell the truth.'

Magnus remained hidden behind Jessie's back.

'What are you doing back there?' Eleanor asked. 'Do you have matches? Did you find matches? You can't be back there. Come out. Come up here where I can see you.'

Magnus remained hidden behind Jessie's back.

Abruptly, Eleanor, who was on Jessie's right hand, launched an attack on Jessie's left arm. Jessie still had Magnus hidden behind her back, so he couldn't be reached by Eleanor on her right hand, but she made Eleanor go up and down her left arm, biting it angrily.

It was an odd display to witness. Jessie appeared completely absorbed in the dialogue between the two bears, but she was, in essence, attacking her own arm with her own hand.

The puppet became so vicious that I sensed we were on the cusp of self-harm, so I put my hand out to calm the bear. 'Eleanor has some very strong feelings, but I don't want her to hurt your arm,' I said. 'So let's see if we can put how she's feeling into words instead of actions.'

Jessie looked down at the puppet as if it were a new thing that she hadn't realized was there. Keeping my hand on Eleanor, I gently slipped the puppet off her hand. I put it on my own hand. 'Wow. That made me angry,' I said for the bear.

I looked at Jessie. 'I noticed Eleanor got angry when Magnus disappeared. Why do you suppose that was?'

Jessie didn't answer. Her brow furrowed; her expression was blank, as if she had just woken up.

'Where's Magnus?' I asked.

He had remained on Jessie's hand behind her back. Even as I asked, he stayed hidden.

'Magnus doesn't want to come out?' I asked.

Jessie shook her head.

I slipped the Eleanor bear off my hand and laid it on the table with the head facing away from us and the hole where my hand had been facing towards us, making it very clear it was just a puppet.

Jessie regarded it. There continued to be an odd, spacey quality to her behaviour, which made me think she had dissociated during the time Eleanor was attacking her arm, that something about Magnus's hiding or Eleanor's anger had proved too frightening to Jessie. Dissociation is a common coping mechanism, particularly with traumatized children, where, when stressors occur, the brain copes by compartmentalizing what's going on. This keeps the child from feeling too much pain.

'How is Magnus feeling right now?' I asked quietly.

Jessie brought her eyes to meet mine. The pupils widened upon making eye contact. There was no spark of recognition.

'It's all right for Magnus to stay hidden,' I said.

Silence between us.

Jessie dropped eye contact, looked down at the table.

The urge was to press onward, to ask again, to try and move us forward from this spot, but as I sat, what came back to me were memories of my long-ago research with selectively mute children, children who did not speak for psychological reasons. One of the great insights to come out of that work for me was an awareness of silence as a force in its own right. Learning to be comfortable with silence, learning to wait patiently within it and not rush through it or away from it had been one of the harder things for me to learn, and indeed I was still learning it. Sitting here now, the impulse to do something was very strong.

But we sat. I don't know for how long. It felt like ten minutes, but it was probably only five.

I could see Jessie coming back into herself. Her posture changed. Her head moved in a less stilted fashion. She looked up again and met my eyes and this time we connected. Slowly she brought her left hand around from behind her back and laid it, still with the puppet on, on her lap.

'That was a bit scary, wasn't it?' I said softly.

Jessie was looking down at the bear puppet. 'No. He hated her.'

'Was it because Eleanor told him to sit down and pay attention?'

Jessie shook her head slightly. 'Because she wanted to take the matches away.'

'Magnus hated that Eleanor was going to take his matches away?' I repeated to ensure I was understanding what she'd said.

Jessie nodded.

'Why did that make him feel so upset?'

Jessie didn't respond.

The room had grown very still. Normally when there was a pause in what we were doing, I would notice noises beyond the door that spoke of life going on around us in the group home. However, now there was nothing except a silence. I listened into it, trying to discern the distant murmur from the television in the playroom. I could hear nothing.

'He was going to kill her,' Jessie said, her voice soft.

'Magnus?'

She nodded. 'He wants to kill. Kill. *Kill*. Until everyone is dead.'

'Magnus has very strong feelings,' I reflected.

'He hates them.' She looked over at me, not moving her head, only her eyes, to meet mine. 'That's why he's got to be here,' she said quietly. 'Because he's got the devil in him.'

This wasn't the first time Jessie had expressed homicidal feelings. We would be doing something quite innocuous, as we had been here playing with the puppets, and suddenly the conversation would turn violent. She didn't appear angry when she said these things. Her voice was quiet, her manner controlled, which made what she was saying unsettling. I'd dealt many times with upset children screaming that they wanted to kill parents, other children or me, but once the storm passed, once we managed to negotiate other ways of expressing frustration and upset, the death threats were seen for what they were:

desperation rather than authentic threats. Jessie, in contrast, expressed a desire to murder so matter-of-factly that I wasn't sure of the best way to respond. As with children who say such things in the heat of the moment, I suspect here too Jessie was using the topic as a means of expressing something she wasn't otherwise able to articulate, but her detachment made it difficult to guess what that might be and how to help her find a more gratifying way of communicating her feelings with us. Most of the time, I chose just to 'hold' the comment, making it clear I heard her but that she had not frightened me nor appalled me, and resisted the urge to contradict her, because I sensed a power struggle might lie that way. The challenge was to exude a calm strength that implied I was in control of myself and would set the necessary boundaries that would keep control of her, when, truth be said, I was unnerved.

At the end of that week Jessie's Social Services team held a formal assessment of my time with her. I had been seeing Jessie for the better part of three months by this point and I hadn't forgotten the team's goal of placing her in a therapeutic foster home, nor that I was there to aid in assessing Jessie's needs and developing strategies to help her cope with a less restrictive environment.

I told them that three things stood out for me in the time I'd spent with Jessie. The first was her need to control any and all situations. This showed itself most clearly in her refusal to do anything anyone asked her explicitly to do, even if they were things she wanted to do herself. Jessie was cagey in how she went about this. She was not the kind of kid to fly into a rage if things did not go the way she needed them to. Manipulation was more her style. A bright, insightful girl, Jessie knew how to smile and flatter, and she was skilled at bait-and-switch, where she called your attention to something small and innocent, so that you didn't realize she had taken you off track until you ended up someplace entirely different from where you'd started out going. Her particular genius, however, was in lying. Jessie spun tales the way Rumpelstiltskin spun gold – easily and manipulatively. Her lies often came complete with backstory and detailed minutiae, and were always delivered with good eye contact and smiling certainty. And she practised this skill relentlessly. Jessie lied to get others into trouble. She lied to stay out of trouble herself. She lied to get what she wanted. She lied to avoid what she didn't. She lied to make people feel sorry for her. She lied to make herself sound smarter, bigger, more experienced than she was. And much of the time, she just plain lied. She lied so much that it was hard to discern if she even knew why she was doing it. Was that a new pair of shoes she was wearing? Did she like bananas? Was it raining outside? Why lie about things like that? But Jessie did.

The second thing to stand out for me during my time with Jessie was how sexualized much of her behaviour seemed. Jessie wanted to sit on my lap, to touch me, to caress me in a way that had, right from the beginning, felt flirtatious. Other children would climb over me, hug and kiss me or want to sit on my lap and it did not set off these same alarm bells. With

Jessie, however, there was an underlying creepiness to her behaviour.

This spoke to me of sexual abuse. I had already brought this suspicion up with staff in the group home, because there had been the incidents when she had inappropriately touched Joseph. Joseph said he had also noticed Jessie's behaviour in the TV room as occasionally inappropriate. She had been disciplined two or three times for touching others' genitals through their clothes. Occasionally, she had been sent to her room for publicly masturbating. When called out on these things, Jessie blamed the other children for starting it.

The team agreed with me that her behaviour was indicative of sexual abuse, but there was no substantiation of this in Jessie's notes, neither in the psychological reports nor the medical records. We tossed back and forth the people who would be the most likely suspects – her father, neighbours, family friends – but there were no concrete leads.

The third thing to come to my attention during my time working with Jessie was that broad category of what I could only term as 'antisocial behaviour', such as the fire-setting and the homicidal talk. As sweet as Jessie often was when in with me, it was clear that she was a deeply angry young girl, who did not yet have a productive means of expressing all of what was going on inside. I mentioned that on a couple of different occasions Jessie appeared to dissociate. If this was happening, it meant Jessie might not be fully aware of what she was doing during moments of intense emotion. This could present an even greater danger, both to herself and others, and it would also make helping her to change her behaviours harder. Furthermore, dissociation was another indicator of having experienced severe trauma. This might have been the sexual abuse, whenever it was, whoever had perpetrated it. It might have been some other factor we were not yet aware of. Whatever, we needed to understand her behaviour better ourselves if we were going to be successful in helping Jessie move forward.

The meeting ended with cautious optimism that we were getting a more complete picture of her, and agreement that I should continue working with her.

chapter eleven

I brought the puppets with me to the next session, but stowed them, still in their black bin bag, under my chair. When Jessie came in she immediately looked for them, and when she finally saw them she gave me a quizzical expression, one eyebrow rising. 'Why are they there?'

'Mrs Thomas has asked me to play a little game with you first.'

Jessie groaned.

'You don't even know what it is, but you make annoyed noises.'

'I want to see if Puppy's all right,' she replied. 'You never take care of Puppy. You've jammed him down in a black bag where he can't breathe and he needs to be taken care of.'

'In a moment. First we'll do what Mrs Thomas has asked.'

'Puppy can't breathe in there. Let me just get him out first.'

'I know you would like that, Jessie, and in a moment you can. But first, we are doing this.'

'You wouldn't like it if you couldn't breathe. Please? Let me just get him out. Just Puppy. *Please?* It will only take a minute.'

'First, we are going to do this.'

'Puppy needs to be *taken care of* . . .' she moaned in a whingy, drawn-out voice.

Bargaining like this was typical conversation with Jessie, but it was made all the more challenging on this occasion, because, as part of her care plan, we were to actively encourage her to see things from other perspectives, to be empathetic towards others, and here she was expressing exactly that. I was also aware that, as a neglected child herself, concern for Puppy might well be an expression of her own needs, and so in reassuring Puppy she was simultaneously reassuring herself as well. *But* . . . master manipulator that she was, Jessie knew these things about us – that we were keen to encourage her to care for others and that we wanted her to feel secure – and by pressing the 'nurture' or 'neglected child' buttons, she could get us to do things that she wanted.

I found constantly having to deal with Jessie in such a structured way hard going. I am a naturally spontaneous person, and if immediate circumstances look like they might lead in a more productive direction than my plans, I am usually quick to switch and follow where the moment takes me. On many occasions this has resulted in wonderful teaching experiences, but not with Jessie. She found an easy tool in my spontaneity, inevitably manoeuvring us into doing exactly what she wanted. This wasn't always a bad thing. Her pathological need for control indicated an earlier life where she had had very little security, and if she was going to reach a healthy place eventually, she needed to be allowed some appropriate moments of autonomy. Moreover, I had learned a great deal about Jessie in following where she took me, and it had been possible to turn some of these experiences into helpful and productive activities. However, the key words were 'appropriate' and 'helpful'. Continually letting Jessie hijack my plans was neither appropriate nor helpful. More to the point, it wasn't an efficient way of working, and we did not have all the time in the world. With each week that passed, Jessie was growing older, more acclimatized to life in an institutional setting and less likely to experience a healthy, happy childhood.

Meleri felt this pressure of valuable time passing acutely and brought it up every time we were together. As a consequence, I'd come out of our meeting the previous Friday with a list of things Meleri wanted me to focus on getting through with Jessie. One of these things was a standardized assessment used to determine how healthy a child's bond was with his or her caretakers. Jessie had already been identified as having an attachment disorder, the condition where children have trouble forming appropriate and trusting relationships. Unfortunately, she had proved a difficult customer to assess. Her formal interview with Ben, the Social Services child psychologist, had gone nowhere, because when he'd tried to administer the tests used to diagnose the disorder, Jessie had given very poor responses, either saying 'I don't know' to his questions or responding with comments completely off the mark. This meant her overall scores were very low, and Ben had been unable to tell if this was because Jessie was being difficult and oppositional or if her personality was genuinely so disorganized. So Meleri asked if I would re-administer some sections of the interview in the less formal, more familiar setting of our room. This session was being videotaped, so that the team would be able to see Jessie's behaviour as well as read the transcript of her answers.

Because of this, I had arrived with an agenda that day that I needed to follow, and consequently Puppy had to wait. This, of course, meant that Jessie was in a less than good mood by the time I finally got her to sit down across the table from me so that I could start the interview.

'I wonder if you can tell me three words that describe what it's like to be with your mum,' I asked as the first question.

Jessie leaned forward. Lifting up her left hand, she walked her fingers across the table top. This appeared to delight her, so she leaned further across the table to make her fingers approach me. 'Look, they are walking,' she said.

'So they are. Can you choose three words that describe what it's like to be with your mum?'

'I . . . don't . . . know. That's three words.'

'They aren't describing words, though.'

'You didn't say describing words. You just said "say three words". I did. I'm done with that question.'

I didn't point out that, indeed, I had used the word 'describe' in my original question. Instead, I just said again, 'Can you choose three words that *describe* what it's like to be with your mum?'

'I want to play with the puppets.'

'Yes, and you may, as soon as we are finished with this. So let's finish it quickly and get it out of the way. This will only take about twenty minutes, if we focus. Then there will be plenty of time for puppets.'

'The puppets are the only nice thing in my whole week. You know that?' she answered. 'All week I look forward to coming in here and playing with the puppets. And now you won't let me.'

I didn't respond.

'Beautiful. Fun. Fantastic,' she said.

'Thank you,' I replied. 'I'll write those down. The first word you chose was "beautiful". Can you tell me about a time you felt your mum was beautiful?'

'Ha, ha!' Jessie laughed delightedly. 'The *puppets*. Those are three words that describe the puppets! And you thought I meant my mum. Ha, ha! I tricked you!'

'I can tell you don't want to do this very much, but this is a task Mrs Thomas has set for us, so until we do it we can't do anything else.'

'Yes, we can,' Jessie replied quickly. 'You don't have to take orders from Mrs Thomas. She's not the boss of you. You can do what you want to do, silly. *Silly.*'

'Even adults have to do things they don't feel like doing. It isn't possible for anyone to do only what they want.'

Sitting back in her chair, Jessie sighed wearily.

'So,' I said, 'let's start again. Can you choose three words to tell me what it's like to be with your mum?'

Silence.

I leaned back in my chair and let the silence linger.

'I don't really remember what it's like to be with my mum.'

'Perhaps if you take a moment longer to think, it will come to you.'

'Okay, here's three. Worrier. Sleepy. Happy.'

'Thank you,' I said. 'The first word you chose was "worrier". Can you tell me about a time when your mum was a worrier?'

'Like, she just does. All the time. She worries.'

'Can you tell me about a particular time when you felt like she was worrying about something?'

Jessie shrugged. 'I don't know. I just said that to give you an answer so you'd stop bothering me. That's all. I'm done with that question.'

'All right, let's think about the second word you chose. It was "sleepy". Can you tell me about a time when your mum was sleepy?'

'All the time.'

'Can you tell me a little more about that?'

Jessie shrugged again. 'No. That's all. You said three words. You got three words. I want to do the puppets.'

'In a moment. We've got a bit more to finish first. The third word you chose was "happy". Can you describe a time when your mum was happy?'

'When I left.'

'Can you tell me a little more?'

'When the social worker took me away that day, my mum said, "I'm happy she's going."'

*

While I managed to keep Jessie more or less on task, getting through even one question had been a monumental struggle, so it seemed wiser to discontinue the interview and reward that small bit of cooperation with the puppet play rather than push her to the point where she lost her temper.

Jessie fell on the bag of puppets like a starving wolf on a sheep carcass. Literally ripping the bag to get it open, she grabbed the puppets, clutching them to her with one hand as she continued to pull the others out. When finally she had the whole lot out, she sat for a minute or two, just hugging them all against her.

'You seem a bit desperate. Were you worried about the puppets?' I asked.

'Yes, I thought maybe you got rid of them.'

'I wouldn't do that. I bring them every time. What makes you think that might happen?'

'Because.'

'That's a scary thought, that someone might get rid of something you especially like.'

'I more than like these,' she replied. 'I love them. They're my friends. They're my family to me. My puppet family.' She was sitting on the floor at my feet and, one by one, she lay the puppets out, some on her lap, some on the floor beside her. 'That happened to me before, you know,' she said.

'What?'

'My cuddly toys were got rid of.'

'When was that?'

'My mum did it. She took all my toys out in the front garden and set fire to them.'

She lifted up the dragon puppet. Up until this point, Jessie had shown little interest in this particular puppet. Now she tried it on and turned her hand in a way that allowed the dragon to face her. It was an especially detailed puppet made in two-tone green felt with leathery wings, pointed gold-coloured claws and a very fierce, sharp-toothed mouth.

'Once I had a dragon toy,' she said. 'It was like this. It was my favourite. I used to take it to bed with me. But my mum got really mad at me and she took it away.'

'Why did she get mad?'

'I don't remember.'

Jessie clacked the mouth open and shut. 'Rowwwrrrr,' she said for the dragon, and reached up to make it bite my arm. 'If I had this, I could make it bite my mum for taking my toys away. She put them in a big pile on the lawn and then she poured petrol on them and lit a match.'

'That sounds dangerous,' I said.

'It was. You shouldn't ever light petrol because it can make a dangerous fire. But she did, because she's crazy. My mum is crazy in the head. The doctors said that. That's why she didn't take care of me when I was a baby. Rowwwrrrr!' The dragon bit me again, not hard enough to hurt but hard enough for me to know it was meant seriously.

Jessie got to her feet, the dragon puppet still on her hand. It was quite a large puppet, so she had to hold her hand at shoulder height.

'I'm going to eat the world!' she said for the dragon, and began to move around the room. There wasn't much space because of all the furniture, so she climbed up on the sofa and swung the dragon above her head as best she could. 'I'm going to eat you!'

Jessie was on the opposite side of the table to me at this point, so there was no danger of her attacking me with the dragon, but she made it swoop menacingly in my direction.

'I'm going to eat my mum and dad! I'm going to eat my sisters! I'm going to eat Mrs Thomas and Joseph and Enir and all the kids. I'm going to eat you. I'm going to eat everyone and then I'm going to eat some fish and chips!'

'That is one hungry dragon,' I said.

'I'm going to eat up Magnus and Eleanor too. And the unicorn. And all the other puppets! And then I'm going to eat the chairs and the table. Eat up this whole room! Nothing will be left! Then I'm going to breathe fire everywhere. Rowwwrrrr!'

Before I realized what was happening, Jessie was up on the table itself. She swung the dragon puppet around and around above her head. 'I hate my mum and dad!' she shouted. 'I hate them so much! I'm going to burn them to pieces, just like my mum did to my toys. Just like she did to me. I'm going to kill her! I'm going to kill my dad! I'm going to set fire to the whole, whole world! That's what I want to do! Yes! That's what I want to do!'

Jessie began to dance on the table, swinging the dragon puppet. I was concerned because a manic quality had come into her actions, and I sensed that she was not fully within herself. It would be very easy for her to go spinning off the table.

Rising, I said, 'Jess? It's time to come down from there.'

She danced on, twirling around and around, the dragon held above her head. Because of its size, it took both her hands to elevate it, and this kept her spinning in a slightly more contained manner than would have happened if she could have extended her arms.

It was hard to reach her properly because of her movements and I was growing more concerned that she would hurt herself. 'Jess?'

'I'm going to burn the world! Rowwwrrrr! I'm the strongest dragon in the world. I'm going to burn everything to a cinder!'

I climbed up onto the table myself and took hold of her around her shoulders. 'Jess, we need to stop now.' She continued to spin between my hands.

I scooped her towards me, and we stood a moment, teetering, because she was not yet completely still. A little worried about the stability of the table under both our weights, I let go and slipped quickly back to the floor. Then I grabbed her around the waist and lifted her down. Jessie didn't resist. In fact, by the time she touched the floor she fell willingly against me, her eyes closed, her expression joyful. She clutched the dragon puppet in against her chest. I held her a moment to ensure she was able to calm down.

Jessie let out a huge sigh. Then she opened her eyes and looked up at me, a smile touching all corners of her face. 'Wow, that was fun,' she said, her voice hardly more than a whisper. 'Wow, that's the most fun I think I ever had.'

chapter twelve

Throughout the time Jessie had been playing with the dragon puppet, the video recorder was running. I was very glad for that, because I was anxious for the other staff to give me their opinion of what was going on with Jessie.

Ben, who had asked me to conduct the assessment interview, wasn't available that same day, but Meleri, Joseph and two other staff members sat down with me later in the afternoon to watch it.

Almost all my career I had used recording devices. In the US, the 1970s had been a time of prosperity in education, and many schools were able to acquire the newest technology. In those days that meant reel-to-reel video recorders and cameras so big and heavy they needed dedicated tripods to support them. Unfortunately, while the districts bought us all this lovely equipment, very little training was given. As a consequence, in way too many schools the equipment ended up collecting dust in AV cupboards for the simple reason that most members of staff had no idea how to operate the items. My geeky love of technology finally paid off, because after a bit of playing around I figured out how things went together and tried the video recorder out in my classroom. I loved it! Up to that point, I hadn't realized how much I was missing in the classroom when my focus was solely on the kids, and found it inordinately helpful to review certain situations again later.

I'd felt guilty for hogging this new resource, but it seemed a shame to let it go unused, and that was what was happening. So I offered to 'store' the video equipment in my special needs classroom until someone else wanted it. My headmaster was more than happy about this, as the audio-visual closet was small and video equipment in those days was bulky. Thus started my long career of recording in the classroom, which I found enormously helpful. I re-experienced this on this occasion, watching the video of Jessie, because it brought home once again just how much I missed while caught up in the situation.

What was unmistakable in the video was how openly manipulative Jessie was. Everything she said, everything she did, was aimed at keeping me on the back foot, and for the most part she succeeded. I grew embarrassed as the other staff began pointing out her behaviour. Their comments implied naivety on my part, that however well intentioned I was in my efforts, I did not have a good grasp of the realities of working with a child with reactive attachment disorder. No one was the least bit nasty about it, but it stung, because I didn't think it was true. I had successfully resisted her desire to play with the puppets at the beginning of the session, and while I had not been successful at getting her to respond appropriately to the interview questions, neither had anyone else in other settings. It was possible her personality was so disorganized that this was the best we were going to get for the time being, and it wasn't my fault or anyone else's that we weren't getting anything more. I wasn't convinced my approach was wrong.

Joseph described my allowing Jessie to play with the dragon puppet instead of doing the assessment as 'going soft and fuzzy', but to me it felt like an appropriate shift of emphasis as the situation evolved. We didn't know what had happened to Jessie in her past, but she had many indicators of serious abuse or neglect. To move forward, we needed more insight into what was going on for her. I did not see how we could achieve this without allowing her a degree of space and freedom within the sessions so that she could communicate some of this to us. Yes, she was manipulative and controlling, and, yes, there were inevitably going to be times when she completely threw a session, but that didn't mean the time was wasted. We still had a learning opportunity. And that's what we needed most – the chance to learn more about how and why these dysfunctional coping behaviours had developed.

When I said that, Joseph replied, 'That's how thinking used to be, back in the day. That as professionals we needed to understand the origins of things in order to change them. You know, Freud and everything. But we're not there any more. I wish that we were. It was a gentler time. But these days, change happens because we engineer for change. And that's how we have to do it, because we don't have the resources to do anything more, much as I wish we did.'

I sat, feeling officially old.

Then it got worse. As we watched the second half of the tape, where Jessie was playing with the dragon puppet, Joseph said, 'Stop it there a moment, please.' It was the section of the tape where Jessie was talking about her mother putting her toys out on the front lawn, pouring petrol over them and setting fire to them.

The tape froze Jessie mid-motion, the dragon held high, her head back, her red hair flying. Her mouth was open, her expression absorbed.

'That isn't true,' Joseph said. 'She's lying there.'

'About her toys being burned?' I asked.

'No. She's right about that, but she's lying about her mother doing it. Toys *were* put in a pile in the garden and petrol poured over them and set alight, but it was Jessie herself who did it. That was the first arson event.'

I didn't reply.

Joseph appeared to take my silence as reproach, which it wasn't meant to be. I was simply attempting to take this information in. However, he turned to Meleri for support. 'Isn't that how it was?'

Meleri nodded. 'Yes, when Jessie was six. And they weren't her toys. They were her sister Gemma's toys. You know, the kind of cuddly toys teenagers keep on their bed. Jessie had had an argument with her, so she put the toys out into the garden and took petrol for the lawnmower from the can in the garage. She poured it over the toys and set fire to them.'

'Ah, okay,' I said, because there wasn't much else to say.

'It's interesting that she said her mother did it,' Meleri added. 'From what we know of her mother, she's extremely passive around Jessie. She's had a hard struggle with depression, and apparently went through periods where she didn't get out of bed at all, leaving Jessie to her own devices. It's interesting that Jessie interprets that relationship so destructively.'

I went home feeling depressed myself. While we had differences between us, all of us were trying our hardest with very thin resources. Our area, geographically large and mostly rural, was one of the most disadvantaged parts of the country. There were too many children in care, too few foster homes, too far apart, and too little in the way of support services. Meleri was tired and overworked in the way social workers everywhere are. Ben was the only child psychologist employed by the local authority and he had almost 2,000 children on his rota. Among the local population, very few who needed treatment could afford private therapy or specially skilled doctors. A number of charities, both large and small, did what they could to take up the slack, but it wasn't enough. Joseph was right. You had to focus on change. Understanding was a luxury.

These kinds of thoughts always brought me back to comparing the culture I'd ended up in with the culture I'd left. I went back to the US every summer because my family were still all in Montana, where I'd grown up. This annual trip had allowed me to stay in touch with many of my old teaching friends. We always went out together and 'talked shop', and if the time was right, I visited their classrooms.

My own memories of working in the US were rosy. Clean, new buildings, appointments with professionals that you got simply by phoning up and making them, doctors who saw you quickly and had a battery of tests at their disposal, which produced precise labels for what was wrong and, often as not, medications to make it better. Even as I was thinking these things, however, I knew they were false memories. My mind had simply edited out the bad bits. The truth was, I'd only worked in one shiny, new school. The others had all been ageing brick behemoths from the first half of the twentieth century, grand in their day, disintegrating in mine and, occasionally, completely decommissioned except for the need to put the special education programmes somewhere. We had often lived hand-to-mouth in the schools I'd worked in, waiting for the annual property tax assessment, called the mill levy, which funded our programmes, to know whether we'd still be there or not. As someone who had the fatal mix of being highly educated but working with only small numbers of children, my programmes were often among the first cut if funding wasn't secured or if there was an administration change in Washington, and I'd find myself job hunting. In a similar vein, while my former colleagues all had access to quick appointments with an array of specialists, they were also paying a fifth of their income in insurance. Many of the families I'd worked with in the US couldn't afford that, and thus they had no insurance at all and, consequently, no access to services. One of my former students told of having his pregnant wife turned away at the hospital door because they had no means to pay for treatment. And those tests and labels, while comforting, had led to an explosion of drugged children. Rosy as the past seemed, I realized it was not so much a case of one culture being better than another but more a matter of picking which set of bad circumstances you felt you could best cope with.

The videotape viewing had upset me more than I wanted to admit, even to myself. I felt annoyed at being duped by a nine-year-old and humiliated at having had it pointed out in a group of fellow professionals. I felt others on the team saw my work as low status because I was a volunteer, and thus not as valid as that of the paid staff. And I felt they saw my approach as 'soft and fluffy' when I believed myself pragmatic and evidence-based. As a consequence, I went into the next session with Jessie intent on taking control.

Jessie arrived in a cheerful mood. She had just had her hair cut. It wasn't a very different style to what she'd been wearing all along, but she liked the way it moved when she shook her head, so upon entering the room she came around to my side of the table for me to admire it.

Then she said, 'I want to show Magnus and Eleanor,' and she reached down to open the black bin bag beside my chair.

I didn't say anything. I thought I would let her get started however she wanted, and then I'd address the whole control issue head on.

Jessie took the puppets out one by one and laid them on the table. She was standing beside me, so the bears, Magnus and Eleanor, were laid out directly in front of me. Then came Puppy. She snuggled Puppy close, kissed the puppet's head and set him up in the middle of the table to oversee things. Then came the unicorn, the monster, the dragon she had played with the previous session, the toucan, the lamb, the hare and the purple ostrich.

'There. That's all of them.' She regarded them a long moment, then she leaned over the table and shook her head. 'See, you lot? I got my hair cut. See?'

I continued not to speak, curious how long it would take her to notice.

Jessie straightened up. 'They are just puppets, you know. They can't actually see anything. They don't know I got my hair cut.'

She picked up one of the bear puppets. It wasn't possible to tell which was Magnus and which was Eleanor until they were brought to life, because the puppets looked more or less identical. Jessie put her hand into it and turned it to face her. She moved the mouth up and down but didn't say anything. Then she looked over the top of the bear's head to meet my eyes.

'What's wrong with you today?' she asked.

'I need to talk to you about something.'

'I could tell that. I could tell you were huffed, because you didn't say anything nice about my hair.'

'I'm not angry, but we do have some serious talking to do.'

'I want to play with the puppets first.' She snapped the bear's mouth together two or three more times and then turned it towards me. 'Magnus says, "You've got a huffy look on your face and it makes you not pretty. Pretty faces smile." Don't they, Magnus? Pretty faces make us want to talk to them.'

'I need to talk to you,' I said, 'and you have a choice of three things. You may keep Magnus on your hand while we talk. You may put Magnus away and use the paper and pens while we talk. Or we can just talk. Those are the choices.'

Jessie regarded me but did not move. Leaning across the table, I began to put the other puppets back into the black bin bag.

This alarmed Jessie. With the bear puppet still on her hand, she reached out for Puppy. 'No!'

'Today we're not playing with puppets. You may keep Magnus, if you wish, but the rest will be put away.'

'*No!* Don't put Puppy away! Let him stay out.'

'Today we're not playing with puppets.'

'No!'

'I hear you. You would like to have the puppets out, but today we are not playing with puppets.'

'Just Puppy. Just leave Puppy out. Please?'

'Today we are not playing with puppets. You may keep Magnus, if you want, but the rest are going to be put away.'

'I'll trade Magnus for Puppy. Okay? You can have Magnus. I'll put him away, but let me have Puppy instead.'

'Today we're not playing with puppets.'

'Please? Just this one thing? Please? Let me have Puppy instead of Magnus. Then I'll do anything you say. You'll see. Please? Please?'

I didn't respond.

'But Puppy gets so lonely. *So* lonely. And scared. He's scared in the black bag. He got shut away when he was little. Shut in the cupboard, and it was so dark, and now he's scared. So *scared.* He needs a cuddle.'

This was such a typical exchange with Jessie, this ever-present bargaining to bring things back around to where she wanted them. It was hard to ignore because she was so good at sussing out what would play upon my sympathies. Had she been an ordinary child, this small request would have been reasonable, kind, even. With Jessie, however, it was sadly all part of the game.

Calmly, I said no again. 'You may play with Puppy another time. Today he goes with the other puppets. You may choose to keep Magnus with you or put him in the bag too, but the rest of the puppets need to be put away.' I held the bag open.

'No. You can't have him. You can't have Puppy.' Jessie dived under the table, pulling the dog puppet from the bag.

I remained seated and did not look under the table to where she was hidden.

'I'm going to keep Puppy. I'm going to stay under here and keep Puppy safe.'

I didn't respond.

'No!' she shouted.

Moments passed. I sat quietly, not looking under the table, not speaking.

'No! No, no, no! I won't do it! NO!'

Angrily Jessie rattled the chairs. She kicked out the one next to mine. There wasn't enough room for it to fall over, so she only managed to knock it back against the sofa. She kicked out two on the opposite side. She screamed.

I didn't respond.

This carried on for the better part of ten minutes, Jessie howling fiercely from under the table, kicking the chairs, bumping the table. Despite the noise she was making, I could tell she wasn't crying. This was anger and frustration.

When I said nothing, she decided to up the ante. 'I'll rip him up. I'll ruin Puppy and you won't have him any more. You want to see me?' she raged from under the table.

'Our time is almost up,' I replied.

She climbed out from under the table to stand at the far end of the room. Her skin was mottled with her wrath. 'I'm going to ruin him.' She had one of Puppy's front legs in each hand and stretched the puppet out tautly. 'I'm going to tear your puppet.'

'You are feeling so angry with me that you are willing to hurt something you love to play with in here.'

'I'll do it.'

'Yes, I know you will. But think how you will feel next week when you come in and Puppy isn't here. Think of opening the bag and seeing that Puppy has been hurt and thrown away.'

Jessie began to cry. 'Noooo. Don't throw him away.'

'Think how you will feel.'

'Nooooo. You're cruel.' She brought the puppet in against her chest in a hug. 'You can't just throw Puppy away like he's nothing.'

'How can you stop that from happening?' I asked.

Her mouth drawn down in a grimace of tears, she shook her head. 'I don't know.'

'Yes, I think you do, Jessie. I think you know what you can do right now to stop that from happening.' I opened the bin bag wider.

Very slowly she released her hold on the little dog puppet. Sobbing, she held it out for a long moment and then finally dropped it into the bag. 'I hate you,' she muttered.

'Yes, I know. That's okay.'

'I hate you so much.'

chapter thirteen

The moment she arrived for the next session, Jessie asked, 'How's Puppy?'

'Puppy is just fine.'

'Where is he?'

'The puppets are all at my house. I didn't bring them in today because I want to have a talk with you. We didn't have a chance to talk last time, because we got distracted by the puppets. So today I left them at home.'

'Noooo!'

'Puppy is safe.' I opened my satchel. 'You may have paper and pens if you want something to do with your hands while we talk.'

'*Nooooo*. You promised you'd bring Puppy. You said last time that this time we'd get to do puppets. You *lied* to me.'

I didn't want to get drawn into a distracting conversation, so I didn't respond. Instead, I took out the packet of pens and paper and laid them on the table. I then closed my satchel and set it on the floor.

Jessie was still standing just inside the door. Her brow

furrowed, she regarded my actions. 'Why are you so huffed with me? I haven't done anything.'

'Please sit down.'

'I just wanted Puppy,' she said in a plaintive voice.

'Yes, I understand. Please sit down.'

Leadenly, she approached the table, pulled out the chair and fell into it. 'You're not nice to me any more. You used to be nice. When you first came. But now suddenly you're always huffed. What's your problem?'

I didn't respond.

After a few moments of frowning, Jessie snatched the paper and pulled it over in front of her. She opened the pens.

'When you and I were together the time before last,' I said, 'you were telling me about something that happened when you lived at home. You told me how your mum took all your toys out on the lawn and set fire to them.'

Jessie had begun to draw down in the lower right-hand corner of her paper. She cupped her left hand around what she was doing so as to shield it from my view. 'I'm not going to show you what I'm drawing,' she said.

'I want to talk about what you said. You told me your mum burned all your toys in the garden.'

'I'm not going to show you this.'

'Jessie?' I said, and reached my hand across to lay it on the paper.

'You said I could *draw*,' she cried in an outraged voice.

I wasn't attempting to take the paper away from her, nor

was I trying to stop her pen. I had simply laid my hand on the paper.

'No! Take it away.' She shoved my hand.

I pulled it back. 'You told me your mum set fire to your toys, but that's not true, is it? That's not what really happened. You were the one who set fire to your toys.'

She leaned close to the paper and began to draw intricately. Despite still shielding her work from my view, I could tell it was another skylark because of the delicate way she made the strokes.

For several moments Jessie appeared intently focused on her drawing. I sat back. I wanted her to talk. I wanted to explore the whole issue of lying and being caught in a lie, but I also knew that if I pressed her there was a good chance that wouldn't happen. The challenge was to keep us delicately balanced between Jessie's taking us off topic and her freaking out over something she couldn't control.

So I sat, and Jessie drew. A minute passed. Two. Five. Ten. I said nothing. Tension began to ease away as the time passed. She let her left hand drop away from shielding what she was doing. Picking up a fuchsia pink pen, she filled in the skylark's delicate wings.

At last I said, 'If you were explaining to the skylark how lies happen, what would you say?'

'What do you mean?' she asked. She didn't look up.

'You said it was your mum who set fire to your toys, but really it was you. That makes it a lie. Usually there are reasons for lies. They don't just happen. But skylarks don't know about lies, because they're birds. So if you had to explain it to the skylark, what would you say?'

She reached over, took a green pen from the packet, and began to colour in the skylark's body. The silence grew so long that I thought she wasn't going to answer.

Then she said quietly, 'I don't lie. It's just sometimes I remember things differently. It's like . . . people think what's in your mind is like a programme on the telly. That all you have to do is turn on your mind and there's your memories and you're always going to see the same thing. Like, there's this one *Simpsons* cartoon, and every time I turn on the TV, that *Simpsons* cartoon seems to be on. It's exactly the same every time. Homer's sitting at the nuclear plant and he's eating doughnuts, and Bart's at school and he's in trouble. And every time I look at it, they're doing exactly the same thing. I've seen it a million times. People think your memory's like that, that you've got the same thing playing over and over. They say, "Tell me about this", and they think all you've got to do is turn on the TV in your mind and that exact same cartoon is going to be playing. Except it isn't. You switch to that channel and maybe there's Homer and there's Bart, but it's a different cartoon and so you say about that cartoon, because that's the one you see. And people say, "You're lying. That's not the cartoon I saw." But you didn't see that one. You saw something different than they did.'

'That's a very interesting idea,' I said. 'And what you've said shows me you've done some grown-up thinking about this subject. Let me see if I understand. You think it feels like people want you to remember exactly the same thing over and over, like the one cartoon that is always on, but when you tell them what you remember, it's different from that, so they think you're lying.'

Jessie nodded.

'So what you're saying is that you remember it being your mum who took your toys out into the garden and set fire to them? But other people remember it as you?'

She nodded again. She was bent very close over the sky-lark, outlining the tiny drawing in black ink.

'It wasn't me,' she murmured.

'It wasn't you who set fire to your toys?'

'She took them out. She put my toys in a black bin bag, like you've got. Just like what you put Puppy in. She carried it out into the back garden where there is this little tree that gets blossoms on at the wrong time of year. It blooms in the winter, when there shouldn't be flowers. She put the bin bag under the little tree and poured petrol on it. I was crying. Crying and crying and crying and crying, because I didn't want her to ruin all my toys, and just pouring petrol on them ruined them. But she lit the match and it went whoosh! And everything burned up.'

Jessie had grown tearful as she told this story. Her head was still down, her voice small and tight.

My own thoughts raced through a maze of possibilities. *Was* this a lie? Were Jessie's manipulative skills so sophisticated? Her cartoon analogy showed me that she had an ability to think abstractly well beyond her years, but it still seemed a stretch to assume she was consciously telling the alternate story purely to lead me astray. Was there a possibility she had dissociated when she set the fires? Had she disconnected psychologically, so that she didn't feel present when she was doing it? Or was she perhaps not lying at all and her mother *had* set fire to her toys at some point? Had her mother possibly retaliated in an eye-for-an-eye way after Jessie started burning things? Or was Jessie's fire-setting a re-enactment of an earlier experience of having had her toys burned?

I wanted to know so much more, but I realized direct questions would lead us into a house of mirrors where it would be impossible to tell what was real, what was imagined and what was somewhere in-between. Consequently, I tried a slightly different tack.

'Why do you suppose that happened?' I asked. 'Why were the toys set on fire?'

'I don't know,' Jessie replied.

'Let's include the skylark in this. Birds don't know anything about these kinds of things. Human actions are a complete mystery to them. The skylark can't understand why we even have toys, much less why they would be taken out into the garden and put under the tree that was blooming. How would you explain what happened to the skylark?'

Bringing up a finger, Jessie stroked the bird on the paper. Then, slowly, she shrugged. 'I don't know.'

'What kind of feelings did the human have, when she gathered the toys together and put them in the black bin bag?' I intentionally didn't specify who 'she' was to avoid the conflict over whether it was Jessie or her mother. 'Remember that day when we talked about the fish and chips? About getting inside someone's head to imagine how it looked from their point of view? To imagine their feelings?'

Jessie was quiet so long I didn't think she was going to reply. She sat, hunched forward, staring at the edge of the table. 'She didn't have feelings,' she said finally, her voice small.

'She didn't have any feelings at all?'

Jessie shook her head. 'No. That's why she did it. The fire felt good because it made her have feelings again.'

Jessie began to cry.

I sat quietly for a few moments to see if the tears would pass, but they didn't. Instead, she began to cry harder.

'Jessie, would you like a cuddle?' I asked.

Nodding, she got up from her chair and came around to my side of the table. I put my arm around her shoulders.

One of the things that had changed the most over the years that I had been working was how we touched children. In the late sixties and seventies, none of us in special education had thought twice about hugging a child close to comfort him or her, changing a child's clothes or, indeed, even bathing the child if there had been a messy accident. Greater awareness of personal boundaries, new definitions of abuse and an increasingly litigious society had changed all that. I was now very careful how I touched those I worked with. So I simply put my arm around Jessie's shoulders and pulled her against my side as I sat in the chair. She stayed in this position for a few moments, but then before I realized what she was doing, she turned, sat down in my lap and lay her head against my chest.

I let her stay. Wrapping both my arms around her, I held Jessie close. It seemed the right response. She was still crying, gasping for breath through snot and tears.

Then I reached across the table and grabbed the tissue box. Taking out a couple, I handed them to her. Jessie accepted them, blew her nose, wiped her face.

We sat a few moments longer then I felt something and looked down. Jessie had her left hand between her legs. She didn't appear to be touching herself, just resting her hand there. What I was feeling were the fingers of her other hand, pressing down between her outer thigh and my lower abdomen. She wasn't touching my crotch, but she wasn't far away.

'Jessie, we don't put our hands there,' I said, and lifted her right hand out and put it in her lap.

'I wasn't doing anything.'

'Stand up, please.'

'I wasn't *doing* anything.'

'No, perhaps not. But we don't touch other people in their private areas.'

'I *wasn't*.'

'I felt uncomfortable when you put your hand where you did.'

'I *didn't*. I didn't do anything. You just imagined it.' Anger was quickly replacing her tears.

'I've noticed you put your hand there other times.'

'I haven't.'

'Sometimes when kids do that, it's because they have been touched that way themselves. Has that happened to you?' I asked.

'*No.*'

'Sometimes when people touch our private areas, they say it's a secret. They say it's your fault it happened. Or that you will get into bad trouble if you tell. Those things aren't true. They're saying that just so they can keep doing what they want. If someone is touching your private areas, the right thing to do is tell a trusted adult.'

The anger had faded. Face blotched from crying, nose glistening, hair rumpled from sitting against me, Jessie looked despondent.

Seeing her forlorn expression, I felt great warmth for her. 'It's hard sometimes, isn't it?'

She nodded.

'But I mean what I said. If someone is touching you in a way you don't like, it is all right to tell on them.'

She shook her head.

'I know it must feel sometimes like things will never get better. But if you start with just one true thing, we can work from there.'

She shook her head again. 'No.'

chapter fourteen

I didn't see Jessie the next week, because I was in Italy on a promotional tour with my most recent book. Jessie had been well prepared for this. We'd talked about my being away. I'd shown her on the map where I was going, and I promised to send a postcard from Rome. Postcards were a valued currency among the kids in the group home, proof that someone, somewhere, was thinking of them. Jessie had three from Blackpool, all from one of her older sisters who worked there, but she longed for a foreign one. Several times she had asked if I'd remember to send her one, and I'd assured her I would. I made sure to send the postcard straightaway, because I knew the change in schedule would unnerve her. Indeed, I sent her one from Milan as well.

Unfortunately, I came home from the trip with an extra souvenir – a stinking cold that had me laid out for a couple of days on the sofa with a mug of lemon, honey and medicinal whisky.

When I realized I was going to miss a second week with Jessie, I phoned Meleri. Recognizing my voice, she gave a sharp intake of breath, and I knew immediately something was wrong. She started casually, saying not to worry about being ill, to take the time I needed to recover. A pause then and she added, 'Jessie is no longer at the group home.'

'*What?*' I knew we had been waiting months for a thera-peutic placement to become available, so I hoped this was good news, but I was caught off guard by its happening with so little warning.

There was a long hesitation on Meleri's end of the phone, and then finally, she said, 'It's complicated. I need to talk to you. I know you're not well, but could you manage coming over to the office for a short while? It's something I'd rather not discuss on the phone.'

I arrived at Meleri's office in the late afternoon. It was heavily overcast, the sort of day when you always need lights on, and was punctuated by periods of sleet. The room, with its government beige walls and government-issue furniture, looked drab and washed out in the wan, fluorescent bright-ness. Not much of Meleri's personal flair had carried over to her office beyond the Calvin and Hobbes mugs she used to make our tea.

'Where to begin,' she said, and fished the tea bags out of the mugs. She examined the one from her cup, judging, I suspect, whether it was worth saving and using again, but she didn't. She flipped one after the other into the plastic bin beside the desk.

I took the tea and sat down in the chair across the desk from her.

'Jessie accused Joseph of molesting her.'

Slack-jawed, I stared.

Meleri met my gaze. Her eyes were dead. No other word for it.

'How? What . . . ?' I had no idea what to say to that.

'It was two days after you left. She told Enir at bed check. She said Joseph touched her after her shower. She said he'd done it before. She said he'd exposed himself to her.'

I stared in disbelief. 'Joseph wouldn't be the staff member overseeing the girls when they take their showers. He isn't even on the evening shift most of the time.'

'I know,' Meleri replied.

'So . . . ?' I said, because this made it almost certain to be untrue, but my first thoughts went immediately to the conversation I'd had with Jessie just before I'd left for Italy. *If someone is touching you in a way you don't like, it is all right to tell on them.*

'He was on that night. But he wasn't supervising the girls.'

'So . . . ?' I didn't know what else to say. Knowing Jessie, it was so easy to imagine that, if Joseph had made her angry, she would hit back with whatever she thought would do the most damage to him, and there would be little regard for the truth. However, also knowing Jessie meant knowing that something had happened to her sometime, somewhere.

'We had no choice but to respond from the assumption she is telling the truth.'

'Oh, please, not Joseph,' I said forlornly, because I really did not want to even entertain the idea that Joseph was corrupt. He was one of the good guys. I had felt that instinctively from the moment I'd met him. He was *good*.

I sat back in my chair, feeling overwhelmed by this news, still trying to take this in. I felt like crying. I really did.

Meleri peered into her mug of tea, swirled it slightly and drank from it. 'So . . . I had to get her out of there. Right then and there. This isn't a good placement, where she's been moved. They're good people, but they are inexperienced. They've only had three kids before Jessie. But it was all we had on the night, and I had to move her then.'

'How's she doing?'

Meleri see-sawed her hand back and forth.

'And Joseph?'

'He was arrested. He's been bailed, and so he's at home. We can't talk to him. I mustn't. You mustn't. None of us can, so please don't try, because it could prejudice the outcome of the case.'

I nodded.

A heavy sigh from Meleri. 'We're in a mess at Glan Morfa. There isn't anyone available with the equivalent experience to replace him. We've had to hire what we could get just to put enough staff in the home. And, of course, we're trying to keep it out of the press.'

A few years earlier, there had been a serious scandal involving group homes and child abuse, and I knew the lurid British tabloid press would like nothing more than to find a new 'monster'. Sudden horror hit me at the thought of this blowing up into national news.

'So far we're okay,' Meleri said. 'The police are being decent. No one is losing their head. But it only takes one comment . . .'

Silence again, and it hung between us like air before a thunderstorm.

'What do you think really happened?' I asked.

Meleri didn't answer straightaway. Indeed, she didn't even react to my question initially. Instead she sat, leaning back in her office chair and staring at her tea mug.

'I have to believe her,' she said at last.

'No, I know that. I appreciate that. And it's right that we do. But what do you think? Really?'

'I *have* to believe her, Torey. I mean that. I can't speculate. I don't speculate.'

'But this is Jessie we're talking about here. What if she just got angry with him in the way she does and said it out of spite? Or what if she just said it for the sake of it, the way she tells so many of her lies? Jessie is such a damaged child. In a million years, I wouldn't want her to be abused right here, under our noses, where she is supposed to be safe, but I also don't want to see an innocent man destroyed. This is going to take down Joseph's whole career, whether he did something or not. He's never coming back after this.'

Meleri didn't reply. She just shook her head slowly.

'For what it's worth, I do think Jessie has been sexually molested,' I said. 'I very much get the sense of that. But is it

Joseph? What if she has projected it onto him because he's here, because he's safe, because . . .' The words drifted off.

Meleri was still shaking her head. 'I *can't* go there, Torey. I'm sorry.'

PART II

chapter fifteen

It ended that easily.

Jessie had been a weekly part of my life for just over six months. I left the Social Services office that afternoon, no longer part of hers. The foster home Jessie had been moved to was over an hour's drive away and the charity outreach I was working for did not cover that area. That was the end of our sessions.

I couldn't get the situation out of my mind. The news had shocked me, not only that Jessie was gone and I wouldn't be seeing her again, but more so the circumstances under which she had departed.

My instant gut feeling was that Jessie had lied. In all probability, Joseph had made her angry or jealous of his attention to other children, and she'd wanted to get back at him. She would never have thought of the consequences. The vast majority of Jessie's lies were impulsive and outrageous, aimed solely at getting a rise out of people. She wouldn't have foreseen how saying that sort of thing would change everything, not only for him, but for her too.

I was deeply upset about Joseph. From the first moment we'd met, I had liked him. He was one of those naturally charismatic people, a quiet extrovert who could put you at your ease and make you feel included with just a few words. There was also something of the old-school lefty about him that reminded me of the long-ago friends of my youth, the ones who'd chosen to be conscientious objectors during the Vietnam War. Joseph had that same mix of compassion and civil conscience, and this, in my opinion, was what had made him just the sort of committed, responsible individual that was so badly needed in social care.

Because he did give off this aura of compassionate conscience, I'd never had the slightest sense of any impropriety from him. Indeed, if anything, he gave the impression of someone who was more highly principled than average. Not moralistic, but the sort of person to whom ethical living seems to come naturally, leaving you a little embarrassed about your guilty pleasures.

Joseph was particularly skilled at discipline and boundary setting. He was kind and considerate towards the children, but he had a strong belief in the need for structure and consistency with these kids, because all of them had come out of chaotic backgrounds of one sort or another. They knew exactly how far they could go with him and what would be the consequences. This did mean he got his fair share of abuse from the kids, because he was often the one enforcing the limits, but I'd never seen him act out of anger. And he knew how to have a laugh with them. He was particularly astute when it came to understanding teenagers, what they found funny, what they enjoyed doing. Every experience I had with Joseph left me with the sense that here was a good guy.

Yet . . . I also knew predators were difficult to spot. They were seldom the greasy-looking, shifty-eyed characters who populated books and films. Sadly, they were much more often the friendly, engaged members of the community who gravitated towards settings such as group homes and activity programmes, where being alone with children was normal and the children's pasts made them vulnerable.

I'd had unfortunate personal experience of this. While teaching in America one of my colleagues had been arrested for molesting little boys. He'd taught first grade in the school where my special education classroom was, a school that was in a deeply impoverished area, situated near both a prison and a migrant camp where there were large numbers of itinerant children. Many at our school came from homes where the men were absent, so we'd all been delighted when John joined the staff. Here at last was a kind, functional male role model, and he was just such a lovely man. We all thought the world of him. Until that day. That day when, like now, I turned up for work and he didn't.

I refused to believe what they said about him too, when they first told me. Not John. Not possible. I did not believe it. But then came the trial and I had to, because it was true. Because he admitted fondling all those little boys he was putting on his lap in his classroom. Because he'd been fired from his previous post for doing the same thing. The school board hadn't known that at the time they'd hired him in our district. This was the seventies. If you got in trouble, you just moved on.

So while my experience of Joseph was of a good man, I realized I didn't know what went on behind closed doors. I'd been wrong once, so I knew it was possible to be wrong again.

I tried not to jump to conclusions about Jessie either, which was harder, because I knew her better. I knew just how clever she was at lying, how naturally it came to her, how difficult it was to pick a way through to the truth unless there was corroborating evidence, and even then she was unwilling to admit her version was untrue. I knew she was perfectly capable of making up something like this. Indeed, it could almost be considered characteristic. Expected. This is what Jessie did best. Cause utter chaos for the sake of it by saying whatever came into her head. Yet . . . I didn't know here, either. *Something* had happened to Jessie. The inappropriate way she caressed me or put her hands where they shouldn't go, her conversations with the puppets about vaginal penetration; these were all markers of sexual abuse. How could the child who never told the truth make herself heard? And what better victim could a predator choose than a child who was never believed?

The next few weeks were frustrating. Confidentiality meant I couldn't discuss what was happening with my family. Being an outsider meant I wasn't encountering people at Social Services often enough to be kept in the loop, and so far it had all stayed out of the press.

I did know that the police were actively investigating Jessie's allegations and, within ten days, I received a call asking me to come to the police station for a formal interview.

Upon arriving at the police station, I was escorted into a claustrophobically small interview room by a sergeant in plain clothes and a female police constable. The room was literally no larger than a closet – only enough space for a small rectangular table with two chairs on either side. The only window looked out onto an internal hallway and had venetian blinds that were closed once we were seated. I was given a Styrofoam cup of instant coffee, lukewarm and the colour of dirty dishwater, but otherwise there were no pleasantries. I felt like a suspect myself.

The sergeant asked me to give an account of my experiences at Glan Morfa. The policewoman emphasised that they were gathering information at this stage; they were not trying to place any blame. They just wanted my observations. The interview was recorded, but about halfway through the recorder stopped working. There was a pause while the constable went to find another one. The sergeant offered me a biscuit.

I worried that I might say something that would inadvertently implicate Joseph, if he wasn't guilty, or prejudice them against Jessie. I said that. I said I was nervous, I explained that Jessie was prone to telling lies, that this was an integral part of her mental health issues. I talked about reactive attachment disorder and how it affected children. The sergeant asked me if I thought Jessie had been sexually abused. I replied yes, then immediately regretted it, because I was afraid they would interpret it as my saying Joseph had abused her. So I backtracked. I spoke of some of the things Jessie had said to me during our sessions together, some of the behaviours she had exhibited, and said that in my professional experience these were indicators of sexual abuse. However, there was no way to tell if this was current or historical abuse nor who the perpetrator was.

'What were your experiences of Joseph?' the sergeant asked. I told him that I hadn't observed Joseph doing anything inappropriate at any point. He asked if, while she was in with me, Jessie had talked about her relationship with Joseph. I replied, 'Only in the usual ways.' Because Jessie did regularly accuse the staff of all sorts of horrid things which I knew to be patently untrue, I needed to speak carefully. I wanted to be honest, and I wanted to be supportive of Jessie without damning Joseph. It was hard to gauge how savvy the sergeant and his companion were. It wasn't a large police force, so I had no idea how experienced they were with child psychopath-ology, and thus how likely they were to temper what I said with common sense. These kinds of worries made me more tentative than I actually felt, and then I worried about how that came off.

The sergeant kept going back to the question of whether or not I thought Jessie had been sexually abused. Each time I said yes, I did. In my professional opinion, she had experienced sexual abuse. Each time, I also said that it was not possible for me to say when the abuse had happened or who had done it.

I don't know if they believed me. Being asked a question over and over gives off the impression that the answer you're giving isn't sufficient, but that may just have been the way they worked.

I returned to my quiet life on the farm. It was time to put the ram out with the ewes. There was a new book to write. My daughter got chicken pox. The immediacy of Jessie and Glan Morfa began to fade as I was pulled back into ordinary day-to-day life.

Autumn turned to winter. Christmas came and went. We had bad storms in January and February that battered the coastline, knocking holes in the sea walls. The big supermarket I occasionally shopped at was flooded with seawater. Nearby roads were covered in sand. This made me think of Glan Morfa, which wasn't very far inland. I knew caravans in some of the holiday parks had been toppled over by the flooding. I wondered how the group home was doing. I wondered how the proceedings with Joseph were going. I wondered where Jessie was and how she was getting on.

Meleri and I didn't speak to each other during this period. This was partly due to the restrictions on discussing Joseph's case, but partly just to the weather, the Christmas season and the fact we both had busy lives. By late February, however, we were missing each other's company, so we arranged to meet for lunch at an ancient roadside inn that was halfway between her office and my farm. Centuries earlier, the road in front of the inn had been a busy thoroughfare, but it was now nothing but a narrow country lane with high hedgerows on either side. We needn't have worried about privacy, because we were the only lunchtime customers.

Meleri was at her flamboyant best that day. Dressed in a red wool cape and matching beret, she whooshed into the pub as theatrically as a film star, and it clearly brightened the day of the young man behind the bar. Too bad the news she bore wasn't as glamorous, because it turned out that things had gone every bit as tumultuously for Jessie as I had feared would be the case. The first placement, in the city on the far side of the county, had ended within a fortnight due to Jessie's peeing. She had peed on the settee, she'd peed on the kitchen chair, she'd peed in the dog's bed. The clincher was when she'd peed on the foster parents' bed.

It was hard not to find this funny, not only for the way Meleri told it, but also because black humour is almost a prerequisite for our work. But it wasn't funny. I knew that. It was dispiriting, because she was moved.

The next foster placement had seemed more promising. The couple were more experienced. There was no random peeing. Jessie seemed to settle into the new school all right. Things seemed to be going well. Until the fire.

Precautions to keep Jessie away from matches and other fire-starting materials had always been part of her programme to the point that checking her school bag, checking her room, checking where she was and what she did were all just things her carers did naturally. And she had done well at Glan Morfa. There hadn't been any fires for several months.

This fire was not serious. It was in a waste bin in a bedroom and had been confined quickly. Jessie insisted she had not started it. One of the couple's former foster children had come back for a visit and this girl smoked. Jessie insisted that the fire was this girl's fault, Jessie had only been trying to put it out after the girl had thrown a smouldering cigarette into the rubbish. No one believed this, of course, but Jessie wouldn't back down. Unfortunately that was it, as far as her foster parents were concerned.

So Jessie was moved once again, this time clear across the county to a very small town about twenty miles inland from the sea.

This news cheered me. While this town would involve a slow journey through a tangle of minor roads across the moors, it wasn't any further away from me than Glan Morfa had been, so I hoped I could resume seeing Jessie, if it was all right with my charity and Social Services. This cheered Meleri. We left our lunch date on a high.

chapter sixteen

Jessie's foster mother, Fiona, met me at the door. She was a young, heavy-set woman with dark hair slicked back in a tight ponytail and a Scottish accent so strong it sounded fake to me. This was an accent that belonged on the set of *Highlander*, not in a new-build bungalow on a Welsh housing estate. It was, however, impossible not to fall instantly in love with Fiona. She was one of those smiley, extrovert people so naturally warm that everyone becomes family.

'Och aye, we've been expecting you. Come into the sitting room. Jessie? *Jessie!*' she hollered. 'Jessie, your lady's here.' Fiona had a small boy about two years old on her hip and she set him down. 'Jessie?' she called more loudly.

There was no response.

'Now, where is she? She's been looking forward to seeing you. So excited she was this morning that she didn't eat her breakfast properly. Och, noo . . .'

The little boy fell over and Fiona bent to lift him up again. She turned to me. 'Have a sit down. You want a drink? Tea? I'm sure she'll be out in a minute. We'll give her that. If not, you can go fetch her, Angus, can't you?' she said to the small boy.

Tea and a couple of biscuits duly arrived but Jessie didn't. Fiona sent the little boy in but he came out, shaking his head but not speaking. This time Fiona herself went to get Jessie. The boy looked longingly at my biscuits.

'Would you like one?' I asked.

He nodded but didn't reach for one, so I held it out. Grabbing it, he ran off behind the settee to where I couldn't see him.

Fiona reappeared. 'Nope. She doesn't want to come out.'

'May I go in?' I asked, because I could tell I was very near to not seeing her at all.

Jessie was under the bed.

'Hi,' I said from the doorway. Sensing fear, I didn't want to encroach on her personal space, so I just stood still a moment. The room was what is called a 'single bedroom', meaning it is only large enough to accommodate a single-sized bed, which was a bit of an exaggeration in this case. If I'd stretched out my arms, I could have touched the wall on either side. The only furniture was the bed, a night table and, at the end, a small wardrobe that could only be reached if you were standing on the bed. The bed itself was still unmade, the duvet rumpled up, not in an airing-out sort of way but in a fight-with-your-bedclothes manner. I pushed it aside and sat down.

'Guess who I brought with me?' I said. I opened my hand-bag and removed the puppet. 'I have Puppy here.'

There was no response from under the bed. No sound, no

movement, nothing. I was taking Fiona's word for it that that's where Jessie was. But who knows? I might have been sitting in a stranger's bedroom on a stranger's bed, talking to myself. It felt that way.

'I expect you're feeling a bit overwhelmed,' I said. 'There's been so much change since we last saw each other.'

Nothing.

'I'm sorry I couldn't come before now. It took me a while to get everything in order again. But here I am at last.'

Nothing.

I leaned down and set Puppy on the floor so that Jessie could see him. 'Puppy's here.'

Nothing.

For several minutes I sat quietly, hoping the silence would smoke her out. Even two minutes in total silence is a long time. I watched the second hand go around the face on my watch to help me stay silent. Each time it passed the twelve, I looked up, around the room, then back to the watch.

A very soft sound started. I couldn't identify what it was initially but then realized Jessie was crying.

'Will you come out and talk to me?' I asked very quietly. I was measuring my words carefully, even considering whether or not to use 'please'. I wanted her to know I genuinely wanted to see her, but I was concerned 'please' might sound more like coercion in the way that adults so often use, couching demands as polite questions.

Still the almost inaudible crying.

'Come sit here with me,' I said. 'With me and Puppy. Come see Puppy. Come hold him.'

'No,' the voice under the bed said plaintively.

'No?'

'No. Make Puppy go away.'

'You don't want Puppy?' I queried and lifted him up off the floor. This didn't make a lot of sense to me, as Puppy had always been her favourite puppet, and I'd thought it would remind her of happy memories.

'No, I don't want Puppy. I'm scared of Puppy.'

'Why is that?'

'He reminds me of that night.'

'Which night?'

'That night Joseph touched me. The night he came in and put his hand on my pussy. He put his finger in me.'

'And Puppy reminds you of that?'

'Yes, because I was having a dream about Puppy. And then he put his finger in my vagina.'

This didn't correlate with what Meleri had told me about the incident. Her account had Joseph touching Jessie during shower time, but perhaps the abuse was ongoing, in which case there would be multiple instances.

I stared straight ahead. The door, now closed, was opposite me. I studied the small chips here and there in the paintwork.

'Are you still there?' came the small voice from under the bed.

'Yes, I'm still here.'

A pause.

'Why don't you come out and sit beside me here on the bed,' I suggested.

'I don't want to.'

'I expect it would be more comfortable than on the floor.'

'I don't want to look at you.'

'Why is that?'

'Because you went away. You said you wouldn't. You said you were going to be my person, but you weren't. And you took Puppy away. And now I don't like you any more. I'm not going to be your friend.'

'I see.' I sat back on the bed. 'It sounds like you have lots of strong feelings.'

'It was your fault.'

'What was my fault?'

'That I got sent away.'

'I'm not sure I understand.'

'You said you'd be my person and you weren't.'

'You feel it was my fault you got sent away from Glan Morfa?'

'Yes.'

'Can you explain that to me?' I asked.

'You said I should tell if someone was doing anything bad to me. So I did, because you said so. That made me get sent away. And I'm here and I hate it.'

'Jessie, please come out from under the bed, so we can talk more easily.'

'I hate Puppy too.'

'Come out from under the bed now, please. Now.' I kept my voice calm and matter of fact, but I spoke firmly.

There was a rustle and the bed rocked gently, as if a small earthquake had happened. Feet appeared, then legs, then Jessie herself. She stood up.

She was a bit mussed from hiding, her expression melancholy.

'Things haven't gone in a very good way, have they?' I said.

Jessie shook her head.

'Everything's got tangled up, hasn't it? Here, sit down with me.' I slid over on the bed. Jessie sat. 'Let's talk about this.'

'I don't want to.'

'Perhaps not, but I'd appreciate it. I'm not sure I know everything,' I said. 'Could you start right at the beginning and tell me everything that's happened to you since we last saw each other? That would be really helpful for me.'

'Hasn't Mrs Thomas told you anything?'

'Yes, Mrs Thomas has. But this is your experience, so I'd like to hear it from you.'

Reaching over, she took hold of Puppy and pulled him onto her lap. Then she shook her head. 'Well, you're not going to.'

Silence descended.

Jessie leaned forward, pressing her face into the puppet's fur.

'Here's what I heard you say just now. When I wasn't there, Joseph came in and touched you. You were asleep in bed and he came in. Is that correct?'

She nodded.

'That's different from what Mrs Thomas told me. She said that Joseph touched you when you were in the shower.'

Again Jessie nodded.

'Are you saying Joseph touched you more than once?'

'He touched me lots of times. Mostly in my room. But once when we were in the car, he had his hand in my knickers the whole time and Helen turned around and she didn't even notice. He had a blanket pulled up, because it was cold.'

This sounded suspicious to me. 'You and Joseph were sitting together in the back of a car? When was this?'

'Once.'

'Why was Joseph sitting in back?'

'I don't know. I don't remember.'

'Were there other children with you?' I asked.

'Sometimes. I guess. I don't know.'

I paused.

'Can I go back to Glan Morfa now?' Jessie asked. 'I don't like it here. Will you tell them that? Tell them that you said for me to tell and now I have, and so can you make it so that I can go back?'

'That isn't something I decide,' I said.

'But you're the one who told me to tell. It's your fault I'm here. You should be able to fix that.'

I paused, wary of what to say. It was awful to think Jessie might have somehow started these cataclysmic events out of some misguided effort to please me. I doubted that it was that simple, but I did suspect she now hoped I would be able to undo it all.

'Unfortunately, I'm not the person who decides those

things,' I said. 'I can hear you're upset and I'm sorry, but it is Mrs Thomas who makes those decisions, not me.'

Jessie lowered her head. 'Why am I being punished?' Her voice was petulant. '*I* didn't do anything. Joseph should have to go away, not me. This is so unfair.'

'Is that what you thought would happen? That if you told on Joseph, he would go away?' I asked.

'Yes, because he was horrid to me. He said I had to wash my hair. I told him I had a cold and Enir had said I could wait, but Joseph made me go do it.'

'Is that what happened that night?'

'It's unfair how they treat kids,' she muttered. 'No one listens to them. Everyone just makes decisions and no one cares what kids say.'

'I'm trying to.'

Jessie hunched forward over the puppet.

'Did Joseph really touch you in the shower?' I asked quietly. 'Or was he just being really, really annoying and you wanted to get him out of your face?'

She turned her head very slowly to look at me. 'Don't you believe me?'

'I'm just asking. And I'm not going to get upset, whatever the answer is. Because I know that sometimes when we get angry with people, we say things to get back at them, and sometimes these things aren't strictly the way they happened. We say them because we want the other person to feel as unhappy as we do. Everyone has done this at one time or another, said something not quite true to get someone else in trouble. That's just how people work. So I was wondering if this was what happened between you and Joseph.'

'*You don't believe me.*' Her voice was low, pained.

Instantly I felt awful.

'You think I'm a liar.' She was starting to cry. 'You say, "Tell somebody, if something bad happens", and then when I do you call me a liar. You're the one who was angry and said things to get back at me, not *me,* because you made it so that I'd get in trouble. You said, "Do this." You said, "Tell someone what's happening." You made me *believe* you. But you just wanted me to get into trouble. You *wanted* me to get sent away. You knew nobody would believe anything I said. This is all your fault and I *hate* you.'

In that moment, I think Jessie genuinely believed what she was saying, that what had happened was my fault and that she had no part in it. As desperately as I wanted to refute it, my sense was that the more her misconceptions were repeated, the more strongly they implanted. Things weren't cleared up by arguing with Jessie.

To make matters worse, my time was almost up. I didn't want to leave on such a low, especially after we had been apart for so long. Taking in a deep breath, I held it and then dispelled it slowly in an effort to bring my own self back to a calm place. I was aware of Jessie looking at me as I did this. It was a fierce look with cat-watching-prey intensity. She was angry. She wanted me to take the bait. I was scrambling for a way to defuse the situation.

'I know what you just said feels true to you,' I said, 'I understand that.'

Jessie continued to glare at me.

'And I'm sorry that telling the truth doesn't feel like a safe option to you, but maybe sometime in the future it will. We'll keep trying, okay?'

Jessie didn't answer, but she dropped her eyes.

'I need to go now, because it is almost five o'clock, but I'll come back next Tuesday.'

'Will you bring Puppy?' she asked in a small voice.

I nodded. 'Yes. See you then.' I rose.

Jessie remained seated and didn't reply.

'See you then,' I said again. '*Ta ra rwan*,' I added, the colloquial Welsh that literally means 'Going now'. It was usually directed at people in shops, but locally it had come more generally to mean 'Bye-bye'.

Without warning, Jessie reached out and hugged me around the thighs. '*Ta ra rwan*,' she wept. '*Ta ra rwan*.'

chapter seventeen

On Thursday we had a team meeting – myself, Meleri, Ben, two other social workers, another representative of my charity, and, because the case with Joseph was still ongoing, a woman from the police, named Ceridwen Davies, whom everyone called Crid.

Very early on in the meeting the conversation turned to Jessie's issues with telling the truth. Ben, the child psychologist, spoke at length about reactive attachment disorder and how lying becomes such an ingrained behaviour for these children. He explained how a baby is totally dependent on others for survival and life is all about getting needs met – being hungry and getting fed, being dirty and getting changed, being upset and getting comforted. When these needs are met consistently, the baby learns to trust adults to take care of him or her. When this doesn't happen or it happens inconsistently, the baby learns that people can't be trusted, that the world is unsafe, that others don't care. Ben said it was during this early childhood period that lying begins to establish itself. The child learns to cope by telling him or herself lies: 'It's okay my mother is gone. I don't really need her. I don't need to eat now. I don't want anyone to play with me. I can take care of myself.' Lying is a way for the child to take control of the situation. It's a survival technique.

Ben said we always had to keep this in mind: Jessie lied to stay alive. Not to be annoying or deceitful, but to survive. And so far, it had worked. She was still here. This meant she was likely to default to it any time she felt threatened. In dealing with Jessie, Ben told us that it was important that she could not play one of us off against the other. We had to assume she was going to tell us many different versions of what had happened with Joseph, that she would tell different versions to different people, and that none of them might agree with what Joseph told the police. Our only recourse was to collect up every single version and see if we could distil any truth from them. Ben said this was the key to working with Jessie. We had to talk to each other. We had to make sure each of us knew what Jessie was saying to the others. We had to trust each other because we couldn't trust her. And one more thing, he said. It was important for each of us to convey to Jessie that while we didn't trust her to tell the truth and wouldn't let her get away with her lies, this did not stop us from being able to care very much about her and wanting to help her.

One of the other social workers then articulated what was going through my mind. What if Jessie genuinely had suffered abuse at Glan Morfa? How would we know?

Ah, Ben said, we must also be alert to the possibility that, for all her lying, Jessie sometimes did tell the truth.

171

What a tangled web. We were to assume Jessie was lying, but we were to be alert to the possibility she wasn't. We were to assume Joseph was the perpetrator, but we were to be alert to the possibility he wasn't. We were to assume we knew what the abusive incident was, but we were to be alert to the possibility that that might not be it. We were to assume the abusive incident was current, but we were to be alert to the possibility that it may have happened long ago. In other words, we were to assume we knew what was going on, but we were to be alert to the possibility that we didn't have a clue.

What started out as quite an interesting, useful meeting slid off into a repetitive discussion of the ins and outs of reactive attachment disorder and the various options within the system for dealing with Jessie. The ultimate goal was to get her back into her family, and an extended conversation then followed about why this hadn't previously worked out. As an outsider listening to this discourse, I was struck by the dissonance between what we thought we knew about this case and what we did know. So much emphasis was put on the fact that this family appeared to be in a better place than most of the children we worked with. They were not homeless. They were not jobless. They were not living in abject poverty. Neither parent was a drug addict or an alcoholic. Yet they had a child with serious mental health issues whom they did not appear to want to take responsibility for. Why? Had Diane Williams's depression been so severe she had never bonded with Jessie? Had this made her so cold and neglectful that Jessie did not learn how to bond with anyone in return? Many mothers suffer post-natal depression and yet bond well with their children in the longer term. And what about the father? Why had he not bonded with her? Was he too busy supporting his wife? Supporting the family? Were there marital issues? Something else going on? Or were they just not that into parenting? I recalled the report about Jessie's older sister being 'feral' and that this was a reflection of the family's permissive beliefs, but how much of it was an actual belief system and how much of it was due to people who couldn't be bothered with the hassle of raising a well-behaved child? Had Jessie been just one too many children for them and they were unable to cope?

I had a very strong sense that Jessie had been sexually molested. While the general focus was on this having happened in the foster system, could it have happened earlier? Could the family's reluctance to take her back be a deflected effort to keep her safe from a predator at home or in the neighbourhood?

During the discussion, the third social worker, the man I had not met previously, asked about the possibility of sending Jessie to a special programme designed for children with reactive attachment disorder. It was at a centre in Kent, south of London, and he had read about the good results they had in rehabilitating children with RAD who, in particular, had arson issues. Someone asked about cost. It was in England and, while it was a government programme, the local authority in Kent had developed it and consequently children in their own area had first choice. They did allow children from other areas to enter the programme, but the cost was considerable.

It was unlikely Jessie's parents would be able to afford to pay for it, so if Jessie went the cost would have to be borne entirely by Social Services, and there really wasn't the money.

The conversation meandered at that point into a more general conversation about treating children with reactive attachment disorder and, from there, speculation on how many children with RAD were sociopathic and were sociopaths made or born. The meeting was growing tedious to me, because no one was saying anything new and we were no longer on topic. I looked over at the other representative from my charity. She rolled her eyes slightly and let out a long, slow, weary breath. I glanced then to Crid. She had a small spiral-bound notebook out, but from where I was sitting I could see she was doodling along the edge where the spiral was. I knew Crid was in the meeting as a liaison person for the police, but probably also to ensure we wouldn't talk about anything that would contaminate the case. She glanced up, meeting my eyes briefly, and I recognized the glazed look. We were all meeting-ed out.

The next time I drove out to see Jessie, it was a very rainy afternoon. We'd passed the worst of winter but the day was so heavily overcast it was dim as twilight when I reached her house.

The door was answered by a small boy in thick glasses, whom I hadn't met before. 'Hello. Come in,' he said, in a manner that made it sound like one word – then he immediately disappeared back into the sitting room to continue a computer game, leaving me to drip in the dim, narrow hallway. I took off my jacket and left it draped over the umbrella stand because there didn't seem to be any coat hooks. I then went down the hallway because I could hear Fiona talking. She was in the kitchen, doing the ironing and chatting to a man at the table whom she introduced as her husband's cousin. The little boy was his son. Fiona explained that Jessie hadn't been to school that day because she had a bad cold, and then nodded her head in the direction of the bedroom where I'd seen Jessie the previous time, saying to go on down.

I was slightly disconcerted by this very casual approach to my arrival, as if I were a regular visitor who knew what to do and where to go, but I carried on, finding the right room and knocking on the door. No one answered on the other side, so I gently turned the handle and opened it.

Jessie was sitting on her bed.

'Oh, it's you,' she said with an air of ennui.

'Yes, it's me. Remember? I said I would come today. How are you?'

'I'm poorly. I have a bad cough. See?' she demonstrated dramatically. 'And snot. Lots of snot. Aren't you afraid you'll catch it?'

'I'll take my chances. How are things otherwise?' I asked.

'Awful. I hate it here. When can I go back to Glan Morfa?'

'You sound fed up,' I replied.

'I hate it here. I hate it. Hate it. *Hate it*. Tell them that. Tell Mrs Thomas that. Tell her it's awful here and I want to get out.'

'Poor you. I'm sorry to hear that it's so awful. What don't you like?'

'Everything.'

'For example . . . ?'

'I don't like that little boy with the glasses. He turns on the TV without asking. He acts like he lives here, and he doesn't.'

'That sounds annoying,' I replied.

'*And* I don't like the way it smells here. Fiona is always cooking fish. It stinks of fish and I hate fish.'

'You like fish and chips.'

'That's proper fish. She cooks kinds that got skin on them. She cooks red fish.'

'Salmon?'

'Yes, salmon. All the time. And I hate salmon. And she knows it, but she keeps cooking it.'

'Poor you,' I said as empathetically as I could.

She sighed. 'I wish I had a bomb, and I could set it off right in this room. Boom!' She threw her hands up.

'I'm not sure that would be a helpful thing to do.'

'It would. Because I'd be dead. And you'd be dead. And Fiona would be dead. And everybody else in this stupid place. I'd like that. I wish I could get a gun.'

This wasn't a direction I wanted to take the conversation, so I reached down for my bag and pulled out a game of Yahtzee.

Jessie said matter-of-factly, 'I think I'm going to kill that little boy. I don't have a bomb or a gun, but I might kill him anyway. Because he's so annoying.'

I looked over at her. I was about 90 per cent sure this was

said to shock, that she was trying to keep control of our time together by engaging me in such a dramatic conversation. I did not want to reward her by getting upset, or into a power struggle over whether she should be bombing or shooting anyone. The other 10 per cent of me, however, was not so sure. Either way, it was not a comment I could ignore. So I said, 'You sound very fed up with things here.'

'I am.'

'I don't think killing people is the way to go. Perhaps we can think of some different things you could do when you are feeling as fed up as you are right now.'

'I could kill myself. I could take my pillow and put it over my face until I was smothered.'

'I don't want you to kill yourself. I would feel so sad if that happened. I would cry and cry.'

She looked over at me for a long moment. 'Would you?'

'Of course I would. That would make me very unhappy. So please don't consider it.'

'No one else would.'

'I'm really sorry you are feeling so down about things. I really am.'

'My mum wouldn't feel sad if I died,' she said. 'She'd be happy. She wouldn't have to hate me any more. Then it would just be Gemma at home, and my mum would stop being depressed all the time.'

'That's a big thought to be carrying around in your head. No wonder you're feeling discouraged.'

Sitting forward, Jessie sighed heavily, then she leaned

against me. I had been careful up to this point not to have any physical contact; because these were our guidelines, but also for my own safety, given the situation with Joseph, because I was alone. Now, however, I put my arm around her shoulder.

'I don't think that's true,' I said. 'Your mum has problems that make it hard for her to be a good parent, but that doesn't mean she doesn't love you. It just means it's hard for her to show it properly. And this is your mum's problem because of things that have happened in her own life. It's not your fault. That's hard to understand when you are little, because that's all the life you know, but it's true.'

Jessie shook her head. 'You don't know. You think you do, but you don't know.'

We sat together for several minutes in silence.

I still had the small box containing the Yahtzee game on my lap. Jessie reached down, took it and threw it towards my satchel. 'I don't want to play any of your stupid games. I hate games. Don't you know that about me yet?'

'I have a different idea,' I said. 'Let's do a visualization together.'

'What's that?'

'Remember that day when we imagined eating the fish and chips? That was a visualization. Let's do another one.'

'I don't want to.'

'That's okay.'

'I said: I. Don't. Want. To.'

'And I said that's okay. I meant that. You don't have to do

it, if you don't want to. You can just sit here beside me. I'll do it instead.'

Mostly, I wanted to reorientate Jessie's thinking, because what was obvious to me was that she'd become trapped in a downward spiral of thoughts. No doubt being ill did not help, but my sense on both visits was that Jessie had become more negative since being in foster care, more inclined to reject efforts to engage her. I suspected she was feeling quite isolated. While Fiona was warm and inclusive, she was an absolute extrovert. Friendship and connection were such innate skills that they took no effort for her. My sense, however, was that Fiona didn't always notice that others didn't find this as easy. What had clued me in was my arrival, when I was greeted by a strange child and then expected to find my own way down to the kitchen and then to Jessie's room. I knew from Fiona's perspective this was a generous and friendly 'my home is your home' gesture demonstrating how welcome I was, and I knew that I could have asked for a cup of coffee or a biscuit, or possibly even helped myself to something, and she would have seen this as natural behaviour. From a less outgoing perspective, however, such treatment wasn't welcoming. This was a strange house full of unfamiliar people, and it would be easy to feel nervous and uncertain about what to do. For someone like Jessie, who had come from a silent, rejecting household where she had been required to stay in her room for long stretches of time, I could imagine this expectation that people would naturally feel accepted and able to spontaneously join in was a big ask.

Jessie wouldn't have much support outside the home either. Making friends had never been a strength for her, even in the group home, where children were constantly present, but she'd also had three changes of school in short succession. Now she was living in a small village where most of the children would have known each other all their lives.

The humour was gone from Jessie's provocativeness. Everything about her now seemed grim. There was, sadly, not much I could do in such brief, erratic visits, but because she had responded so well to the visualization back at Glan Morfa, I hoped this might prove a skill I could teach her to use to soothe herself, or, at the very least, it would give her a brief bright spot in an otherwise dreary afternoon.

'Okay, here's how I'm going to start. First, I get comfy,' I said, leaning back on the bed. 'Remember, it's okay if you don't want to do this. I'm just saying these things for myself.'

She ignored me.

'Next, let's breathe in, way in. So our tummy goes in and our chest goes out. Then let it out slowly. All the way, so that when we get to the end of the breath, we go a "Haaah".' I demonstrated, taking in a deep breath and letting it noisily out of my mouth.

'You're not fooling me. I'm not stupid. I'm not going to do it, and you can't make me.'

'I'd never want to make you. I'm just talking out loud to myself because it makes this easier to do.' I was slightly behind her, relaxed back against the wall.

Jessie sat primly on the edge. 'I've got a cold. It wouldn't be good for me to breathe that way anyway,' she replied, not turning around to look at me. 'It'd make me cough.'

'That's fine. It's okay if you don't do it. You can just listen.'

'I don't want to listen either. I don't want to do it. I said that a million times now. And I'm not fooled by what you're doing, because you're trying to make me do it anyway.'

'Okay, that's fine. But I am doing this for me. It makes me feel good. First, I've taken nice, deep breaths and I'm sitting comfy, and now I'm going to close my eyes.'

Jessie put her fingers in her ears.

'In my imagination, I'm standing outside a door. It's an inside door and I'm looking at it. What does the door look like? Is it big? Is it little, littler than I am? What colour is it? Brown? Or white? Maybe green? Or red? Look very carefully at the door, at the details of the door . . .'

Jessie was being so obstinate about not participating that I was half expecting her to start singing la-la-la to block out my voice, but instead, she removed her fingers and laid her hands more gently over her ears. I carried on speaking in a soft voice.

'This door is inside a house. On the other side of it, there is a room. This is a very, very special room, not like any room you've ever been in before. This is your dream room, a room you have created just for yourself. You have designed it to be exactly the way you want it, and when you open the door, you know you are going to see this lovely room that is all yours.'

There was no response from Jessie. She kept her back to me.

'The door is big and sturdy, because it keeps the room safe. How do you open it? A round doorknob? A handle? What is it made of? Is there a lock that only you have the key to? Or is it a door your friends can go through too?' I said all this very slowly in a lulling voice, giving plenty of time to imagine.

I could see Jessie's fingers slipping down the sides of her head. She was still giving the impression of blocking her ears so that she could not hear me, but I could tell only the middle finger of each hand was touching her ears, and these were not pressing inward. She was listening.

'Open the door now and step inside. Here is your special room. You have chosen the colours. The walls and the floor are exactly right. Everything is very, very safe in this room. Nothing can happen here that you don't want. This is your safe place.

'Start to walk around your room and look at the things that you have chosen to be there.' I paused to give her time to imagine this. 'What is under your feet? What colour is it? How are the walls decorated? Are there pictures? Is there a bed? What colour are the covers? Are there things on the bed to make it nice? Are there toys in the room? Or books? Or something else? How have you specially designed it to make it your perfect room?'

I continued on with the visualization, very slowly, suggesting things to look at, to feel, to smell, to listen to. I drew the visualization out over the remaining twenty minutes of the visit, gently shifting the focus from the imaginary room to noticing how relaxed her muscles felt. Finally I suggested we open our eyes and rest a few moments longer before it was time for me to go.

Jessie had remained on the edge of the bed, her back to me, the entire time. As I slid forward to stand up, I saw she had her eyes open, but tears were streaming down her cheeks.

'This has made you cry?'

She nodded.

'That's okay. Can you tell me why?'

'I don't know.'

'It gave you strong feelings?'

Jessie nodded. 'I had an aquarium. It was over there in the corner,' she said, as if she were indicating somewhere in her bedroom, but her gaze was inward. 'There was a big, big window and the sun was coming in the window and shining on the aquarium. And I had Puppy sitting on my bed. I had a turquoise duvet cover with rainbows on it and a big floofy pillow, and the sun was shining everywhere. And in the corner, I had an aquarium with angel fish in it.'

'What a wonderful room,' I said.

'It made me happy to be there. And that made me cry.'

chapter eighteen

School had always been Jessie's strongest area. This seemed to be the one place she was able to focus her considerable energy and, more importantly, the one place she had connected good behaviour with positive consequences. She was a competent student who was often near the top of her class. She loved being praised for her work and was insanely keen to win stars and certificates. The frequent moves meant she hadn't bonded closely with any particular teacher, but she had engaged well with the curriculum, which was the same all across the county, enabling her to fit in smoothly.

Jessie's social skills with peers at school didn't fare quite as well. She found it hard to share positive attention and harder yet to lose out to someone else, so there was a tendency to get theatrically upset if she didn't achieve top scores. And, of course, she lied. At school, this mostly took the form of boasting about experiences or talents she did not have or lies to save face or avoid trouble. In other words, normal lies, albeit more frequent and flamboyant than other children told them. For the most part, however, Jessie functioned close to a normal level in this environment. Even during the changes over the last few months, Jessie had managed to hold things together at school. Her work remained in the upper quarter of the class, and her behaviour was acceptable, if a bit melodramatic.

Out-of-school life had always been more problematic for Jessie, whether in her own home, the group home or a foster home. In Meleri's opinion, the placement with Fiona's family was working better than the previous ones. While this was not a therapeutic foster home – the council was still waiting for an opening in one of those – Fiona and her husband were knowledgeable and admirably unflappable.

I did not have enough experience of visiting children in the foster setting to judge. Jessie was clearly not happy, but it was impossible to discern how much of this was due to the foster home, how much to the disruption and change, how much to the circumstances around the incident with Joseph and how much to Jessie's ongoing issues. I would have preferred to work with her in a more traditional setting than her bedroom, but at least I could see her.

Then, yet again, everything came crashing down. A few days after I'd last seen Jessie, Fiona went into her two-year-old son's room unannounced and found Angus had been stripped below the waist and Jessie was playing with his penis. Jessie was removed immediately.

Jessie returned to Glan Morfa. As Joseph was no longer there, it seemed the best solution after so many fraught attempts at fostering.

I sighed when Meleri told me. This was the hardest part of this new kind of work for me, this constant chopping and changing. In the old days, once the kids were in the class-room with me, I had them those six hours, five days a week, and I could pretty much count on our being together for the next nine months. I could get on with the task of creating the close-knit community that was as important to my success as I was. Most of the variables, and hence the behaviours, could be controlled by the natural consequences of the classroom structure. Consistency meant that routine did half my work.

The set-up I was now in was a completely different matter. There was no chance of sustained structure or consist-ency. I had limited authority and very little control. Indeed, in this case, I spent most of my time running to catch up, almost literally, because Jessie seemed to be in some different far-flung corner of the county practically every week. If this was hard on me, it must have been a hundred times harder on her.

The saddest part, however, was that it was no one's fault. We all saw what was wrong with the system, but it couldn't be helped. There were not the programmes locally. Jessie's family did not have the resources to pay for one of the spe-cialized programmes in far-off London, and even if they had I'm not sure they would have paid for it. My sense was that they were not bonded to Jessie at all and were happy to be free of her in whatever form that took. The local authority did not have the resources to pay for what Jessie needed either. There were hundreds of children in care who needed focused, specialized attention, but the money and the programmes just weren't there. Meleri, the other social workers and the child psychologist were all doing the best they could with what they had; they genuinely were. As was I. It just wasn't enough.

So, back to Glan Morfa we went.

More than six months had passed since Jessie had accused Joseph of molestation. We'd gone through the dark months of the year and now it was mid-March, still inclined to be snowy up on the moors where my farm was, grey and rainy down the coast with a strong, cold wind coming in off the sea. As I drove down the long single-track lane towards the group home, I noticed the road had never been resurfaced since that first visit nearly a year ago. The potholes were almost car-sized now. The small, scraggly trees, permanently braced against the sea wind, reached twigs out to skitter excitedly against my side windows as I passed.

Glan Morfa stretched out long and low in the overcast light. This was my first time back since I'd left for my trip to Italy. I noticed there was a car in Joseph's parking space, so I assumed a new manager had been hired.

Helen was at the front desk. She waved excitedly with both hands and then made an upward gesture with one hand that I knew as the signal for 'Want a cup of tea?'

'Catch you later,' I said, because I wanted to get organized in the room before Jessie got there. I had brought the puppets with me, as I thought Jessie might want to see them all again.

There was a welcome familiarity to the small, overcrowded room. Someone had stacked chairs on the sofa, so I took them down and put them in the corner, but otherwise nothing had changed. I opened the black bin bag and took Puppy out and set him on the table.

Jessie arrived within moments, opening the door with a flourish. 'I'm baaaack!' she said with a smile.

'Yup, here we are.'

'And there's Puppy!' She snatched the puppet up and cuddled it to her chest. 'I love Puppy so much. He's just like a real dog, but he isn't.' She looked up. 'I can't have a real dog.'

'No, it wouldn't work out very well here,' I replied.

'I can't have one because I tried to strangle ours,' she said cheerfully.

Not easy to respond to that, so I smiled and nodded, as if she'd mentioned something about the weather.

'You know what I did this week?' she asked, and set Puppy down on the table. She pulled out the chair next to me and sat. Reaching a hand up, she caressed my face. 'I really do like you. Even though you've started to get wrinkles.'

I gently removed it. 'Why don't you tell me what you did this week?'

'I got interviewed.'

Jessie slid her chair back and then bent forward to pull out the black bin bag from next to my chair. She started to open it.

'The lady's name was Dr Hughes and she said I will get three interviews and then they put it on TV! So, like, maybe I will be on *Real Crime*, or something!'

'I think what they mean is that they will make a video.'

'Yes, that's what I said.'

'Video is a recording. TV is a broadcast,' I said. 'This will be for your testimony, if it goes to trial. Do you know what a testimony is?'

'Do you think I'm stupid?' she replied. She pulled out the two bear puppets from the black bin bag and put one on each hand. A moment or two was taken up with manipulating the mouths up and down. She made the bears bite each other and tussle a bit.

'This one is Magnus,' Jessie said, indicating the bear on her left hand. 'I don't forget. People think I forget things, but I don't. Sometimes I just don't want to talk about them.'

'I see.'

'Dr Hughes asked me lots of questions. That's the lady doctor. Except she's not a real doctor. She didn't know anything about sore throats. And she asked stupid questions, so I didn't like her very much. She had a hair growing out of a mole on her neck, and it made her look like she might be a witch.' Jessie made one of the bears grab the side of her own neck.

'Do you know what her job was?' I asked.

'Yes. Psychologist. Like Dr Stone is, only different. I don't like him either. I don't like psychologists. It's a stupid job. They ask stupid questions.' Jessie paused, not looking up. 'She had these dolls . . .' She exaggerated the word 'doll' into 'daaaww-wwllls' to indicate her irritation. 'They had bits on them. Dirty bits, and she wanted me to play with them. She wanted me to do dirty things with them.'

'I'm guessing that she wanted you to show her what happened between you and Joseph.'

'She said, "Put his penis in her mouth." She meant the boy doll. He had a big willy. With *hair*. It had black hair all around the willy. And the willy wiggled up and down when you moved the doll.' Jessie demonstrated by flapping one of the front legs of the bear puppet. 'She expected me to *play* with it.'

'My guess is that she wanted you to show her what had happened,' I said again.

'I don't play with dolls. I'm too old. And I'm certainly not going to play with those dolls. They were gross. The man doll had this big floppy willy and the girl doll had a *vagina*. No clothes on at all, and a vagina that you could stick your finger into.'

'Those do sound like quite exceptional dolls, but they are important to Dr Hughes's work. They help her understand what happens when someone says they have been touched in their private areas.'

'She told me to make sex with them. So I did. I stuck his willy into her vagina and went like this.' She made the two bear puppets bump against each other, belly to belly.

I sat back. 'Okay, so first you are telling me you didn't play with the dolls, and now you are telling me that you made them have sex. Which is it?'

'What I said,' she replied irritatedly.

'You said both things.'

'Yes, well, that's how it happened.'

'And the psychologist told you to do this? She told you to put the boy doll's penis in the girl doll's mouth?'

'*No!* That would be gross!'

'She told you to have the boy doll put his penis in the girl doll's vagina?'

'God, you've really got a perverted mind, don't you? You should have played with those dolls. You'd like them.'

'I'm just trying to understand what happened when you were with Dr Hughes, because I am hearing that she told you to do these things, but I also know that isn't usually how these interviews work. I'm hearing that you didn't play with the dolls because they were gross, but I'm also hearing that you did play with the dolls.'

'Why don't you ever listen properly when people tell you things?' Jessie asked. 'Here I go, explaining the whole thing to you and you're still like, explain this to me again. Explain that to me. Why don't you just listen the first time?'

Not wanting to get sucked into one of Jessie's conversations-without-end, I didn't reply but just sat back in my chair.

Jessie opened the bag again and took out the unicorn pup-pet. She had never previously played with this one, deeming it too childish. Putting it on her hand, she fingered the rainbow-coloured crown and arranged the mane around it. She clapped the jaws up and down, first in front of her own face, then in front of mine.

'This would be good for a birthday. It looks like a party animal.'

I nodded. 'Yes, it would be good for that.'

'My birthday was last month. In February. February twelfth.' She petted the nose of the unicorn, feeling gently around its cloth horn. 'That's why I wanted to be back here. Because we get a cake from the Swiftie Bakery.'

'Didn't your foster parents remember your birthday?'

She shrugged. 'I wanted a cake from Swiftie's because they are really good. They put these sugar roses on them when it's your birthday and they taste soooo nice. And if it's your birthday, the staff let you have the roses. You can eat as many as you want and you don't have to share.'

'Do you know why you left your last foster home?' I asked.

'I was going to ask for a turquoise and white cake. Melanie had one like that and it was really pretty. It had turquoise icing and white roses all around it, and it said "Happy Birthday Melanie" on it.'

'Do you know why you left Fiona's house and moved back here?' I asked.

'Because I wanted to have a cake from Swiftie's for my birthday. That's what I said already. Why do you keep asking me questions you know the answer to?' She looked over at me, her expression faintly challenging.

'Because I am here to help you, Jessie. That is my job. And it means sometimes we have to talk about difficult things. Sometimes it is all right to chatter about things that are on our mind, even if they aren't the topic at hand. Sometimes we need to stick to the topic.'

'I am sticking to the topic. The topic is my birthday cake, and you are the one who is trying to talk about other stuff.'

A pause came then, and it grew.

Jessie still had the unicorn puppet on her hand. She examined it carefully, fingering through the polyester fur and the mane, around the horn, into the mouth. Then she pulled it off in a rough, disapproving manner and chucked it back into the bag.

'You know how to ruin things, you do,' she muttered. 'Did you know that about yourself? Because you should.'

I remained quiet, curious if my silence would get her around to the more important topics at hand.

Instead, she reached for the bear puppets again that had been left lying on the table. She put them on her hands.

'Hello, Magnus. Long time, no see.'

'Long time, no see, Eleanor. How are you, old bear?'

'My bones ache. How about you?'

'My bones ache too.' Jessie brought the two bears together. She had their jaws open, so as they met up together, it appeared as if they were biting each other, but the legs embraced. For a moment or two, she moved the bears back and forth with each other in this manner.

'I missed you,' the Eleanor bear said, as they broke apart.

'Yes, I missed you too,' Magnus replied. 'I thought you went away for good and I'd never see you again. I thought that was forever.'

'I wanted to say I would see you again. I wanted to say bye. And ask you to wait for me. But I didn't, because I didn't know . . .'

'Who touched you?' Magnus said.

'It doesn't count if it doesn't go inside you.'

'Who did it? Was it Joseph?' Magnus asked.

'Don't tell. They won't believe you.'

'Fingers down there. Down between your legs. Tickle, tickle, tickle. And nobody sees,' Magnus said.

'I know,' Eleanor replied. 'When I'm asleep. Asleep in my cave for the winter and in it goes. Tickle, tickle, tickle in the dark. And then there's baby bears. They happen in the dark.'

'I know,' Magnus said.

'Yes, I know,' Eleanor echoed. 'Fingers down there. It always happens in the dark.'

chapter nineteen

On the next visit, I brought a small cardboard box about ten inches square. The outside was a glittery, laser-cut metallic purple and the inside a pristine white. Originally it had been the gift box for a birthday present, but seemed much too beautiful to throw away after the present was opened; so in the way of such things, it had sat collecting dust in the back of my hall cupboard.

'What's that?' Jessie asked with interest. Not waiting to be invited, she snatched the box up and opened it. Her face dropped. 'Well, that's rubbish. It's an empty box.'

'Ah, but this is a special empty box. This is a "Me Box".'

She grimaced, as if I'd just told a particularly bad dad joke.

'In a lot of cultures, people create a special bundle or box of things that are important to them. These are things that express who they are, things that are precious because of what they mean, things that, when you look at them or touch them or listen to them or even smell them, help you feel good.'

'Puppy's not going to fit in there,' she said dismissively.

'No, Puppy won't, but you've got the right idea. You under-stand how nice Puppy makes you feel. When something important is too big for the box, we represent it symbolically in the box. For example, you could take one of these small pieces of paper here and write "Puppy" on it to put in the box. Or perhaps you would like to draw a picture of Puppy on the paper to make it extra special . . . ?'

Still unconvinced about the value of what I was doing, Jessie shook her head. I went ahead and dropped a piece of paper saying 'Puppy' into the box.

'While some things are too big to fit in here, the thought of them isn't. So we write the thought down and put it in. Some important things will fit just fine. Maybe you have a special necklace or a photograph, or maybe a CD that makes you feel calm when you listen to it. Or maybe a special stone that looks pretty or a pressed flower or a piece of cloth that is nice to feel.'

'This is stupid. I don't want to do it.'

'The me box is personal. You don't have to explain it to any-one. You don't have to show it to them. You fill it with things that feel special to you. And when you are feeling upset or stressed, you can open it and use the things to help you feel happy again.'

'I don't want to do it.'

'Maybe not, but let's try just a little bit of it. Let's put three things into the box. Then we will stop and do something else,' I replied. 'And you've already put one thing in. You chose Puppy, so we put the paper saying "Puppy" in. Next time you are feeling worried or lonely, you can take the paper out and envision Puppy in your mind. You can imagine Puppy's fur and think about how cuddly Puppy feels and this will help with the bad feelings. Puppy is a good thing to put into the box. What else can go in?'

'I don't know.'

'Take your time.'

'I don't need time. I don't know.'

Silence. Initially it felt hostile. Jessie was doing her usual control thing where whatever I suggested had to be opposed, but as we continued to sit quietly it mutated into a more thoughtful silence. A couple of minutes passed without any words.

Then Jessie tipped her head. 'Can I have one of your pens to put in the box?' She shrugged slightly, as if to deflect the fact she was allowing herself to take part in this activity.

'Which pens?'

'One of these.' She stood and leaned over to open my satchel. She took out the packet of felt tips. 'Could I have one of these for my box? Because they make me happy. They remind me of drawing.'

'All right,' I said.

'I wish I could have them all,' she said, her tone wheedling. I didn't respond. She fingered through them and finally picked out a dark green one. 'Know why I took this one?' she asked, holding it up.

'Tell me.'

'Because it's the first pen I used in here. Remember? That

first day you came. You let me open the packet and it was brand new. And I drew with this one first.'

'That's a nice memory,' I said, despite the fact that my memory of the green pen was as an instrument for exorcising the devil.

She put the pen into the purple box. 'And I know what I really want to put in' She leaned over my satchel again and sorted through it for the drawing paper. 'One of my pictures. Are any of them in here?'

Jessie was referring to her skylark drawings, but I only had blank sheets of paper with me, so she decided that she would draw a new one to put into the box. Taking out a clean sheet and the packet of felt tips, she sat down in the chair next to me and began the drawing.

The small bird soon took shape down in the right-hand corner of the page. Jessie seemed more focused than she usually was. There hadn't been much belligerent behaviour, and now when she settled on the drawing she stayed on task.

As always, the bird was brightly coloured. The body was a vibrant yellow and the wings the dark green colour of the pen she had selected for her box.

'Have you seen many skylarks?' I asked as she worked. I kept my tone casual because I didn't want her to take my query as disapproval of what she was doing, but I was curious if she was consciously choosing to colour them so brightly.

'Yes, of course I have,' she replied dismissively.

I didn't respond immediately, and when I didn't, she looked up. 'Of course I've seen skylarks. Don't think I'm stupid.'

'I've never thought you were stupid, Jessie. I was asking, because we have many skylarks up where I live. I was thinking that maybe you would like to come see them sometime. But if you have seen them many times, then I expect you wouldn't be interested.'

'It would be okay to do that sometime,' she replied, not looking up from the drawing. Her tone was still faintly dismissive.

Silence.

'Where do you live?' Jessie asked, her focus still on the drawing.

'Up beyond Llanfair. Across the high moor. We aren't on the moor ourselves, but you have to go across it to get to our farm. When it is spring and summer, the skylarks all fly up as the car goes by. You can hear them, if your window is down.'

'Do you have a husband?'

'Yes. And a little girl. And two dogs and two cats and some ducks and some turkeys and some sheep. And a grandpa.'

Jessie looked up. 'A grandpa?'

'Yes, my little girl's grandpa lives with us. And his little dog too.'

'How old is your little girl?'

'Five.'

Jessie bent back over the drawing. Several moments passed in silence as she coloured in the bird and added depth to the surroundings.

Then she said, 'I've been up on the high moor.'

This seemed questionable to me. The moor remained an

entirely natural area, treeless, boggy and windswept. There were no developments for sports or outdoor activities, and consequently they weren't a popular destination for outings, not even for walkers because of the bogs. So I asked, 'When did you go there?'

'Joseph used to take me out in the minibus. You know, that one they use to take us to swimming. Sometimes we went up on the moors. We saw the places you saw. We probably even saw your farm.'

This sounded unlikely to me, but I didn't challenge her.

'Sometimes Joseph sexed me up there.'

'What do you mean?' I asked.

Jessie kept her focus on the bird drawing. She was making a much more elaborate drawing than she usually did with the skylarks. There was grass and trees and flowers, all in vibrant colours. 'When Joseph wanted to do sex with me, he took me to the moor. We went there lots of times.'

'Just you and Joseph?' I asked.

'Yes. Me and him. It was a date. And then he sexed me. Behind the picnic shelter.'

That was patently false, because there were no picnic shelters on the moors. There were no picnic tables, no parking areas. I was also highly doubtful that Joseph would try to take any child out alone in the minibus because that was a serious breach of policy. Someone would have noticed.

Indeed, the whole event seemed fabricated. The moor was a long drive from the coast. Both people and vehicles would have been missed if they'd made the journey, and even if she had gone there Jessie couldn't have been molested behind a picnic shelter, because there were none. My sense was that she was attempting to show a connection to me by saying she had been in the same places I had. What about the rest of it? Had she chosen to talk about Joseph for the same reason? As shorthand for wanting to show she had a connection to him? Or was it because she knew talking about sex with him was a good attention grabber? People paid attention to her when she was on that subject. Or was there truth threaded through her story? Had the picnic shelter, wherever it was, been a genuine site of rape? Was the rapist Joseph? Or had someone else been transmogrified into Joseph because he was safer to talk about?

All these thoughts went rapid-fire through my mind in the few moments of silence that followed as she worked on her picture. I wasn't to discuss Joseph with her. I wasn't to ask leading questions or draw her out. In the end, all I could think to do was reflect back to her what she had said in the hope that it would encourage her to clarify herself.

'So, you and Joseph went on a date, and you and he had sex behind the picnic shelter on the moors?'

'Yes. And there was this other man there and he had a girl-friend. I think her name was Alice. And me and him and them, we all sexed together.'

That took it a step too far. 'This sounds like a story to me,' I said.

'It's *not*.'

'Generally, stories are okay. It's fun to imagine life different than it is,' I said, 'but we have to be careful what we tell, because stories can have consequences.'

'You don't believe me,' she said accusingly. 'No one ever believes me.'

'What I believe,' I said, 'is that telling stories is sometimes a way of talking about difficult things. Sometimes when we can't say things straight out, we can do it in a story.'

'My story is *true*,' Jessie insisted.

'Yes, I believe you. I believe that someone has touched you in a way that they shouldn't. I believe you didn't want it to happen. I believe it upset you a lot. And I believe that's what you're trying to tell me.'

Jessie raised her head and looked over at me. Her brow furrowed, a faintly bewildered expression on her face. 'But you just said it was a lie.'

'No, I did not say that. That's what you heard, but it isn't what I said. I said going on the moor with Joseph and Alice and this other person sounds like a story to me. And what I've just explained is that sometimes, when something true is very difficult to tell people, we wrap it up in a story because it is too hard or too scary to say outright.'

Jessie's frown deepened. 'I don't get what you're saying.'

'Let me tell you about when I was a little girl,' I said. 'I used to love horses. They were my very, very favourite thing in the whole world. Our across-the-street neighbours were a couple named Mr and Mrs Fox, and they didn't have any children. This meant they had a house full of all sorts of wonderful, delicate, breakable ornaments. One of these ornaments was a horse statue. I don't know exactly what the horse was made of, but it had a real hair mane and tail and looked very lifelike. It also had all this miniature gear on it – a Western saddle and some saddlebags made out of real leather and a tiny lasso – and all of these things were so lifelike that it was magical. I so wanted to play with it, because it would have been just the right size for my dolls, but, of course, I could only ever look at it up on the shelf when I visited.

'Then one day when I was about your age and it was very near my birthday, Mrs Fox invited me into her house. She told me she couldn't give me this beautiful horse statue because it had been made for them by a very special friend, but she knew how much I loved it. So as a birthday present to me, she told me she was going to let me take the horse home for a little while and I could set it up in my room. She wrapped it up well and put it in a cardboard box, so that I could safely carry it home. I was *so* thrilled.

'Then, as I was about to cross the street, this big boy named Lawrence came up to me. I hated Lawrence. He was a horrible bully and I'd had lots of trouble with him in the past. When I saw him, I hid next to a parked car, but he saw me. He was on his bike and he started to pedal towards me like he was going to run me over. He didn't, of course, but he came very close to me and I tripped over the kerb, trying to get out of his way, lost my balance and fell over. I fell right on the cardboard box with the horse in it and I heard it break. There was just this rattly noise of bits knocking about in the box.

'You can imagine how upset I was. I started to cry, and

I cried and cried, because I knew I was going to be in such bad trouble for ruining Mrs Fox's horse. I didn't want to get blamed for it because it really wasn't my fault, but I was so scared of Lawrence. I didn't know what he'd do to me if I told on him. So when I got home and my grandmother asked me what had happened, I said that a little girl named Susan, who lived a block over from me, had been riding her bike too fast and knocked me down, and that made me break the horse. I was too scared to say who had really done it.'

Jessie had sat riveted to her seat throughout my account. '*Wow*, that was really bad,' she said. 'I would have punched Lawrence in the nose. I would have given him a black eye. I would have took care of you, if I'd seen that happen.'

'Thank you. That's very kind of you. But why I'm telling you about this is to show what I mean about telling stories when you're frightened of what will happen,' I said. 'Sometimes telling the truth is too scary, so we explain things with a story. In my case, I was so scared that Lawrence might beat me up if I told on him, that I blamed Susan instead. I told the grown-ups that Susan had been riding the bike, when the truth was that Susan wasn't even there that day. It wasn't a good story to tell, because it could have got Susan into bad trouble, and she was innocent, but I was too scared to think about how it would affect Susan. I thought instead, "Well, *part* of the story is true." The horse got broken because someone made me fall over. And it was important to me that people understood it wasn't my fault it happened. I *was* being careful with it. But I was too worried about what Lawrence might do to me if I got him in trouble to say who had really done it, so I made up the story about Susan.'

Tears welled up in Jessie's eyes as I spoke. They clung to her lower lashes without falling. 'I feel sorry for you,' she said.

I reached an arm out and put it around her shoulders. 'You're being very kind-hearted right now. Thank you. But I'm wondering if anything like that has ever happened to you?'

She shook her head. 'No, I've never seen any horses like that.'

'No, I mean about telling stories because it's too hard to tell facts. I'm wondering if someone has done something, maybe touched you in a way you didn't like, but you find it scary to talk about the actual person who did it.'

Jessie lowered her head. She brought a hand up and wiped her eyes.

Silence came then and it stretched out between us, a brittle, noticeable absence of words.

I lowered my arm from her shoulders, ever conscious of how careful we needed to be about touching children, even without the added weight of accusations.

Jessie looked at me. 'I wish you were my mum,' she said in a small voice.

'Yes, that would be nice, wouldn't it?' I replied. 'Unfortunately, it didn't work out that way. But I can be your friend who cares what happens to you.'

'Can I call you Mummy? Just for pretend?'

'I can understand how nice that would be, but I think we need to stick to Torey.'

'Just in here? Please? It wouldn't hurt just in here.'

'I think we need to stick to Torey.'

Rising up, Jessie reached across the table for a tissue. Once reseated, she opened it up flat, put it on the palm of her hand and wiped it over her face. She blew her nose. Then turning her attention to the drawing of the skylark on the table, she pulled it over. 'You were going to take me out for fish and chips once, but we never got to go. Will you take me out on the moors instead? So I can see the skylarks?'

'Yes, sweetie, I will. I promise that.'

Folding the skylark drawing up into quarters, she placed it in the purple box. 'I'm going to put this in here for now, but that's just for today. I'm not sure I want to do this box thing. It makes me sad.'

'What feels sad about it?'

Shrugging, she stood up. 'I want you to bring the puppets with you next time instead. I like them better. They're our best thing in here and that's how I get happy. Not this box.' She slid it in my direction.

'Okay.'

Jessie started for the door, but when she reached it, she paused and turned. 'And I'm sorry.'

'For what, sweetie?'

'That the horse you liked was broken. That the boy was bad to you. I feel sorry for you.'

chapter twenty

On Friday, I met up with Meleri for lunch. She couldn't get away from the office for any length of time, so I drove into town to meet her there and we went to a nearby pub. Although it was March, the day was unpleasant in the way only late winter days can be, with a bitter wind tugging at our clothes and slushy snow underfoot. The pub, an old building tucked into the arches of a disused railway viaduct, was warm and dark, the air heavy with the yeasty fug of draught ales and stale tobacco smoke. We took a booth in the corner where we could have privacy to talk.

Mostly I wanted to touch base with Meleri, because we were seeing less and less of each other outside the regular team meetings at Social Services. Her caseload had grown bigger and was covering a wider area, so it was harder to schedule a meet-up, and when we managed it Meleri was often tired and stressed. As a consequence, we usually ended up not talking much about work at all. My sense was that Meleri needed a break more than anything else, because when she did talk shop it was mostly to let off steam about her boss and his increasing demands, or about the scandalously over-stretched services. It was so much more pleasant talking about our dogs or our families, or even the irascible weather.

So it was on this occasion. We chatted. For me it was all about getting ready for lambing on the farm, which was always a demanding time of year. I also told her about our sex-mad ducks. They began feeling amorous while my young daughter was feeding them, and how *did* you explain a drake's infeasibly long corkscrew of a penis to a five-year-old? Wide-eyed with curiosity, she had wanted to know what it was and how on earth he stored such an amazing thing when he wasn't using it. Meleri and I both fell about laughing at the silliness of it all.

Our food arrived, interrupting our merriment. Meleri looked down at her bowl of soup and it was as if a curtain fell across her face. Her shoulders dropped and she looked over at me, her eyes sad.

'I can't do this,' she said very quietly.

I wasn't sure what she was talking about – the food? Our meeting? Life? So I looked over questioningly.

'Whenever we're having a conversation about Jessie, there is this huge elephant in the room. In every bloody room I go into. This huge elephant.'

I was still not quite following the abrupt change of conversation.

'*Joseph*,' she said with emphasis. 'I cannot keep going on, meeting up with everyone, laughing, carrying on, and never acknowledging Joseph. I have no idea where he is, what's happening to him, how this is all affecting him, but I can bloody well imagine. And here we all are, having to act like nothing is happening, like he isn't there.'

I knew exactly what she meant.

'I'm just so depressed this is even happening,' she continued. 'In one corner, we have this lost, mixed-up kid, who pisses people off as a way of connecting with them. We all know she's a pathological liar, that she spews the most vile stuff out, and probably doesn't even mean it herself, but she just doesn't know how else to be. And then in the other corner we have this good, kind man, just the sort of man we need in the world, certainly the sort we need in Social Services. But is he? Is he innocent and about to have his life ruined? Or has he ruined Jessie's? I don't know what to think any more, and my heart's sick of trying to figure it out.'

I understood Meleri's quandary. In my heart of hearts, I felt Jessie's allegations were probably something said in the heat of the moment, something to get attention. My gut said Joseph was innocent, but . . . what if? I'd been wrong about my colleague who'd taught first grade. What if I was wrong here, now, too?

When I arrived at Glan Morfa, Jessie was waiting for me at the door. Excited that I had brought the bag of puppets with me, she offered to carry them into our room.

'It's so good to see these,' she said brightly, as she opened the bag. 'These are my friends. My good friends. Hello, Mr Toucan! Hello, Mr Hare!'

Abruptly, her mood changed. 'Have other children been play-ing with these? Because where's Puppy?' she asked accusingly.

'He's in there. Everyone's in there. Keep looking.'

Jessie dug through the black bin bag with a sense of urgency. 'Puppy's right at the bottom! He'll smother! And here's Mag-nus right at the bottom too. And Eleanor! Someone else has been playing with these.' She didn't disguise her outrage at this possibility.

'No,' I reassured her. 'No one else has touched them. The bag just got knocked about in the car.'

'What about your little girl? Did she get into them? Did she think they were her toys?'

'No, my little girl has her own puppets. Her favourite is a bunny puppet we call Super Rab.'

'Maybe she got into these when you weren't looking.'

'No, I don't take them in the house. My little girl doesn't play with these.'

Jessie scowled. 'I should hope not,' she said pertly.

Slipping one of the bears onto her hand, she then reached into the bag and took out the hare puppet and handed it to me. 'You wear this one.'

This was a change. Previously Jessie hadn't wanted me to participate in the play. She preferred 'doing shows' for me to watch or just playing on her own with the puppets. How-ever, I obliged and pulled the hare puppet on my hand.

Dropping the usual Magnus/Eleanor identity for the bear, Jessie made it gallop along the table in a fairly realistic man-ner. She made growling noises.

'Okay, I'm a bear going through the woods, and you're the bunny. Make the bunny go around.'

I started to move the hare along my side of the table when Jessie suddenly attacked it with the bear puppet. She flew at the hare, hitting my hand quite hard. There was a moment's wrestling and then she had my hand with the puppet flat on the table top.

'That wasn't very good,' Jessie said. 'Didn't you know the bear would eat Super Rab? Because bears do, of course. They eat rabbits right up. Didn't you know that? So try to get away this time. Try to run so the bear doesn't catch you.'

Again, Jesse caught and killed my hare within seconds, and then wanted to do it again, and once more instructed me to defend myself better. On the fourth or fifth repetition, I succeeded in getting my hare around the edge of the table and out of sight, and, because my arms were longer, out of reach of her bear puppet.

The game had become increasingly lively, leaving Jessie panting with exertion when my hare disappeared to safety. I was curious to understand the purpose of the game and wanted to find out if winning was important, and if she'd get angry when I'd 'won' by getting away from her bear. She didn't. Not being able to catch my hare brought her up short, and she gave me a long wordless look, as if perhaps I didn't know how to play the game properly, but she didn't get upset. Instead, she leaned down and pulled the second bear puppet out of the bin bag and put it on her other hand.

'Two bears against my one little hare?' I asked. 'Do you think that's fair?'

'Sometimes things aren't fair,' she replied grimly. 'Being a rabbit isn't fair. It doesn't matter if you have one bear or two bears chasing you. Mostly you're going to get et.'

Then, unexpectedly, Jessie changed the game. After two times pouncing on my hare and killing it, she paused, pulling a bear off her one hand. She reached into the bin bag and pulled out the lamb puppet. 'Here, you can have this one too, so that we both have two puppets. That makes it fairer.' She put her free hand back into the other bear.

'So you have two bears and I have a lamb and a hare.'

'That's right. And I'm going to kill you.'

'I'm hearing an angry voice. When I first arrived, you were excited to play with the puppets, but something's changed.'

'That's right. So run away. See if you can get yours away.'

It became a strangely primal game, a game of chase-and-catch that you'd expect only a three- or four-year-old to enjoy, but I discovered it was full of unspoken rules, like our not being able to stand up or move the puppets any further than our arms could reach.

I began to vary my side of it. I hid the lamb puppet behind my back where it couldn't be reached, and when the hare was savaged, I brought the lamb out to take care of it. 'Aww, poor hare, you're hurt badly.' The lamb stroked the hare's head.

Jessie pounced on the lamb. 'There. I killed it too!'

My sense when we first started to play was that Jessie was staking out her territory with me, that she had been worried my daughter might be playing with 'her' puppets. Finding out that my daughter had a bunny puppet named Super Rab, Jessie had given me the closest thing she could find and then proceeded to 'kill it', giving her a sense of control over our relationship and over my daughter's claim on me.

As it progressed, however, the nature of the play had changed, becoming more about her strength and my weakness. I tried to introduce the concept of empathy and caring by having the lamb comfort the fallen hare, but this simply made the lamb vulnerable in Jessie's eyes. Each time I did, she immediately pounced on it and killed it. I found this interesting in light of our previous meeting when she had spontaneously empathized with my being bullied as a child, because that did show Jessie was capable of empathy.

Jessie got fed up with my making the lamb so vulnerable. 'Try to get him away from me. Pretend you have a gun. Pretend to shoot my bear when he comes near.'

'But the lamb is worried for his friend. He wants to help his friend. Hare is hurt. Lamb wants to make Hare feel better.'

'No, that's not how it goes. This is war. Your lot are at war with my lot. I want you to fight me. Pretend you've got a gun. Shoot me. Shoot my bears dead, if you can, because otherwise they are going to kill you.'

'I'm not comfortable with guns,' I said.

'Well, then, just *kill* me,' she said in frustration. 'Make your lamb kill me with his bare hands. Like this.' She shot one of the bears out across the table and whacked my lamb to the table top.

We went back to the bears chasing my lamb and hare. I let the bears win. While the lamb and hare made a spirited effort to get away, they didn't fight back, and inevitably the bears caught up with them and gobbled them up. No mercy was shown if one puppet attempted to comfort the other. That one too was eaten. Jessie was matter of fact about my demonstrations of empathy. 'If you're going to do that, it's going to get killed,' she said. 'That's war.'

'We could make peace?' I suggested.

'Nope. Bears never make peace with lambs or hares. That's just how life is.'

The entire session was taken up with this game. I kept questioning myself as I was playing, because the game felt as if it were right on the boundary between what might or might not be helpful. I couldn't decide, so I kept going. And Jessie, whose energy seemed endless, kept going too. The rule about staying in our seats was abandoned. She whooped and hollered and ran around the table, pounding my puppets repeatedly.

At last I gave the five-minute warning that our time was nearly at an end. Jessie expelled air in a long, noisy sigh and fell forward on the table top. 'Whew!' she said, and pulled the puppets off her hands. 'That was *fun*. That was the most fun I ever had with you.'

'Good, I'm glad,' I said.

'Did you like it?' she asked.

'I liked spending time with you,' I said.

'Did you like getting beaten up all the time?' She grinned mischievously.

'Well, I could see *you* were having fun!' I replied with a smile.

'But did you like it? Did you like getting beaten?'

'No, not especially. You wouldn't like it, would you? If you were in my place?'

'But I didn't have anybody that was weak.'

'But how would you feel,' I asked, 'if you were playing and always lost? Always got beat up on? How would it make you feel?'

'It wasn't me that got beat up. It was them.' She pointed to the hare and lamb.

I could tell Jessie wasn't quite in the right place at that moment to see things from my point of view. The fact that she'd asked me if I liked it made me think she was aware of my perspective and that she knew that, no, I wouldn't like it, but I suspected this was also the point of it. Insisting she change viewpoints at this time would do nothing but ruin what she was working through. So I tried to reframe the comment. 'This would have been more fun for me if we could have been friends.'

'That's not how it works,' she said. 'Bears are never friends with hares.'

'Couldn't we change that?' I asked. 'Maybe the hare would realize that the bear was being so nasty because he was very hungry. Or maybe the bear had hurt himself in some way. What if the hare said, "Can I help you?" Maybe if he helped the bear not feel so bad, then the bear wouldn't be as angry.'

'Noooo, silly,' Jessie replied, and flapped a hand at me. 'That is not how it works. Bears just hate rabbits, that's all. And hares. And lambs. They just hate them and always want to eat them up. And that's okay, because that's how bears are.'

I sat, regarding Jessie.

'It's true,' she said to my unspoken challenge.

I didn't reply.

'It's *true*.' She came closer and flapped her hand near my face, as if she were slapping me. 'It's true, it's true, it's true. Say that. Say it's true.'

I grinned at her.

She grinned back. 'I beat you up a million times today, so I'm right. I'm right and you're wrong. So say it. Because I proved it.'

'A million times wasn't enough to change my hare's mind. I still think your bear can be a different bear,' I said. 'I think he's just scared to. It's easier for him to eat my hare than listen to him.'

'A million and one times. A million million times. That's how many more times the bear will eat him.'

'That's a lot,' I said, 'but it's not enough.'

'A million, million, *million* times,' Jessie said, laughing. She sat down on my lap and wrapped her arms around my neck. 'That's how many times I'm going to beat you up. A million, million, million, *million* times. And you will be dead and an old lady.'

'And it still won't be enough.'

She laughed. 'I love you.'

chapter twenty-one

Jessie had news when I next came to see her.

'Guess what? My mum and dad took me out. They came on Sunday and we went to Dragon World. Have you ever been to Dragon World?'

This was a local themed tourist attraction based on Celtic mythology. The 'experience', as it was labelled, relied heavily on darkness, smoke machines and animatronic dragons, witches and other fairy-tale folk for its effects. I had been once, or rather, almost once. My young daughter had pestered and pestered us to take her, but when, just inside the front door, the first witch popped up out of the smoke, she went running back outside and that was the end of our visit. I told Jessie about this and she laughed heartily.

'*I* wasn't scared. I liked it. I said to my dad, "Bring on all those dragons!" I said that, because I wish I lived when there were real dragons. I wouldn't be afraid of them.'

'It sounds like you had a good time.'

'My mum works at Poundland now. She takes people's money when they want to pay, and sometimes she puts stuff on the shelves. That's when it's not busy. My dad got laid off from the factory. He says that's all right because he didn't really like it, but I can't come home yet. He says that's because there isn't anyone to look after me. He's going to job interviews all the time, and Gemma is taking a catering course, so she's mostly not home either. And my mum has a proper job, did you hear that? She's not hanging around the house all the time now. So that's good.'

'I see.'

'Gemma didn't come. It was just me and my mum and dad, just by ourselves,' Jessie said. 'And we had a burger from a stand on the front. I wanted to go to McDonald's, but my dad said that was good enough. And then we went to Dragon World. My dad said it was too expensive for what it was, but I thought it was good. But it's not for little kids. No wonder your little girl didn't like it. You need to be, like, ten or so to like it. Probably lots of kids my age get scared too, but I didn't. I thought it was brilliant. Brill-iiii-aaant. I want to go again. I want to punch that big green dragon in the nose, the one that comes out and scares you. It's the biggest.'

Jessie paused to catch her breath. All this had been conveyed to me immediately on arrival. She hadn't even sat down yet. Looking around the room before she pulled out a chair, she asked, 'Did you bring the puppets this time?' She knew I had, because the black bin bag was there.

I smiled.

'You're getting to know me at last, aren't you?' Jessie said in a good-humoured but faintly patronizing tone, as if I were a dog who'd successfully performed an intricate trick.

Opening the bag, she began to take out the puppets, cuddling Puppy, as she always did, and setting him up to watch over us benevolently. Then she lifted out the dragon puppet. 'This really is good, this puppet. Look how it's made, so that it's shiny like gold. Dragons love gold. Did you know that? I did. This one looks like it's made of gold. It looks as good as any of the ones at Dragon World. I said that to the man. I said I know where there's a dragon that's as good as those there, and I meant this one.'

She took it off her hand and set it on the table. Out came the toucan, the unicorn, and they too were laid on the table. Then came the lamb puppet that had been so abused by the bears the previous week. Jessie slipped her hand into it and turned it so that its face was right in front of hers. 'Larry the Lamb,' she said to it. 'Lambs can't do anything. A dragon would eat a lamb up in one bite.'

She kept the lamb on her hand, kept looking straight into its face. 'I saw Dr Hughes again,' she said, more to the puppet than me. Then she looked over. 'She's the sex lady. The one with the dolls. Remember?'

'The psychologist. For the police,' I gently corrected.

Jessie nodded and looked back at the lamb. She turned the puppet over. 'Do you have any sex bits?' Jessie asked it and fingered through its fleecy wool. 'You do not.'

Suddenly she looked around. 'They're going to have a trial, these puppets.' She grabbed the dragon. 'He's going to be the judge.' She set him up in the middle of the table. 'And here's Mr and Mrs Bear. They're the parents. And here's Lambie and Unicorn and . . . where's the hare? That's another one of their children. They've got three children. And Puppy's going to be the child psychologist. No. Puppy's going to be these kids' social worker. Let me get that big ostrich puppet out. That can be the psychologist, who says, "Make sex to show me what happened."' Jessie leaned over to me and said in a stage whisper, 'I think she just wants to talk dirty all the time and this way she gets paid for it. I'm not going to fall for it. I'm not going to get in trouble for that kind of talk.'

She arranged all the puppets across the table and then put her hand into the lamb puppet again. She cradled it a moment with her other arm. 'So they are going to have a trial. To decide if Mr and Mrs Bear can have their children back. See, they got their children taken away. They got sent to a home. Mr and Mrs Bear were doing heroin. They were doing smack and laying around all day and not feeding their children. Lambie just about starved to death. He got put in hospital because he was dying, but Mr and Mrs Bear didn't care. So now the judge is deciding if they will get their children back. Hare hopes they won't. Hare says, "I'll take care of you other two." See, Hare is oldest. Hare is, like, fifteen. Unicorn is, like, ten or something. But Lambie's just a baby. Just little. And everyone forgets to feed Lambie.'

Jessie was quickly absorbed in her play. Despite her other issues, she had a remarkable ability to focus at certain times, and when this happened then everything else seemed to disappear for her. Within moments she had created a court trial room, the sort seen on TV, not what Jessie would actually experience if the case with Joseph came to trial.

'Dragon Judge says, "Are you off the junk? Have you cleaned up? Do you have a proper job yet?" Daddy Bear is just lying there. See? See?' Jessie poked my arm and pointed at the puppet lying on the table top. 'He's still stoned. He's doing smack and pot and heroin, all at the same time. So he's just lying there and Dragon Judge says, "You bad father. You bad, bad father, 'cause you're not paying any attention to your kids. Anything could be happening to them."'

Jessie leaned over and pushed the other bear puppet across the table. 'And Mama Bear is just lying there too. Has she done smack and heroin as well? Or is she just lazy? Has she got depression because it's too much for her? All Too Much? She wants to give her kids away. She says that to Daddy Bear. She says to the children bears, "I want to be rid of you. I wish you'd die. Here, have some heroin. Smoke some heroin, so you die."'

I watched silently as Jessie played with the puppets. To my knowledge her family did not have drug problems, and her slight confusion about drug names and methods of use made me think that she was not revealing that there was drug use in her family. Many of the children in the group home did come from backgrounds where heroin addiction was a major issue, so my guess was that Jessie had picked this up as a reason for abuse and neglect. Tangled into her conversation with the puppets, however, were the tendrils of her own family dysfunction, in particular parents who did not take care of their children. It was interesting to me that she should ascribe this to heroin addiction in the puppet family. Was she trying it out as an explanation for her own parents' lassitude? I also found it interesting that she should explore this after a weekend when, to our knowledge, her parents had spent focused time with her.

Jessie pulled the unicorn puppet over and put it on her hand. She ran her fingers through its mane and then fingered the rainbow-hued crown. 'I don't like this puppet,' she said to me.

There was an expectancy to her comment that demanded a response, so I asked, 'Why's that?'

'I don't like its horn.' She fingered over the soft, silver material of the unicorn's horn. 'You can tell it's a girl unicorn, because it's got all girlie colours. It's like My Little Pony, only it's girlier. I don't like My Little Pony either. I don't like girlie girlie things. I'm tougher than that.'

'I can see that.'

'Girlie girlie stuff is for soft people. Soft in the head people.'

'You don't feel they are for you,' I said.

'Little children like things like this. Little children who don't know better. And girls. Girls like Melanie, who's got blonde hair and blinks her eyes like this.' Jessie did an exaggerated flutter of her eyelashes. 'She used to do that at Joseph. She'd go "Jooooseph" and blink her eyes and flip her hair, because she thought it was sexy. She'd love to play with a rainbow unicorn.'

'What did Joseph do when Melanie acted like that?'

Jessie shrugged. 'Nothing. Melanie was being stupid. He knew it. He just ignored her. But it didn't stop her. Melanie said, "Joseph's going to marry me." She properly thought that. I said, "He's not. He's already married." She said, "I've got some fishnet stockings. I got them at my mum's house last time I was there." She showed them to me. I said she was stupid. She should know better. Joseph isn't going to marry her.'

'No,' I said, 'that wouldn't happen.'

Jessie still had the unicorn puppet in her hand. Again, she felt along the conical horn. 'This puppet shouldn't have anything that pokes on it,' she said.

'The horn is made of fabric,' I replied. 'Even though it's pointed, it can't hurt anyone. It just folds up, if you press it. See. Try it on your hand.'

'But it's a girl unicorn. It shouldn't have anything that pokes at all. Girls aren't supposed to do poking.' She grabbed up the lamb puppet with her other hand, not putting it on, just holding it. She began to stab the unicorn's horn between the lamb's back legs. 'See, it can poke in the wrong spot.'

Lifting her head, Jessie looked over across the table. 'And see there. Nobody notices. Mama Bear is still lying there. Daddy Bear is still lying there. Pokey! Pokey! Pokey! Stop it! Stop it! Stop it! That's Lambie saying that. Lambie's getting poked in his vagina and he doesn't like it. Nobody notices. Unicorn says, you shut up or I'll poke right through to your heart. I'll poke through to your brain and it will explode and you will die.

'And now the judge comes. Judge Dragon. Judge Dragon says, "I'm going to put you in jail, Unicorn." But Unicorn says, "You're just pretend. Dragons are pretend. No one has to be scared of dragons because they aren't real." The End. I'm done now.' Jessie whipped off the unicorn puppet and threw it on the table top.

'That ended suddenly,' I said in surprise.

'Trials do,' Jessie replied.

The puppet play had stopped so abruptly that a noticeable silence flowed in around us in its wake.

'I'm finished for today,' Jessie said, and surveyed the table. 'We need to put all those away.' She grabbed the black bin bag, and in one big swoop she pushed the puppets off the table towards the open bag. A few fell in but most went onto the floor.

I bent to pick the hare up and put it into the black bag.

'I don't know why you make me do this,' Jessie said.

'Make you do what?'

'Play with these puppets. You're just like the sex lady. That's what you want, isn't it? For me to tell you sex stuff. You wanted me to tell you about Melanie and Joseph, huh? You wanted me to talk sex to you. You were thinking that if you brought these along, I'd make the puppets do sex.'

I sat back in surprise. 'Jessie, I haven't made you play with the puppets. You chose to play with them. You chose to stop.'

'You're all perverts, you know. You and Mrs Thomas and the police psychologist lady. You want little kids to do sex stuff in front of you.'

'You feel like you're being made to play with the puppets?'

'Stop repeating everything I say. You always repeat stuff and it drives me nuts.'

'I'm just trying to make sure I understand what you're saying,' I said.

'Well, then here. Here's what I'm feeling. I hate these puppets. I only play with them because you make me. Because there's nothing else for me to do while you're here. Because it's super boring when I'm with you, so I've got to do this. *You* brought them, so you know that's true. You pervert. You *want* me to do sex stuff in front of you.'

'The puppet trial seems to have brought up some strong feelings,' I said. 'Can we name how you're feeling right now?'

'You pervert.'

'You came in very excited to tell me about your time out with your parents. We talked about that for a few minutes. Then you wanted to play puppets. You wanted to make a trial. Now you are upset about sexual matters. It feels to me as if we've done things this afternoon that have caused feelings that are hard to handle.'

Jessie's expression was fierce, an angry thundercloud of a face, and I expected her to scream at me, but she didn't. She glared for two or three moments longer and then looked away.

'Let's put words to some of what's going on inside right now,' I suggested. 'When you first came in, we talked about going to Dragon World with your family. How were you feeling when you were telling me about the outing?'

Jessie let out a long sigh and with it went a small amount of the tension that was electrifying the air around us. She shook her head, as if answering an unasked question.

Silence.

'Okay, I have a different idea. Let's get out the measuring stick.' I opened my satchel and took out the long, narrow piece of plastic with the numbers on it that Jessie and I had used in our early days together. It hadn't had much of an outing since we'd resumed seeing each other. I grabbed a handful of draught pieces.

'Now, ten, up at this end, stands for "It made me feel really wonderful, really happy". And one, down at this end, stands for "It made me feel really awful. I hated it. I was very unhappy". So, when you first came in, we talked about your trip to Dragon World with your family. Here's a marker. Where shall we put it?' I asked, keeping my voice as undemanding as I could while still making it apparent I expected an answer.

Jessie looked directly at me, giving me a beady stare.

'What?' I asked.

'Why do you *always* say "we", like you think you're the Queen? You always say it. *Always.* I'm the one who's putting the marker down, not you. So stop saying "we".'

'I'm sorry it annoys you, but let's talk about this now. I asked, When you first came in—'

'*Shut up!*' Jessie cried angrily.

I stopped. Sitting back, I folded my hands together and waited quietly.

'Shut up!' Jessie shouted again.

I didn't respond. Instead, I shifted my gaze away from her and settled instead for looking at the measuring stick.

'Shut up and don't talk to me! Just be quiet!' she shouted, not appearing to notice that I had already stopped talking to her.

Then she did notice and this seemed to anger her even more. 'I hate you! I don't want to be here because I hate you! I hate you!'

She was already on her feet but now she left the table and went to the door. 'I'm going to leave.'

'I'd rather you stayed, but that is your choice. You may go if you wish.'

'I am going to leave.' She opened the door. 'I'm leaving.'

I didn't say anything further.

Jessie went out into the hallway and shut the door right up to the point where it would engage the latching mechanism, but no further. A moment's silence reigned, and then she said through the door, 'I'm going to go.'

I didn't answer.

Jessie cracked the door open. She looked at me briefly, then down at the floor.

'Would you like to come back in?' I asked.

'No.'

Silence.

'You're having lots of difficult feelings today, aren't you?'

Jessie didn't answer.

'Are you sure you don't want to come back in?'

'I didn't mean that about the puppets,' she said in a small voice.

I nodded.

'I like the puppets.'

'Okay.'

'I don't want you to take them away.'

'Okay.'

'I didn't mean it when I said I hated them.'

'No, I know you didn't.'

Jessie came back into the room. Coming around to my side of the table, she knelt down and opened the black bin bag to peer in at the puppets. 'It's just that I don't want to do sex stuff.'

'You mean with the puppets?'

She nodded.

'You don't have to do sex stuff with the puppets. You may play with them any way you wish, as long as no one gets hurt.'

Jessie didn't answer.

'When you were playing with the puppets, the sex stuff seemed to come up as part of the trial with Judge Dragon.'

'I don't like having someone putting fingers down my knickers.'

'No, I can understand that.'

'Feeling my pussy.'

'When has that happened, Jessie?'

'Saying to me, "Don't you tell. Don't you tell or I'll beat you up. Don't you tell or I'll take your baby bear and rip it to shreds. I'll ruin everything you've got."'

'Who's saying this to you? Who's putting fingers down your knickers?'

'That sex doctor. That police sex doctor lady.'

'You're telling me that Dr Hughes has touched your private parts?'

Jessie nodded. 'She put her fingers in my knickers. She asked me to touch her pussy. She says if I lick her, I'll get twenty pounds. If I don't, I've got to stay here forever and never see my mum and dad again.'

chapter twenty-two

After Jessie had gone, I sat a few minutes longer at the table, hand over my eyes, head braced in my palm. I was going to have to report what she had said about the police psychologist, because the law demanded it.

I felt like a bit player in *Alice's Adventures in Wonderland*. Caught up in that weird world down the rabbit hole where up was down and down was up. How did I decode all this? Jessie just kept saying these things, but *was* she just saying them? What was fact? What was fiction? What had really happened to her? When had it happened? Who had been involved? Was it historic? Or was it current? How would we ever, ever find out?

I remembered back to my early thirties, when I was working at a private clinic in the US. I was a research psychologist there, but most of my colleagues were psychiatrists, deeply steeped in Freudian theory. At the time, I'd been dismissive of Freud's murky world of dreams, desires and sexual fantasy as a means of explaining human behaviour. It had seemed archaic to me. I was all math and science, sticking resolutely to observable behaviour and measurable outcomes, believing this was the way to go. Indeed, as it turned out, we were going that way. Schools, programmes and therapy all moved away from Freud, away from Jung, away from humanism, and off towards behaviourism, towards practical means and methods, towards drugs.

Older and wiser, I now knew that none of us had the magic bullet. Everything worked occasionally; nothing worked all the time. As I sat contemplating the best way to go forward with Jessie, I longed to be back in the staff room at the clinic with my Freudian colleagues. I could have done with some of that expansive, interpretive thinking they were so good at, because I needed a new way of understanding what Jessie was trying to tell me.

The next morning, I phoned Meleri to talk over my session and make her aware of Jessie's comments regarding Dr Hughes. Meleri agreed that this was almost certainly Jessie being Jessie, but that, yes, the allegation still needed to be formally recorded. She'd put the pertinent paperwork in the post for me.

Meleri then brought up Jessie's visit with her parents. This had been the first time in over six months that they had spent time with her, and Meleri had a very different version of what had happened to the one Jessie had given me. Yes, the family did go for a burger and then to Dragon World. However, at the burger stand, Jessie had specifically asked for onions on her burger, but when it came she decided she didn't like the look of them and stood picking them off and dropping them on the ground where others were queueing. When her father told her to pick them up and put them into the bin, Jessie became angry and threw the whole burger on the ground, stomping it into the pavement. Her parents had been encouraged to use natural consequences as a way of dealing with Jessie's reactive attachment disorder, so her father said, right then, if she didn't want her burger, that was fine, but ruining it meant she only had her chips to eat. He said he was sorry about that, because there weren't very many chips left and she would probably feel hungry. Jessie became distressed when she realized she would not have a burger and had to be taken to the car to calm down.

At Dragon World, she ran ahead into the venue, squeezing through the barrier while her father was still paying, and disappeared down the narrow, cobweb-strewn passageway. When her parents went through, they couldn't find Jessie and ended up spending no time at all looking at the various displays, but hurried straight through to the end, trying to find her. Jessie wasn't there. The staff allowed them back through again and still they couldn't find her, but when they came out she was with the cashier, sobbing that her parents had left her and now she was lost. More worryingly, she was covered in blood. Jessie claimed she had been attacked inside the venue. Her father determined that the blood had come from her arm, where a scab had been pulled up, and in all likelihood Jessie had spread the blood around herself. However, the staff had already called the police. Fortunately they were understanding about the incident.

Meleri sighed. 'Needless to say, her parents have declined to schedule their next visit.'

When I next came to Glan Morfa for our usual Tuesday session, Jessie was in the quiet room. Enir explained that Jessie had stolen a small teddy bear that belonged to Melanie, whose room was across the hall from Jessie's. The toy had gone missing two or three days earlier and, while a search was done at the time, it couldn't be found. Then this morning, the staff discovered Jessie playing with the teddy in her room. She was adamant that it was hers, that her parents had bought it for her on her day out, and if it looked anything like Melanie's bear that was just coincidence. The staff were certain that the teddy was not Jessie's, as there had been no record of her returning with a gift from her outing with her parents, and no, despite Jessie's protests, this wasn't an oversight on the staff's part. The teddy bear was not hers and she needed to give it back to Melanie. That had precipitated a tantrum and time out in the quiet room. Enir said they thought that was the end of the matter. Not so. Later in the morning, when the girls were in the toilets, Melanie had teased Jessie about the bear. Enir wasn't present when it happened, but one of the other girls told her that Melanie had said how Jessie had to make up stories about getting gifts from her parents because her parents would never give her presents, because they were so glad to be rid of her. Jessie had exploded, grabbed Melanie by the hair and cracked her head against the sink.

I let myself into the quiet room. It was a small space, not much larger than a storage closet, with numerous large and small pillows. Some children crawled under them, finding the weight of the big pillows calming. Some made comfortable nests to rest in. Some, like Jessie, pummelled them angrily until energy was spent. Having beaten all the pillows into submission in the corner of the room, she sat cross-legged on the floor, eyeing me beadily as I entered.

'Why are you here?' she asked, her tone bitter.

'Today is Tuesday. This is our time together.'

'No, it isn't, because I'm in here,' she muttered. 'Because I'm a *horrid* child.'

The utter annoyance in her voice made it hard not to smile. I loved Jessie. I really did. Crazy-making as she was, I couldn't help but fall for that fierce, impossible spirit.

Sitting down cross-legged on the floor in front of her, I asked, 'So what happened?'

'I don't have to tell you.'

'No, you don't. But sometimes it's nice to have someone listen to your side of the story. So I'm thinking maybe you'd like to tell me.'

'Well, as always, you think wrong.'

I got back to my feet.

This surprised Jessie. 'Where are you going?' she asked, looking up.

'If you don't want to talk, that's okay. You are free to choose that and I don't mind. But I am here to talk, so if you don't want to talk, I will go.'

Her expression darkened. 'See? You're just going to leave like that. You don't really want to know my side of things. You're just saying it, because that's what you're supposed to say. But really you want to clear out. You're just like everyone else. You're going to get out of here as fast as you can, if you don't have to stay.'

'I'm sorry you feel that way. Especially as it isn't true. I come because I like coming to see you. I feel sad when you don't want to see me.'

'Don't lie to me. You come because you're paid to come. Nobody would see me if they weren't paid good money. I know that's a fact.'

'Well, that's false news then, because I'm not paid. I'm a volunteer. I come because I want to. I enjoy seeing you.'

A moment's silence followed. I don't think Jessie had expected that answer and it was taking her a moment to think how to respond. She scowled at the floor. Finally she said, 'I didn't say I didn't want to *see* you. I said I didn't want to talk.'

'Ah, okay. My mistake. So shall I stay a while and we can sit together and not talk?' I asked.

'You're making fun of me now.'

I drew a deep breath in. 'I'm sorry you feel that way. I'm not making fun of you. I asked because I thought you might like to do that, but I wanted you to feel free to decide for yourself.'

'I'm fed up deciding,' she said. 'Everything's a decision and there's too many.'

'I see. Perhaps I shall just sit down then, and we can go from there.'

Lowering her head, Jessie nodded slowly. 'Okay.'

I came down on the floor again, this time sitting beside her so that we were both facing the door.

Silence. Jessie had her head hung down, her red hair falling forward, obscuring her face. I noticed how long it had grown. I remembered Jessie saying once that she was growing it out so that she would have enough to donate to a charity that makes wigs for children when she next had it cut. I didn't know if that was true or not, but her hair was definitely long enough now, so I wondered if I should chance that as a topic of conversation. Would it defuse the tense atmosphere in the quiet room? Or should I just sit, letting the silence pool around us? This was the challenge with Jessie. You never knew what was going to set her off and what was going to work.

We were silent together for perhaps five or six minutes when I realized Jessie had begun to cry. She hated to cry, hated to be caught crying, so I didn't want to call attention to it, but I said, 'Would you like a cuddle?'

She nodded, so I put my arm around her shoulders.

'Things feel a bit overwhelming?'

She nodded again. 'I'm thinking about my teddy,' she said tearfully.

'The one you had to give back?' I asked, assuming she meant the teddy she had stolen from the other girl.

'The one I had when I was little.'

'Ah. One you had long ago.'

'Yes, before I came here.'

'What did it look like?'

'Brown. And about this big.' She measured with her hands.

'A lot like Melanie's teddy, hey?'

'Mine was better than Melanie's. Mine had a blue coat on, like Paddington Bear. But he wasn't Paddington Bear. It was a different kind of coat. You couldn't take it off.'

'Did he have a name?'

'Lester.'

'That's a good teddy name,' I said.

We fell silent. I listened to the sounds beyond the quiet room door, the comings and goings of children arriving back from after-school activities.

'I miss my teddy so much,' Jessie murmured. 'I miss him because my mummy gave him to me. He reminds me of my mummy.'

'You have special memories of your teddy bear.'

'When I was in my room, I was lonely. But Mummy said, "Here's Lester to play with," before she shut the door.'

'She gave him to you to comfort you. Do you remember how old you were?' I asked.

'No. I was little. I didn't know my numbers yet. Me and Lester played together. He was, like, my brother that I pretended with. My mummy gave him to me because I asked for a brother, but she gave me Lester instead.'

'You wanted a brother or sister to play with?'

'A brother. I already have sisters and they were horrid to me. I wanted a baby brother. But Mummy said no. She said her body was too sad to have more children. She had to stop having babies after me, because I was going to be the death of her.'

'I think she was saying she was too old to have babies any more.'

'No. She said if she died, it would be my fault, because I was going to be the death of her.'

'That's not quite what that phrase means,' I said.

'I've got the devil in me. The devil jumped into my mummy's vagina when she was asleep and that's how I got born.'

'That isn't true, Jessie.'

'Yes, it is. My mummy told me.'

'It still isn't true. If she said that, she's mistaken.'

'It *is* true. That's why I'm so bad. The devil makes me act like this.'

'Sometimes when people get very upset or frustrated, they can say cruel things that they don't really mean. That doesn't mean it's true. It doesn't even mean that the person meant what they said. I'll bet you've done that yourself sometimes, said things when you were angry that later you realized you didn't mean. Yes? I know I have.'

Jessie didn't answer.

'No one has the devil in them. That's just an expression people use when they're really in a nark.'

'No, you're wrong. Because Daddy got the exorcist man to come to our house. His name was Pastor Jones. When he saw me, he said I was full of demons that the devil put in me. That's why I act like I do. I was born out of my mummy's vagina that way.'

Was this one of Jessie's stories?

'When he came, he made me lay down on the kitchen table, because it was made of wood. There was a tablecloth on it and Mummy had to take it off, because Pastor Jones said I had to lay on bare wood, because demons couldn't go through wood. He put a Bible on my chest. He said words to make the devil show himself. That way the demons could come out of me.'

'Where did this pastor come from?'

'The church.'

'Your church?'

'No. I didn't go to church.'

'Had you seen Pastor Jones before he came to visit you?'

She nodded. 'He came to see Mummy lots of times.'

'How so?'

'Mummy got the screamy-meemies sometimes and it was because she had demons. Daddy would make me go in my room, and then Pastor Jones came to be with Mummy. Daddy would lock the door and tell me to talk to Lester and not listen.'

I knew Jessie had spent many hours of her early child-hood alone, locked in her room, but my understanding was that it was related to her mother's depression. The religious aspect was new to me. It seemed odd to me that Social Services had not logged such an important detail, and this made me think Jessie was making this up, but, at the same time, it seemed an odd story for Jessie to create. I would need to talk to Meleri.

'This one time Mummy got the screamy-meemies really badly in the middle of the night,' Jessie said. 'It woke me up, so I got up to go see, because everything was so noisy. She was in the sitting room on the settee. Daddy was trying to keep her from falling off. She was screaming and writhing around and she wouldn't settle down at all, so Daddy rang Pastor Jones. Pastor Jones came and he said prayers to get the demons out of her, because that's why she was screaming. I saw Mummy bumping around. Pastor Jones put out three Bibles and he lit two candles and started to call on Jesus to come down and face the devil and all the demons of Hell, because they were in my mummy. Pastor Jones started praying louder than she was screaming, telling the devil to go back to Hell. Mummy fell off the settee onto the floor.

'My sister Gemma came and got me then. All the noise woke her up. She came out of her room and down the hallway and got hold of me. She said I shouldn't be in the sitting room. She took me into her bed with her and comforted me.'

'That sounds like a scary experience,' I said.

'Gemma comforted me and comforted me, so that I wouldn't hear the demons coming out of Mummy, but it didn't do any good. The devil had already got into me when I was in Mummy's tummy.'

chapter twenty-three

Was it true? The entire drive home from that session with Jessie, this was the question that returned to me again and again, as I considered what she had told me.

Fundamental Christian churches were not as common in the UK as they were in some areas of the US where I had worked previously, although the evangelical movement was becoming more popular. For the most part, however, people who attended church regularly in the UK tended to stick to the established denominations – Anglican and its counterparts, the Church of Scotland and the Church of Wales; Roman Catholic; the Free Church or Presbyterian in Scotland; and, in Wales, Methodist. As I had not heard Meleri nor, indeed, Jessie previously mention her family's religious activities, this made me think Jessie was creating this 'memory' for dramatic effect. The constant accusations of sexual abuse were starting to lose their attention-grabbing power. How better to regain this ground with therapists and other helping adults than a lurid tale of exorcism?

More to the point, such stories were not without precedence in society in general. We'd gone through a period in the late 1970s and early 1980s when we were only just starting to wake up to the extensive nature of child sexual abuse and did not yet have an understanding of false memory syndrome. For several years there was a strong belief in the existence of widespread satanic cults. I suppose we just didn't want to accept the grubby reality that child sexual abuse was common, because, for a while, even professionals found it easier to believe there were implausibly large, hidden congregations of devil worshippers abusing our children rather than ordinary men.

The television habits of the children at the group home were well supervised, so I didn't think Jessie would have been exposed to horror films like *The Exorcist* that could have given her the grist for her story. However, there was no way to know what she had seen during her time in the foster homes, nor what could have simply been overheard in conversation with other kids. I had long since learned it was not judicious to rule things out based on 'she couldn't have seen anything like that' or 'she wouldn't know about it'. Kids knew about all sorts of things, and often from a shockingly young age. So that, alone, was no test of whether or not Jessie was making up the story.

What we did keep coming back to was Jessie's mother's mental illness. We knew that Diane had suffered post-natal depression, and now her depression was chronic. From what I'd pieced together between Jessie, Meleri and the notes from Social Services, Diane had been ill for years. This had had a two-fold effect. The first was that Diane had not bonded with Jessie. This was reflected in her lack of care when Jessie was small, but also in her willingness now to let Jessie go into the foster system. The second effect was that, as a consequence, Jessie had been neglected.

I did feel sympathy for Diane. It was easy to blame her behaviour for this situation, but there was no point. No one wakes up in the morning, thinking, 'Hey, I'll choose absolute black-dog depression over enjoying my child and taking care of her.' Everyone wants to be happy. Everyone wants to live a fulfilling life full of love and connection. No one chooses to be unhappy. If someone is unhappy because of what he or she is doing, this is not the intended result. For whatever reason, they thought what they did would help them feel better. They didn't set out purposely to make themselves unhappy; they just weren't able to do better at that moment. To change the situation, the focus needed to shift away from blame and towards support.

My biggest handicap was never having met Diane myself, so I had only a filtered version of her through Meleri and Jessie. The more I heard, however, the more I suspected she suffered much more global mental health problems than the catch-all 'depression and anxiety' that was in the notes. This wasn't the first time Jessie had referred to her mother's 'screamy-meemies'. In the beginning I'd considered whether Jessie was possibly fabricating this for dramatic effect, given the rather silly name, but I didn't think so now. This was the first time I heard of her father interacting to stop the 'screamies'. So what might be going on for Diane? Schizophrenia? Bipolar? A personality disorder? A drug problem? Just because we didn't think the family was involved with drugs didn't mean we were right. Could there have been truth underlying Jessie's puppet tales of drug abuse at her house?

Meanwhile, the situation with Joseph dragged on. He had been interviewed – 'helped the police with their inquiries', as they euphemistically called it – and subsequently arrested. The initial police visit had caught him totally off guard. Thinking it was just a case of Jessie being Jessie, he'd assumed the police were just a formality. Procedures that had to be followed. As a consequence, Joseph had spoken freely with the police, eager to clear his name, and didn't think to get a solicitor first. Meleri had grimaced when telling me this and said, 'That thing, that spiel about "anything you say can be used against you", well . . . it's true.' He should have waited for counsel. He should have done all the things you know from TV detective dramas that you are supposed to do when being arrested, but, because you are not a career criminal, you don't realize they're for real.

Now bailed, Joseph was at home, his life in tatters. He had been suspended straightaway from work, of course, which was expected. However, he had also been involved in other community activities – a driver for a programme that delivered groceries to the elderly and housebound, and a cricket coach – and as a consequence, the police had informed both the delivery charity and the cricket association of the allegations.

The biggest worry for everyone was keeping all this out of the press. There had been a major sex abuse scandal in group homes some years earlier and the tabloid press would jump eagerly at the chance of another lurid tale, regardless of whether or not the accused was guilty.

While they were still investigating, the police were under no obligation to tell Joseph any details about the progress of their work. Our guess was that the police were combing through Joseph's background, as well as trying to establish the veracity of what Jessie was saying. That it was taking so long worried me, because it made me think that they might have found something worth investigating, that there might be other children.

This was the challenge for the rest of us. We had all started out certain that Joseph was innocent, and Jessie, the tale teller, was just being Jessie, and surely the police would see this. As the weeks went by, however, and there was no sign that the police did see this, uncertainty began to seep in. What if . . . ? My husband was the worst one for planting seeds of doubt. I'd told him someone had been arrested and he commented, 'There is seldom smoke without fire.' And he continued to say it. Any time I mentioned the investigation, he said it again. There is seldom smoke without fire. And that's true. There seldom is.

Normality had resumed at Glan Morfa. A new manager, a woman in her fifties, named Lin, was now in situ. She seemed humourless and rule-bound when I first met her, coming in to interrupt the camaraderie around the kettle in the staff room and hint that staff should be out on the floor. However, as time passed and I got to know her, I found her nice enough. She didn't have that special spark that Joseph had, but she was fair and worked hard, and I could tell she was good-hearted.

When we were next together, I asked Jessie, 'Do you ever think about Joseph?'

She was drawing a skylark that afternoon. Sitting at the table, hunched over a piece of paper, she sketched the bird with outstretched wings as if it were jumping up out of the grass.

A moment or two with no answer. Then she shook her head. 'No.'

I didn't say anything further. We were still restricted on the topic of Joseph, and I appreciated the reasons for this. However, I didn't think what I was asking could be construed as a leading question, and I was curious what was in Jessie's mind regarding Joseph.

Stretching her arm out across the table, Jessie chose a turquoise pen for her skylark. In doing so, she lifted her head. Our eyes met. 'Why do people keep wanting me to talk about Joseph?'

'I think you know.'

'Unh-uh,' she said and shook her head, before bending back over her drawing. 'Because I'm done with that. I've said everything I'm going to say.'

'But Joseph isn't done with it. The police aren't finished investigating. And you aren't done with it either, because if it goes to trial, you will need to give your side of the story about what happened.'\

'Unh-uh,' she said. 'Because I don't have to if I don't want to. And I don't want to. I'm fed up with this.'

'Yes, I think we're all fed up with it. But until the police are finished, we've got to keep going with it.'

'Unh-uh,' she replied, not taking her attention from the bird drawing.

Her offhand 'unh-uhs' were irritating me, but I could tell she wasn't in the mood for talking, and I suspect she was being purposefully annoying. Putting me on the back foot by evoking an emotional reaction shifted the control into her court. I took a deep breath.

'You're just as bad,' Jessie said, still not looking up from what she was doing.

'Just as bad as what?' I asked.

'You said you'd take me to see the skylarks. You told me that last year. And you told me again when I came back. But you've never done it. You've never taken me out once. Not even for fish and chips, and you promised me that too.'

'You feel that my not taking you to see the skylarks is just as bad as what Joseph did?'

She nodded.

'Did Joseph promise you something and it didn't happen?'

She shrugged.

'What did he promise?' I had to stop myself from associating it with her allegations of sexual abuse, as in asking if he had promised something in exchange for sexual activity. This would definitely be a leading question, but also it may not have been what Jessie had in mind. I didn't want to influence her response accidentally.

'I didn't say he promised me anything. I didn't say that, did I?'

'No, you didn't. I'm just trying to understand what you did say,' I replied. 'You told me I am as bad as Joseph and I want to know in what way. Perhaps I can do better, if I understand what went wrong.'

'You didn't take me to see the skylarks. You said you would. You said we would go out on the moors together and you would show me them.' There was a brittleness to Jessie's voice as she spoke. She had stopped her drawing and was staring down at the paper.

'I'm sorry you feel upset. The reason I haven't done it is because it isn't the right time of year yet. It needs to be later in the spring, when it is warm. The moors are high up and the skylarks don't come until it is warm and sunny. I will take you then. I promise.'

Before I finished speaking, Jessie began to scribble on her drawing. She had the brown pen, and suddenly it shot back and forth across the paper in such angry strokes it was coming off the edges to leave small brown marks on the table.

'Whoa!' I said in surprise. 'Can we get some words here? What's happening?'

'I hate you, that's what!' she screamed and threw the pen at me. She scrabbled up the paper, tore it into small pieces and threw them at me. 'I hate you so much, I could kill you! I wish I had a knife. I wish I could stab it through your heart!'

The sudden viciousness of Jessie's anger caught me off guard. There was a different, more bitter timbre to it that seemed out of character, even by Jessie's standards. After our session was over, I spoke with the staff to find out if anything was going on in the group home that might have upset Jessie before she came in to me. They said no. They were not aware of her being upset.

The incident bothered me enough that when I later ran into Ben, the Social Services child psychologist, I asked his opinion.

Jessie appeared to believe I'd broken a promise to take her out, I said. In reality, I hadn't. We'd made plans a few times, but they had always been scuppered by Jessie's bad behaviour. I suspected self-sabotage was involved, that for some reason Jessie couldn't cope with the reality of going out with me and ended up doing something that put her into the quiet room. A trip to see the skylarks, however, hadn't happened for exactly the reason I said – it wasn't the right time of year. How did she connect this to Joseph?

Ben mooted a connection to Jessie's going out with her parents. There had been several occasions when they had made plans to take her out and never followed through. Could she be displacing that anger onto me? But again, how would this be connected to Joseph?

The only thing I could think was that Jessie longed to be the centre of attention with each of us – with her parents, with Joseph, with me – and she was repeatedly thwarted, either by us or by her own actions. Was her anger frustration that she could never be that special person to any of us?

chapter twenty-four

Meleri phoned me the following week to say she was going out to meet with Jessie's parents in their home and asked if I'd like to come along. I jumped at the opportunity. In the time I had been working with Jessie I had never once met her parents, which felt like a most extraordinary situation, although this was often the norm for us in the voluntary sector.

Jessie's situation was unusual insomuch as she was a voluntary placement in the foster system. Most children come into care through a Care Protection Order, meaning they are removed from the home against their parents' wishes, usually by the police or Social Services because of abuse or neglect. There then tends to be regular interaction between parents and Social Services either to rehabilitate the home situation enough that the child can return to his or her family, or to move forward with a permanent care order and eventual adoption. In contrast, Jessie's parents had relinquished her willingly. The hope was, of course, that she could eventually return to her own family, but thus far there hadn't been much progress in that direction. Jessie's behaviour continued to be difficult and the parents remained reluctant to interact with her. They only rarely turned up to see Jessie, and they came even less often to meetings and reviews. It was clear to Meleri that they intended to move on without their daughter.

Jessie's account of her day out with her parents, along with the episode with Melanie and the teddy bear, spoke to me of a child who was very aware of what kind of relationship she wanted to be having with them. However, while she portrayed herself as belonging to a family who bought her gifts and showed her a nice time, this wasn't the reality. Perhaps this explained why she ended up sabotaging her time together with her parents, ruining things before they could go wrong. How else could she control the heartbreak? Indeed, perhaps it also hinted at why Jessie had been so angry with me the previous session. Perhaps it was less scary to express her resentment with me for not doing things with her than it was to face her feelings towards her parents on this account.

Jessie's parents lived in a small village only a short distance inland from one of the large seaside towns. Originally, the village had been part of a private estate, but the manor house was now a country hotel, hidden from view up a long private lane snaking through heavy plantings of rhododendrons, and the village was reduced to a long string of cottages that were mostly second homes and a gentrified gastropub called the Rat and Carrot. Beyond the old village on the north side of the road was a long string of semi-detached council houses built in the 1950s.

Jessie's parents were in the third-to-last house. Most of the garden was to the front, running from the house down to the road, and it was meticulously kept. We were into April by that point and daffodils were giving way to tulips and wall-flowers. Some bedding plants had already been put in. The soil was freshly turned and weed-free. The garden looked over-manicured to me. As I walked up the long path from the road to the front door, I noticed creosote had been applied along the edges of it to keep the plants from overstepping their boundary, a practice that was uncommon these days because of the poisonous nature of creosote. It seemed a finicky thing to do in such a small garden.

Meleri knocked at the door.

We waited.

Meleri knocked again.

Again we waited.

At last came the sound of movement beyond the door. Gwyl Williams opened it, smiled, said hello to us and invited us in.

We entered a short hallway, and he then opened a door into a modest-sized sitting room with a welcoming coal fire burning in the grate. At the far end of the room, under the picture window, was a dining table. Two well-worn chairs and a small sofa were arranged in front of the fire.

Gwyl went off to make us all a cup of coffee, and returned with tray, coffee and small, sweet treats known as Welsh cakes, which are a cross between a pancake and a scone. His wife Diane followed him in. I don't know where she'd been up until that point, because we hadn't heard her moving about.

Her faintly reluctant manner made me think she had been hiding in the kitchen, panicked at our arrival, and Gwyl had only now managed to charm her out, but who knows? Perhaps she had simply been preparing the Welsh cakes, which were home-made and invitingly warm.

Diane nodded at us and sat down in the chair diagonal to me. Gwyl poured the coffee, offered us the cakes, and then sat down next to Meleri on the sofa.

The conversation was just small talk at first. Meleri asked about Gwyl's artwork, as there were several paintings on the walls, and I think it was a way of introducing me into the conversation, because she suggested he tell me about his latest project. Then the three of us discussed the weather, always a popular topic in Britain. Meleri asked about the garden and how it was coming on.

Then Meleri began to talk more generally about the Williamses' home situation. Gwyl was no longer working at the factory, which meant they were living on benefits. At this point, Meleri asked if his attendance allowance had come through yet, and I was surprised at this. Attendance allowance is a benefit paid to a carer, and Gwyl's claiming it indicated that Diane's mental health was more debilitating than I had been aware of. As Meleri hadn't mentioned it to me in the car on the way over, this was unlikely to have been a recent change.

Meleri then asked about their other daughters. There was a long conversation about the two older girls, who were in their late twenties. Diane joined in for the first time and talked with some animation about both girls, their partners and the grandchildren. One daughter's son wasn't all that much younger than Jessie, and Diane spoke with pride about this boy's accomplishments at school. Gwyl said he had artistic ability.

I studied Diane as the conversation continued. She gave off an air of vulnerability. It was in the way she waited pointedly for Gwyl to answer questions or take the lead, but it was also in her bearing. She was thin and fine-boned with long twitchy fingers that wrapped and unwrapped around her arms. Her eyes were a nondescript colour and her hair was that light, ashy brown colour we called 'dirty dishwater' in my youth. It was parted in the middle and pulled back in a low ponytail, which made her look younger than I suspect she was. She had nice skin, but it was sallow. I looked for Jessie in her features, and wasn't sure I found her.

The conversation turned to Gemma, who was now eighteen and still living at home. Except she wasn't, Gwyl said. They'd had a falling-out a few weeks earlier, and Gemma had moved in with her boyfriend. Gwyl expected she'd be back soon, because this had happened before, and because the boyfriend still lived with his mother. Gwyl said the mother would kick them both out before long, but for the moment she was gone.

'How do Jessie and Gemma get on?' I asked.

Diane turned her head and looked out the window, which overlooked the front garden. I could tell she wasn't going to speak; I wasn't sure she was even paying attention. Gwyl shrugged. 'They're not close in age. Gemma isn't close in age to her other sisters either. She's been the odd one out, poor duck. Gemma's the one who's had a hard time.'

This caught my curiosity, so I asked, 'How's that?'

'Being in the middle as she is. Having Kate and Nesta so much older. They were together all the time. Only eighteen months between them. Then ten years and along comes Gemma. So she was on her own. Almost an only child. Then eight years and along comes Jessie, so Gemma wasn't the baby any longer. Not that we spoilt Gemma. But Jessie was so poorly when she was a baba, and so was Diane. Our Gemma had to grow up then.

'Not saying that Gemma didn't love Jessie,' Gwyl added quickly. 'She adored her. A proper little mother to Jessie, wasn't she, hen?' He looked to Diane. 'Gemma always wanted to be doing with her, didn't she? She loved taking care of Baba. Always holding her, carrying her, giving her a feed. And she did a good job. Didn't she, hen?' he said to Diane. Diane nodded.

'So Gemma was responsible for Jessie quite often?' I asked.

'When Gemma came home from school, she made tea and bathed Jessie and put her down. We were so proud of her. I know it was a lot to put on a young girl, but it helped us so much. It wasn't for too long, was it, hen? Just until you got back on your feet. And it made them close. That's a good thing, isn't it? Sisters being close.'

The conversation continued with Meleri asking questions about Gemma's current schooling and her plans.

'To change the subject for a moment,' I said after several minutes, 'may I ask if either of you attend chapel?'

Both Diane and Gwyl looked at me blankly. Gwyl then shook his head. 'Not for many years. At Christmastime, maybe. To the carol service, but that's about all.'

'Jessie was telling me about someone named Pastor Jones visiting the house, and I was wondering if you could tell me more about him.'

Gwyl and Diane exchanged querying, slightly confused looks, and then Gwyl shook his head. 'Everyone's named Jones around here, you know,' he replied and smiled.

'So there was no Pastor Jones?'

Again they looked questioningly at each other.

'I'm just trying to understand something Jessie was talking about, trying to sort out if it's a story or a memory. It sounded like she was describing a non-conformist church, and I was wondering if you'd ever attended one. Nothing wrong with it, just trying to get things straight in my mind.'

'There may have been,' Gwyl replied, his voice uncertain. 'Down the road, there was a community church for a while that was happy-clappy. They were very friendly towards everyone, always wanting to help you. A woman named Pauline brought us cakes and biscuits occasionally, just to cheer us up, and she might have been the pastor's wife. But that was a long time ago. Jessie wouldn't remember that.'

I nodded.

'It is often dreams with Jessie, you know,' Gwyl said. 'She's always been a vivid dreamer. She'd tell us the wildest tales that had a little bit of truth and then a huge, huge bit that was dreamed. She's never really outgrown that.'

The following Tuesday, I brought the puppets with me. I'd taken the two bears out of the bag before she came in and one of them was on my left hand.

'Look!' she cried from the doorway when she appeared. 'I've cut my hair for the children's wig charity! Look at me!'

Indeed she had. Her hair had been a couple of inches below her shoulder blades when I'd last seen her and it was now in a bob just below her ears.

'Some little girl with cancer is going to get my hair. She's going to have a wig now and she'll look just like me! I bet we could be twins!' Her excitement was unbridled. Dancing around the table, she fluffed up what was left of her hair with her hands.

'What a nice thing to do. I'm sure whoever gets a wig will be pleased. And I like your new style. It suits you well.'

'She'll get a ginger wig. Because I have ginger hair. They'll say, "Hey, Ginge!" But it won't hurt her feelings because she'll be so proud to have hair again. And my hair will grow. It won't stay short like this for long, and then I'll cut it again. And again. I'll donate a hundred wigs, and they'll be so happy to have them. They'll say, "That Jessie's doing good again!"'

Her pleasure was contagious. I couldn't help but laugh with her. 'Yes, you are doing a good thing, aren't you? I'm proud of you for wanting to help.'

Suddenly Jessie noticed the bear puppet on my hand.

She'd been on the far side of the table, but stopped abruptly. Placing her hands flat on the table top, she leaned way over to see the puppet better. 'How come you've got Eleanor on your hand? Where're the other puppets? Why isn't Puppy out? You know Puppy doesn't like to be in the bag where it's all dark and nasty. And what about Magnus?'

She came around the table to where I was sitting, and before I realized what she was doing, she had pulled the puppet off my hand. 'Those aren't for you to play with. You're too old. I didn't give you permission.' She sat down beside me and put the bear puppet on her own hand.

I didn't want to get distracted from what I wanted to discuss. I'd intended to do it with the puppets to make it less 'face-to-face', because I hoped that would encourage Jessie to be more uninhibited, but her taking the puppet off my hand had scuppered that. So I just went ahead as it was and said, 'I went to visit your family this week.'

The bear puppet came up in my face. 'I don't care,' it said to my nose.

'Mrs Thomas and I went together. I saw your house and met your mum and your dad.'

'I don't care,' the puppet said again.

Jessie opened the bin bag and searched through to find the other bear puppet. She put it on her other hand. 'What do you think, Magnus? Do you care?' The other bear rose up. 'Nope, I don't care. I want to eat carrots and lounge in the sun. That's what bears do.'

'I heard about Nesta and Kate and their families, and about Gemma. They said Gemma is living with her boyfriend now.'

'Boyfriend, schmoyfriend,' Jessie made one bear say to the other. 'We don't care, do we? Nope. We don't care.'

'And I asked about Pastor Jones, the one who came to see your mum when she had the screamies.'

'Jones, bones. We don't care.'

'Your parents didn't remember Pastor Jones. They weren't sure they ever went to that church.'

'Jones, bones, we don't care. Church, smurch, we don't care. Bears, bears, bears don't care.'

I paused, because it didn't appear I was going to get far with this conversation. Jessie sat with the two bear puppets on her hands, making them play fight and race around on the table, while she repeated the sing-song over and over, 'Bears, bears, bears don't care.' It struck me as sort of a puppet version of sticking your fingers in your ears and singing 'la-la-la'.

Reaching into the bag, I took out the hare puppet and put it on my hand. Before I had time to do or say anything, Jessie's bears attacked my hand, pulling off the hare and smashing it against the table top. 'There, you're dead.'

I reanimated the hare. Again it was savaged by the bears.

'Once there was a little hare . . .' I said, and brought him back to life.

'And the bears killed him!' Wham, she attacked my hand again.

'And this little hare was very afraid . . .' I said.

'Because he was going to get killed by bears!' Jessie

screamed at full volume and attacked my hand with such violence that I was pinned to the table.

'Because he has a big secret . . .' I said, straightening the puppet back onto my hand again.

Jessie paused. 'What is it? What's his secret?'

'What do you think it is?'

'That he's Super Rab!!' she screamed. 'And he's going to kill those bears and mush their guts all over the table! Make him do that. Make him fight my bears.'

'No, that's not his secret. He's very afraid to tell his secret. That might give you a clue,' I said. 'Look, he's so scared, he's hiding.' I put the puppet under the table.

'Tell me,' Jessie replied. 'What's his secret?' She leaned over. 'Whisper it in my ear.'

'He's afraid to tell his secret. It's about something very bad that happened to him. Something that happened when he was little.'

'*What?*'

'I'm not sure,' I said. 'I'm having to guess it, because he's too scared even to tell me. What do you think it might be?'

'Make him come out so I can see him.' Sitting down, Jessie brought the two bear puppets in against her chest, as she watched me bring the hare out.

'I don't know what his secret is either,' she said after several moments of regarding him.

'No, I don't either,' I said and waited.

'Well, he doesn't have a girl hole. So it wouldn't be that.'

'Wouldn't be what?'

'That someone stuck their fingers in his girl hole.'

'He wouldn't like that, if it did happen, would he? He wouldn't like getting his privates touched. He's just a little hare. No one should touch little children's private areas.'

'It's okay in the bath,' Jessie said.

'Only if someone is washing the little child because he's too little to wash himself. Even then, the person shouldn't stick fingers where they don't belong.'

'They could do it in bed,' Jessie said. 'That's how you make love.'

'No, not with little children,' I said. 'Hare's just little. That's why he's scared to tell, because someone's said he'll get in bad trouble. They've said no one will believe him, and he'll get in bad, bad trouble if he tells what has happened to him. But he hates that someone touches him. He wants it to stop.'

'Yes,' Jessie said and her voice was softer, more uncertain.

'Poor little Hare,' I said. 'Do you think he can tell his secret? It hurts him a lot. Could he tell his secret to Eleanor?'

Hesitantly Jessie held out her right hand with one of the bear puppets on it, as if offering it to Hare, but there was no animation in her action. The bear puppet just hung there.

I made the hare cross the expanse of the table towards Jessie's hand, when suddenly she withdrew it and took the puppet off. 'I'm fed up of this game,' she said.

I looked over at her.

'Can I go now?'

'Right now?' I said in surprise.

Nodding, she pulled the other bear puppet off and laid it on the table.

'I don't feel well. I might have a sickness bug. There's one going around. So I want to go now.'

I regarded her.

'Please?' Jessie said, and rising from the chair, 'I need to go.' And with that, she left.

chapter twenty-five

May arrived and with it the long stretch of warm, dry weather that was so typical of that time of year. Lambing was past, meaning we weren't quite so busy on the farm, and my mind turned to skylarks. Driving up across the moor one afternoon, I pulled the car over onto the grass beside the small lane and turned the engine off. Rolling down the window, I listened. Countless skylarks were rising all across the moor, one after the other, a multitude of liquid songs filling the air. The time had come to bring Jessie out.

The next time I saw her, I told her it was time to come to the moor and Jessie exploded with delight. 'Yay! When are we going? Can we go today? Can we go this afternoon? Just me, huh? Are you going to take just me? Please, let's go now! Please? Please-please-please?'

'It's too late today, because it's almost teatime. I'm thinking Saturday.'

'Can we get fish and chips as well? Will you take me for fish and chips and then up to see the skylarks?' she asked eagerly.

I didn't think this was a good idea. Jessie had a very poor

track record when it came to going out. The excitement had got the better of her every single time I'd tried to arrange something. Inevitably, she would end up misbehaving just before I arrived and, as a consequence, wasn't allowed to go with me because she was in time out. I wanted to minimize the chances of this happening yet again by not planning too big an event, so I explained that we would go to see the skylarks this time, and we would go out for fish and chips another time.

'What about a picnic then? Could we take a picnic? Please? I haven't been on a picnic since I was little. *Little* little. And everybody else gets to go on them. Just last week, Ffion's dad came to visit her and he took her for a picnic at the dinosaur park. And they went on the pedalos. I never get to do that stuff.'

'This will just be a little outing,' I said, bringing my voice way down low in hopes of calming her down. 'We will drive up onto the moor and watch the skylarks. Maybe we can get an ice cream to take with us. But I want to be careful not to make it into something really big, because we don't want things to fall apart.'

'They won't. I'll be good. I promise. I'll be good at school all week and do everything I'm supposed to. And I'll do everything here too. I won't backtalk anyone. I won't get the red mist in my eyes. I *promise*.'

Of course, that's not what happened. I was fully prepared for it, prepared for the possibility that Jessie just couldn't help sabotaging herself when something good was due to happen, and consequently I'd arranged with the staff to take her out anyway. That seemed the only way around this issue. If I could remove the connection between her behaviour and doing something enjoyable, I thought this might get us past this problem. So I asked the staff to have her ready regardless of whatever she'd got up to, and I'd take her out on the Saturday.

Unfortunately, I underestimated just how creative Jessie could be when getting up to trouble. During the night she'd decided to have a midnight feast. The kitchen was off limits to the children without a staff member, and numerous precautions were taken to ensure it stayed that way, including locks on the door, the cupboards and on the fridge. This didn't stop Jessie. She had managed to steal a key from one of the temporary kitchen staff, and she then invited two other girls to join her for her 'feast'. They got into the kitchen but were not able to get into the cupboards or refrigerator. Jessie found a fork and bent it in an effort to pick the lock on the fridge. The other two girls appeared to have chickened out at this point and returned to their rooms, but Jessie persisted. Frustrated at not being able to get any food, she proceeded to smash up the kitchen until noise alerted the staff, who subdued her and returned her to her room rather than putting her in the quiet room, given it was the middle of the night. Jessie's anger heightened and she started to smash up her own things, tipping the bed over, throwing things around and eventually breaking the lightbulb in the overhead light. The situation was worsened by her tying her door handle to the bed, using her sheet, so that initially no one could get in to deal with the mess.

Lin phoned me early Saturday morning to say she was sorry, but Jessie simply could not come out. She understood our programme and my reasoning in wanting to take Jessie regardless of her behaviour, but it just couldn't happen this time. Too much damage. Jessie was confined to the home to clean up the considerable mess she'd made, and would not be able to participate in outside activities for the next fortnight as punishment. So, we didn't go see the skylarks.

Tuesday afternoon, and there we were as usual. Jessie looked a little sheepish when she came in for her session, or maybe I was just imagining it, because the fact was that normal cause and effect didn't usually work for Jessie. She desperately wanted to go out with me. She knew getting into trouble would stop that happening. The logic of how those two fit together continued to elude her.

Sitting down across from me, Jessie didn't make eye contact. Instead, she studied the table top for several moments, bringing a finger up to trace along the edge of it. At last she said, 'I dreamed about you last night.'

I nodded.

'I dreamed you were going to foster me. Lin gave me a bin bag to put my clothes in but, when I looked in it, the puppets were in there and there wasn't any room. So I thought maybe you didn't want me to bring my own stuff. I had to leave everything of my own behind.'

There was a long pause.

'Then you took me to your house. I thought we'd see sky-larks when we went there, but your house wasn't on the moors like you said. It was down by the chippy. But then I thought we could go for fish and chips instead. Except Joseph was there. When we came up to your house, he opened the door. Joseph was your husband and he was holding your little girl. He was her daddy.

'Joseph didn't want me there. He was really angry to see me, and he said he already had a little girl and he didn't want me.'

Jessie paused a long moment. 'I thought it was going to be okay when I saw him open the door. I thought it would be all right for you and him to be my foster parents, because I knew you'd be nice to me. But then he was horrid to me. He wanted me to go away. I started crying.'

'I can understand why you were upset.'

She nodded. 'I wanted you to tell him it was okay for me to be there. I wanted you to explain that you and him were supposed to be my foster parents, and I could live with you forever, because that's what you'd told me. You said it would be okay.'

I sat back in my seat. 'And that's not what happened?'

Jessie shook her head. 'You were horrid too.'

'What an upsetting dream. I'm sorry that dream-me was awful to you, but it's important to remember that it *was* a dream, because what happens in dreams is imaginary. Dreams are just stories our mind makes up. They aren't real.'

Jessie fell silent. She had slid down in the chair opposite me and now sat with her arms wrapped around herself. 'I don't want to tell you what you did to me,' she murmured.

'You mean in the dream?'

She nodded. 'I can't say, because you did dirty things.'

'I see,' I said. I was uncertain if I should encourage her to go on. Children with reactive attachment disorder can be highly manipulative if they sense they have found a 'soft spot', and it was possible that Jessie had surmised that sexual abuse was something that would keep me engaged. As a topic, it was beginning to dominate our conversations, and I was unsure if this was because Jessie was working up the courage to reveal abuse or because she was playing me for all I was worth.

Jessie didn't appear to notice my limited responses. 'I was crying,' she continued, 'because of what Joseph said to me. You put your arms around me. You were going to comfort me. You said you were sorry because we weren't able to see the skylarks. And then you did that,' she said.

'Did what?'

'I can't say.'

I didn't answer.

Jessie looked up and we made momentary eye contact. She snapped her gaze away the instant we did, far too quickly for me to assess what she was thinking.

'You put your finger in my pussy.'

'This is in the dream?'

She nodded. 'To comfort me.' A pause. 'You felt bad for me, because Joseph was being horrid and I was crying. You were trying to make me feel better, but I didn't like it.'

'No, that's not how to touch little girls, is it?'

There was a very long pause. Then Jessie said, 'It's all right for comforting.'

'No, it's not all right for comforting,' I said. 'Little girls should not be touched like that. Ever.'

'I didn't *like* it. I wanted it to stop.'

I watched her.

'Gemma wouldn't stop it. Even when I asked her to. Gemma took me into bed so I wasn't so scared, and she comforted me.'

'Your sister would put her finger in your pussy and she said she was doing it to comfort you?'

Jessie nodded.

'Did you tell anyone that Gemma was touching you like that?'

'Gemma said not to. She said it was our secret, and if I told I'd get taken away. But I wanted her to stop. It made me hurt when I took a wee.'

Jessie had her head down. Her hands were in her lap, her fingers intertwined, and she stared down at them. I didn't say anything, so she lifted her head and looked at me. For a brief moment our eyes locked and then she looked down again.

'Gemma did it,' Jessie said softly. There was a long pause. 'It wasn't you in the dream,' she murmured. 'I just said it was. I don't know why. It wasn't true.'

Silence.

'I wanted to tell you. I wanted to tell you last week because of Little Hare, but I couldn't. It gave me bad dreams to tell you, but I wanted to. I wanted to say Gemma hurt me and she wouldn't stop. I hated her, because she did it all the time.'

'I'm glad you have told me.'

'I tried to tell my mum once. I said, "Mam, Gemma hurt me," but she got cross. She said, "You little bastard, anybody'd fuck you up."'

When Jessie said that, I was thrown into doubt. Having met Diane I couldn't imagine her speaking that way, and as a consequence I was immediately on my guard. Was any of this true? Was Jessie playing me?

As if she could read my mind, Jessie raised her head and looked over. There was a long moment of eye contact after what had been a session largely without any at all. Her look wasn't challenging, nor was it imploring. Truth be said, I didn't know how to interpret it.

'You don't believe me, do you,' she said in an emotionless voice. It wasn't a question.

'I believe you,' I said. 'But I'm going to need to say something about this to Mrs Thomas.'

'No, don't.'

'If this is what's happened, it's not your fault, Jess. You are not to blame. But some secrets I cannot keep. It's Mrs Thomas's job to keep you safe, so we need to tell her.'

'Don't say anything. Please don't tell.'

Of course, I had no option except to tell. Even if this proved to be one of Jessie's stories, I wasn't the person to make that judgement. I had to take it seriously, and the first person who needed to hear this was Meleri; so after the session was over, I phoned her. I told her of the allegations Jessie had made, and said that it was just so hard to know how to take anything she said, but that this felt different than the allegations she had made about others, like Dr Hughes. There hadn't been the heartiness with which Jessie delivered most of her out-rageous pronouncements, nor had there been the elaborations that often accompanied her lies. As a storyteller myself, I rec-ognized in many of Jessie's accounts her glee at a good tale. She understood how details gave life to a story in a way that facts alone did not.

'Ahhhh,' Meleri said in a long breath, as I finished. 'For so long, I've been looking for a key to unlock this family, because they just don't make sense to me. I hadn't considered Gemma. I mean, I *had*, but mostly in terms of thinking Gemma was possibly a victim as well. There had to be more happening behind closed doors than they were telling. I've considered physical abuse, but saw no evidence. I've suspected Gwyl of gaslighting, something like that, between him and Diane. Gemma, however, was flying under the radar.'

'So you believe Jessie is telling the truth?' I asked.

'Yes,' Meleri said. 'In this instance, I do believe Jessie.'

chapter twenty-six

The craziness started all over again. Given that Child Protection was already involved with Jessie, and that Gemma was over twelve, there was no option except to involve the police. Thus started a new round of interviews and investigations. Other than a brief conversation with Ceridwen Davies, I didn't have direct contact with either the family or the police, so all the information I received over the next week came second hand.

Revealing Gemma's abuse finally cracked this difficult case. The turning point came during the police interview, because rather than the denial we'd all expected, Gemma confessed to sexually abusing her sister. She then went on to reveal in detail just how dysfunctional the family was.

The full extent of Jessie's neglect and the mistreatment became clear. Because their mother had been totally para-lysed by post-natal depression, Gemma, aged eight, had been Jessie's only carer during the day when Gwyl was at work. Jessie had been fed all sorts of drug cocktails, some from her mother's prescriptions, some from mixtures Gemma had cre-ated herself, in order that Jessie would stay quiet and not upset

Diane. Jessie had been left in her cot without being washed or changed, because Gemma couldn't find what she needed for the task or, in some instances, just because she didn't understand how frequently it needed to be done. Gemma said there often wasn't appropriate food in the house, so she would make toast and open tins of baked beans and spoon these into her six-month-old sister because it was the only thing she could find to eat.

I'm not sure if it was an issue of control for Gwyl, as Meleri had surmised. It was sounding more to me as if he had an unhealthy over-investment in Diane's mental issues, almost a type of Munchhausen's by proxy. Consequently, his focus was entirely on Diane, and he seemed to pay very little attention to either Gemma or Jessie. Diane reported when interviewed that she had had a normal relationship with her two elder daughters but had found both Gemma and Jessie 'hard to like'. The neglect appeared to have started with Gemma. The two older sisters were young teenagers at that point, and between them they had mothered her, although Gemma claimed that her relationship with the younger of her two older sisters, Kate, had been abusive. Kate had targeted Gemma emotionally, telling her their mother's depression was her fault, that she had ruined the family by being born. Kate would verbally attack her over little things such as how she was 'sitting wrong', and use these things to point out how worthless she was. This formed Gemma's template for treating Jessie, except that she was less interested in the caregiving part, so mostly left Jessie shut in her room.

Gemma didn't remember when the sexual abuse started. She said that she had begun to take Jessie into bed with her when she was three or four, because Jessie suffered night terrors and Gemma didn't want to risk upsetting their parents. This had led to sexual exploration and finger penetration. Comforting, I thought, when Meleri was telling me this. I remembered Jessie telling me quite early on in our time together, 'Gemma used to take me into bed to comfort me.'

I was startled by the amount of information that Gemma so suddenly provided. In my experience, fear and embarrassment tend to make the process of uncovering abuse slow, and it isn't always a straight road. Gemma's confession was so quick and fulsome that I was suspicious at first, concerned that perhaps Gemma was as good a storyteller as her sister, and we were being led down a new primrose path; however, the police and Child Protection were skilful in establishing the veracity of what Gemma was saying. Indeed, much of it could be corroborated by Jessie's stories, which we were now realizing were not always so fantastical after all. This rapid disclosure made me think that Gemma had been as desperate as Jessie for help, and just as the arson had allowed Jessie to escape, the sexual abuse and resultant police interviews finally gave Gemma the safe space she needed to talk openly about her family.

I didn't see Jessie between the time when she revealed the abuse and our next session, but I knew she had been interviewed two or three times by the police and Social Services.

Consequently, I was expecting the dramatic events surrounding Gemma's corroboration of what happened to be our main conversation. It didn't go that way.

Jessie's usual bounce was missing when she arrived. Coming into the room, she closed the door quietly behind her, came over to the table, pulled out the chair and sat down without making eye contact. Reaching out, she grabbed my satchel, unbuckled it and took out drawing paper and the pens. She said nothing.

'You're quiet today,' I said.

'I want to draw.'

'A lot has been going on, hasn't it?'

She didn't answer. Choosing a black pen from the pack, she began to draw one of her minute skylarks down in the bottom left-hand corner of the page. It couldn't have been more than an inch high. Jessie leaned down very close to it to work.

'How are you feeling about things?' I asked.

'I want to draw.'

Several minutes passed with Jessie absorbed in her art. She made the skylark blue and green, but it almost faded into the long grass that she began drawing around it. I watched the clock, following the second hand around two, four, six times without us saying anything.

'You don't feel like talking today,' I observed.

'No. I don't feel like talking.'

'Why is that?' I asked.

'Because I. Don't. Feel. Like. Talking.'

'Okay.' I sat back.

More minutes passed.

'Can you help me understand why?' I asked. 'Because I'm not sure what's going on here.'

Jessie looked up at me and her eyes narrowed. 'Because I might never feel like talking to you again. I might never come here again.'

'You sound angry. What happened?'

Putting the pen down, Jessie sat back. 'You told.'

'You mean about Gemma? I said last week that I would need to share what you'd said to me with Mrs Thomas. Remember? What happened with Gemma wasn't your fault, and I'm very glad you did tell me. But it wasn't a secret I could keep.'

'But you *told*.'

'I'm sorry that you didn't want that to happen.'

Jessie began to cry. Her mouth dragging down in a grimace of tears, she leaned forward and covered her face with her hands.

It was hard to watch her cry. Regardless of what she said, Jessie no doubt did love Gemma and her other life, however inadequate, and it was apparent that she hadn't wanted to be the one to break the silence.

After a few minutes, Jessie sat back. She wiped her eyes with the back of her hand. I passed the box of tissues over in her direction. She took one and blew her nose. 'What's going to happen to Gemma now?' she asked.

'I don't know exactly, because I'm not one of the people who will be dealing with her, but she has already told the police about things that have happened in your family.'

'Are they going to arrest her?'

'No. The police understand this is related to problems in your family. There will be some legal things to iron out over this, and hopefully Gemma will then get some help too.'

'Will she go in care, like me?'

'No. Gemma's eighteen. She's an adult now.'

'She can't get me, can she?' Jessie asked, her brow furrowing.

'How do you mean?' I asked.

'She can't take me out of here and be my foster mum, can she? Now that she's an adult? Because that's what happened to Becky. She went to live with her sister, who's in Manchester.'

'No,' I replied. 'Becky's sister is in her twenties and she's married and settled.'

Jessie fell silent. She picked up the skylark picture and stared at it for a long minute. She sighed. Then with one loud clap, she crumpled the picture up and threw it across the table. 'I don't know why I do these. They look stupid.'

I didn't respond.

'Have you got the puppets with you?' she asked. 'Have you brought Magnus and Eleanor?'

I pulled the black bin bag over. Jessie rooted through and found the two bear puppets, putting one on each hand.

She regarded them a long time and then said, 'Once upon a time, there were two bears in the forest.' She lifted her head and looked at me. 'This is the story I'm going to tell. I'm going to make up a fairy tale about bears.' She returned to the two puppets. 'They didn't have baby bears. It was just them. "How are you, old bear?" this one says. "Fine. How are you, old bear?" "Fine," this one answers.'

For several minutes Jessie had the puppets speak back and forth, making small talk about life in the forest. The puppets didn't seem to take on their usual personas of Magnus and Eleanor, even though that was how Jessie had asked for them. Jessie kept pausing as she went along to explain to me what she was doing, how this was a fairy tale, and how the bears lived in a forest on the side of a mountain and so forth. There was very little life in this fairy tale, which seemed to consist largely of going up and down the forest path, eating berries and asking each other if they were fine.

Then one bear said, 'I'm bored of this. I could do with a tasty rabbit.'

'A hare,' the other bear said. 'And I know where to find one.' Both bears dived into the black bin bag.

'Mmm. Good. Here's Little Hare. Gobble, gobble, gobble.' One bear puppet clutched the hare puppet between his jaws.

The other bear puppet grabbed the hare's leg. 'Rip! Gnash! Gobble. We're eating him all up. All gone!' Jessie tossed the hare puppet across the room so that it disappeared behind the sofa. 'Now, some lamb!'

The two bear puppets proceeded to work their way through almost all the puppets in the bag. Only the dragon and the ostrich were ignored, possibly because they were too big. The rest were gobbled up and the remains tossed in various directions.

'Ahhhhh,' Jessie said in a satisfied way and leaned the two

bear puppets on their backs. 'That was good. That was a tasty feast.'

'Your bears were very hungry,' I observed.

'They were. They ate up everything.'

'Sometimes it feels good to get rid of everything.'

She nodded contentedly and studied the bears on each hand. Then she said, 'I wish I was a bear.'

'You'd like to eat everyone up.'

She nodded. 'I'd make everything go away just by eating it up.' She grinned. 'Chomp, chomp!' A bit of her usual cheekiness was returning. 'Chomp, chomp!' she said, extending one bear to bite my arm.

'You'd like to eat me up too.'

'Yes! Chomp, chomp!'

A pause came then. 'Except if I was a bear, then I'd have to have babies. Because when bears go to sleep, the babies get born without them knowing. I wouldn't like that. Waking up, finding out I had kids.'

Jessie pulled the bear puppets back close to her and made them go mouth to mouth for a moment. Then she held one up at eye level and stared at it. 'That's what happened to my mum,' she said. 'She went to sleep and when she woke up, she had me.'

'Your mum went to sleep, because she had an anaesthetic. The doctors needed to do a Caesarean very quickly. That's a kind of operation. They gave her anaesthetic so she wouldn't feel too much pain. But your mum knew she would have a baby when she woke up.'

'She didn't *want* to have a baby when she woke up,' Jessie replied. 'But there I was and she had to take care of me. Because my dad stuck his willy in her vagina. That's how it happens. She wanted to go back to bed all the time, back to sleep, so that maybe I wouldn't be there the next time she woke up. But it doesn't work like that, does it, Eleanor?'

Jessie made the bear puppets come together, body to body. She pulled them apart and then put them back together, mouth to mouth. My sense was that she was depicting the sexual act but she gave no explanation.

'Unless she could fly away,' Jessie said. 'Like a skylark. Because they fly up high. That's when they sing. See, that's what this fairy tale is about. Eleanor eats some fairy dust and suddenly she's turned into a skylark.' Jessie shot her hand up high above her head, making the bear puppet sail through the air. Rising from her seat, she held it even higher. 'See, she's a skylark now. You're seeing a bear because you don't have fairy dust on your eyes. But really she's a skylark and she's flying all over. She's left all her cubs behind. She's left the cave behind. She's even left Magnus behind. See. He's gone.' Jessie flicked off the other puppet. 'Eleanor's a skylark now. She's happy. The End.'

'I'm glad Eleanor got her happy ending,' I said.

'That's how it works in fairy tales.'

'I expect that Eleanor's cubs felt bad that she flew away and left them though, don't you?' I ask. 'It wouldn't be a happy ending for them, because they'd want their mummy. They think maybe they did something wrong and that's why Mummy

281

doesn't want to be with them. They are thinking maybe it is their fault she's gone away.'

'No,' Jessie said with certainty. 'That isn't how it works. Eleanor's happy. The fairy dust, like, makes everything else disappear, and she doesn't have to worry about it.'

I persisted. 'Maybe that's how it is for Eleanor, but I'm worried about these little cubs. If you're born, it's not your fault. You can't then just disappear because someone else wants a fairy-tale ending. These little cubs need someone to take care of them. They will cry and feel lonely. The cubs aren't to blame for being little babies who cry and need someone to take care of them.'

'*I* blame them,' Jessie said nonchalantly. 'They shouldn't have been born if they couldn't take care of themselves. They shouldn't have come out of Eleanor's vagina when she was sleeping.'

I picked up the discarded bear puppet and cradled it in my arms. 'Poor little cub. I will hold you and cuddle you.'

Jessie regarded me, and for a moment I thought she was going to burst out laughing and tell me how silly I was being, but the pause drew out. Jessie sucked her lower lip between her teeth. Then she reached for Eleanor. Tentatively, she brought the puppet up against her body.

'Yes, you cuddle that one and I'll cuddle this one,' I said. 'And we'll tell them how sorry we are that they were left all alone and crying. No one will hurt them. Nothing bad will happen to them.'

'No one will stick fingers in their pussies, because that's not cuddling, is it?' Jessie said. 'Because look. This could be, like, their pussy.' She lifted open the hole where the hand went into the puppet.

'No, that's not cuddling. Cuddling means we just hold them tight, so that they feel warm and safe. That's what we do with babies. That's how babies should be treated, because that's what babies need.'

Jessie smiled and clutched the puppet close, rocking it back and forth. 'Yes, that's what babies need.'

chapter twenty-seven

'I've got something to tell you,' Jessie said when she came in the next Tuesday. She sat down across the table from me. 'Melanie's going to get adopted.'

Melanie was the now twelve-year-old who lived in the room across the hall from Jessie. The two girls had a rather fraught relationship. Melanie was a very attractive girl with long blonde hair and angelic features, and she was canny, one of those people who hides their intelligence to their advantage. This put her in a position of power in the group home, because she knew exactly how to manipulate both. She and Jessie were the only girls close in age to each other, so it was natural they hung out together, but their relationship had always seemed unequal to me. Jessie wasn't naive, but she was younger than Melanie and not at all good at seeing when she was being set up, and Melanie took advantage of this. So I was always a little wary of her.

This news, however, came as a surprise. While I didn't know a great deal about Melanie's background, I did know she had a mother and a younger brother. The brother was in a foster home and apparently well settled, but that family hadn't been able to take Melanie too. During the time I'd been working with Jessie there had been one attempt to return Melanie to her mother, who had ongoing issues with heroin addiction, but it hadn't worked out and Melanie remained at Glan Morfa.

'Are you sure it's adoption?' I asked, because I'd assumed Meleri had been planning a foster placement for her in the same way she was for Jessie.

'Yes. Melanie said her mum got her rights taken away. Now Melanie and her brother can be adopted.'

'What's Melanie think of that?'

'Well, it's going to be fostering first, to see if they get on. But she's going next week. And if it works out, Melanie said they might adopt her. She'll get to take their last name, if she gets adopted. It's McKie. That's a Scottish name. Then Melanie will be Scottish.'

'Her name would be Scottish. Melanie would still be Welsh because she was born here.'

'But guess what?' Jessie said, her tone low with titillation. 'They're *gay*! It's two ladies! I met them. One is named Ruth and one is named Sylvia. Do you know what "gay" means? It means she'll have two mums instead of a mum and dad.'

'Yes, I do know what "gay" means. And isn't that lovely for Melanie? I bet she will enjoy being in a foster home.'

'Not fostering. She's going to get adopted.'

'Which is Melanie's take on it, I expect, but it will be fostering to start.'

'She said she's going to call herself Melanie McKie right away. She's going to start school like that.'

'How do you feel about all this?' I asked.

Jessie shrugged. 'I don't care really.'

'Won't you miss her? She's been a good friend.'

'She hasn't. And besides, I don't care. And now I think it's time for us to do something in here. Can I draw? Where's your case with the paper in it?'

She rose from her chair and went to my satchel. She took out the pens and three or four pieces of paper.

'When are you taking me to see the skylarks?' she asked, as she sat down again.

'Perhaps next week. Instead of doing our usual session, I can take you up to the moor. How would that be?'

'Do you think it's okay for gay people to adopt Melanie?' she replied.

'Yes, of course I do.'

'You don't think, like, anything would happen, do you?'

'How do you mean?'

'Well, I know what "gay" really is.'

'And you're worried for Melanie because they are gay?'

She shrugged. Spreading out a piece of paper Jessie began to draw, but for the first time it was not a skylark. She started sketching a figure. I was so surprised to see her drawing something different that I was momentarily silenced, watching her.

A girl took shape on the paper. Black trousers, pink blouse, blonde hair and I knew it was Melanie. This intrigued me, that

Jessie would be compelled to draw Melanie. Then another figure beside her, a woman with short brown hair.

Jessie wasn't quite as talented drawing people as she was her skylarks, and the woman came out with unequal length arms. Jessie noticed this as she added the fingers. 'Look, I drew that wrong. It isn't good.' Then she paused. 'Look how long her arm is right next to the girl. She could put her finger in the girl's pussy.'

'Are you worried that will happen to Melanie?'

'No,' she said firmly.

'Being a gay couple means they will have a sexual relationship with each other, just as a straight couple would have a sexual relationship with each other. In both cases, the couple would care for their children like loving parents. Loving parents don't touch their children sexually. So while Ruth and Sylvia will have a relationship with each other, they wouldn't be sexual with Melanie. She will be safe.'

'I know,' Jessie said casually, and continued with her drawing.

A minute or two went by with no conversation. Now there were two women standing beside the girl and they took on more detail.

'I wish I could draw this right. I'd like to do it better.'

'I like it the way you're doing it,' I replied.

'Can I ask you something?'

'Yes, Jess, of course.'

But she didn't. She became absorbed again in the drawing

for several moments before finally saying, 'Do you think a gay couple might adopt me?'

'Are you wondering about getting adopted? Or about it being a gay couple?'

'One of the boys was saying that you never get a mum and dad if you're older, because mums and dads only want little kids. Babies. Big kids are too wrecked. But sometimes, like with Melanie, a gay couple wants you. Do you think a gay couple might want me?'

'What are your thoughts?' I asked.

'I'd be okay with it. I think I'd like it.'

Silence then, as Jessie became absorbed filling in small details on her drawing. Then she said, 'Mrs Thomas was talking to me last week, and she said now that they know about Gemma, maybe I can go back home soon. Because I could get supported and it would be okay.' She paused over the drawing, but didn't look up. 'But . . .'

She lifted the pen. The moment drew out.

'But what?' I asked.

'I mean . . . well . . . what I want to know is: how did Melanie get so that she didn't have to go back home? How did she make it so that her family couldn't get her back? Because I think I want to do that. I want to be somebody else's kid.'

And then there we were, back with our old nemesis: the outing. Jessie and I had decided that I would take her up on the moor the next Tuesday afternoon, as long as the weather was good, but how were we going to get past Jessie's sabotaging it?

'I really, really want to do this with you,' I said, 'but we keep running into difficulties.'

'We won't this time, I promise. I promise, promise. Pinkie promise. Here, give me your pinkie so I can pinkie promise and then it will happen.' She wiggled the little finger on her right hand at me.

'No, I don't doubt that you do mean it, Jess. It's just that whenever we get close to going out together, something always happens.'

'No, it doesn't.'

Raising an eyebrow, I looked at her.

'Well, it's not my fault something always happens. That's them. Helen and Enir. They hate me. And Lin most of all. She's so picky. Everything I do, she comes after me. Like on Saturday night, she said I took Baban-Dai's fifty pence piece. And I didn't. I *didn't*. But she said I did and I had to sit at the table until it was found. And that was so unfair. So super unfair.'

'I'm not concerned about whose fault it is,' I said. 'I'm concerned about how we can prevent things from happening that stop us going out.'

'People get me in trouble all the time. It's so unfair.'

'What can we do to make sure you stay out of trouble this week?' I asked.

'I just won't get in trouble. I promise. And you need to make Lin be fair to me. Then I won't get wound up. Because that's what she does. Wind me up. If you do that, then I'll be able to go.'

'I'm not sure this is my responsibility. It seems to me,' I said, 'that when we make plans to go out and the time gets close, you find it harder to behave. This is something that has happened to other kids I've known too. They really, really want to go out with me, but they aren't sure what is going to happen and how they will feel, and so they start to feel anxious. Quite often, when we're feeling scared, we misbehave. Not on purpose. It just happens.'

'I'm not scared. I'm not scared of anything,' Jessie asserted.

'Well, maybe not, but what I'm thinking is that it might be helpful if we practised going out together. I'll arrange the chairs, and we'll take a pretend journey together.'

'That's daft. I'm not a baby. I don't play pretend.'

'"Pretend" was maybe the wrong word. "Role play". Let's role play going out together, because it's a good way to practise new things.'

'You're weird,' Jessie said dismissively.

'Maybe so, but we're still going to do it.' Standing up, I moved two of the chairs side by side. The room was so small that doing this meant one chair was against the table, the other against the sofa. Jessie was still in her chair on the other side of the table, and she watched me sceptically.

'Okay, this is my car. I'm the driver, sitting here. Come around and get in. Let's go to the moors to see the skylarks.'

Jessie remained where she was.

'Come on,' I said. 'Come get in the car.'

She stood up and came around the table, but there wasn't room to get into the chair beside me without climbing onto the sofa first, so Jessie hesitated.

'Okay, so there's the first situation. What would happen if you came out to my car but you weren't sure how to open the door to get in.'

'I'd say, "You need to move your sofa out of the way of your car."'

I laughed. She was determined to be obstructive, but it was too funny not to laugh. This made Jessie giggle too.

'It's a pretty crap car,' she said.

'Yes, you're right. But get in anyway.'

Jessie climbed over the sofa and sat down on the chair next to me.

'So what would you say, if you came out to my real car but couldn't get in?'

'"Could you help me, please?"'

'Good, that would work, wouldn't it? So, now, here we are driving. What might be the next worry? What kind of problems might we encounter?'

'I don't know.'

'Some children get travel sick. They aren't used to riding on country roads. Does that ever happen to you?'

'No.'

'That's good. But what if it did? What if you started feeling sick while I was driving? What could you do?'

'Say, "I'm going to go blaaaaaaa!"' and she did a fake vomit.

'Say that we didn't want you to go blaaa inside the car? How could we handle that situation?'

'I don't get car sick.'

'Okay, but what if you ate too much ice cream on the way and got a bad tummy and it made you feel sick. How could we handle that situation?'

'I could catch it in my frock, like this! Blaaaaa!' She lifted up the edges of her dress to demonstrate.

Clearly Jessie was finding this scenario entertaining, which I didn't mind, as it gave us some much-needed comic relief. I hoped it was also making the outing sound fun and doable instead of scary. We role played several other versions of dealing with a vomitous child to much laughter and gross sound effects.

'Okay, so now we're driving up onto the moor. What could happen next?' I asked.

'I don't know. I've never been to the moors,' she replied.

'You don't know what to expect. It's pretty normal to feel anxious about something that is new. It helps to explore it in the context of things we do know. Are you worried about the sharks?'

Jessie hooted with laughter. 'You're being so ridiculous! There's not going to be any sharks there. It's land.'

'See, you do know something about where we're going.'

'Maybe I'm worried about the skylarks,' Jessie said mischievously. 'Maybe I think *they* are going to eat me all up!' Putting her arms together, she made jawlike movements. 'Like this!' She made her hands bite up and down my arm.

'I think we've got a silly game going on here,' I said.

Jessie leaped up suddenly. 'Change places with me. I want to drive.'

I looked at her. She was a wreath of smiles, her eyes dancing. Yes, she was controlling the session. No, I wasn't accomplishing what I'd hoped to, but this didn't feel like a battle of wills. It felt like having fun.

I slid over onto the other chair. Jessie sat down in my seat. She reached down and grabbed an invisible gear stick. 'I'm going to put it in fast gear. Vrooom! We're going to roar. See, look. Goodbye, houses. Goodbye, town. I'm going to drive us to the moors.' Several car-going-fast noises followed.

'Are you feeling sick?' Jessie asked me. 'Because I'm going so fast? Up the winding roads, all the way to the moors. What do you do, if you feel sick?'

'Tell you so that you can stop the car.'

'No!' she cried delightedly. 'Too bad! I'm not going to stop. Puke out the window!'

She yanked the pretend steering wheel to the far left. 'Around the corner. We're going to my house. I'm going to take you to my house first. "Hi Mam! Hi Dad! Look at me, I'm driving Torey's car! Look at me! I'm driving her Porsche!"'

'I wish my car were a Porsche,' I said.

'"Hi Melanie!" I'm driving by her new house now. "Hi, Sylvia and Ruth! I hope you have a nice life!"' Jessie turned to me. 'See, I said that, because I'm a nice person.' She turned back to look out the invisible window '"Bye, Melanie! See you never again!" I'm driving my Porsche to the moor. Driving a hundred miles an hour. Got to change gears. To super-fast gear.' More car noises.

We spent a rather magical ten minutes or so driving around in the invisible Porsche. We didn't do much beyond go by the house of every person Jessie could think of, say hi to them, point out the posh car, and announce our intention to drive to the moors. This seemed enough for Jessie. It filled her with joy. I went along for the ride.

chapter twenty-eight

At last the real day arrived. Tuesday afternoon. Our trip up to the moor. It was late May and warm for the time of year, but overcast with high cloud. As I'd crossed the moor on the way to work, I'd paused my car in a lay-by to listen for skylarks. They rose, one after the other, across the broad expanse of heather and purple moor grass. It was a perfect time to visit.

My plan was to pick Jessie up, stop and get ice cream cones at a little cafe on the seafront and then head up into the hills. It would take about forty minutes to reach the area I was planning to take us. If Jessie was in the mood, we could get out and walk a bit, and then it would be time to return. The outing was purposely low-key, nothing more than ice cream and a car ride, because I knew even this could well prove more than Jessie would be able to handle.

Despite how silly our play was the week before, I hoped it had adequately covered what the outing would entail, so Jessie would know what to expect, and that the silliness had helped the therapeutic aspect take effect. We'd also discussed the more practical details, such as wearing everyday clothes, boring, sensible shoes, and bringing a rain jacket, just in case, because you should never really go anywhere in Wales without one.

Even with all this preparation, however, Jessie couldn't hold it together. She'd got into a fracas at school that had ended in a bruised knee and cut lip, and had been threatened with the quiet room soon after returning to Glan Morfa because she'd thrown one of the boys' school papers out in the road after the bus had let them off and then mouthed off to Helen when told to collect them.

I expected this. At this point, I didn't think it was possible for Jessie to keep herself together when anticipating something that made her feel special and the centre of attention. Her defence against disappointment was to ensure it didn't happen at all. Consequently, as before, I'd asked the staff not to tie our outing to her behaviour, and if her misbehaviour wasn't too ghastly I would go ahead and take her anyway. So, even though she'd been annoyingly naughty, off we went.

Jessie's immediate reaction to being sprung from the group home wasn't positive. Her issues so geared her towards control and keeping herself safe that going through the front door of Glan Morfa and out into the car park with me unnerved her. Jessie looked nervously back over her shoulder at the building, then around the car park, as I unlocked the doors to my car.

'Are we going in *that*?' she asked when she saw the vehicle. 'It's *crap*.'

She wasn't far off. A seven-year-old Volvo in mud-splattered racing green, it normally transported a five-year-old, two Labradors and the occasional sheep, so was very much a working car.

Jessie wasn't having it. 'This is *horrible*. I'm not going to ride in this. You said it was a Porsche.'

'I did not. *You* said Porsche. When we were playing last week. I never said it. A Porsche wouldn't be very practical for me.'

'Because you're too poor to have one.'

'Well, that too.'

'This car is *dirty*. I don't want to get in it.'

I knew this was Jessie's anxiety speaking, so I didn't try to defend myself further. Or my car, which was never particularly clean, given the dirt track down to the farm. If Jessie was genuinely too anxious to make this trip, my car was a face-saving way of letting her return to Glan Morfa. Otherwise, I needed to just grit my teeth, listen to the complaining and wait for her to get into the car.

'Do you want to sit in the front or the back?' I asked as a way of moving us forward.

Jessie walked around the car one more time, kicking the back tyre as she went, as if she were a used car salesman. 'It's filthy where you live,' she muttered. 'And there's scratches here. Did someone key your car?'

'No, that's just from branches sticking out from the hedge-rows. It's not really damage. They'll go away when the car is waxed. Front seat or back seat?'

Jessie felt the marks for another long moment, then she said, 'Front. Because that's like what we practised, isn't it?'

Getting into the car seemed to cheer her up. She pulled at the gear stick. 'I could drive. Would you let me drive?'

'No.'

'My dad used to let Gemma drive. He put her on his lap and she steered.'

'Yes, well, we're not going to do that. Buckle up.'

'Why not?'

'Because my insurance wouldn't cover it. Buckle up.'

Jessie grabbed the gear stick again and endeavoured to shift it. 'Vroom!' she cried, turning an invisible steering wheel.

'*Buckle up.*'

On the way over to the cafe for our ice cream, Jessie said nothing. Perhaps it was this silence that allowed my mind to drift back into my early years of teaching, when I'd taken another capricious little girl named Sheila out for ice cream. I was flooded unexpectedly with memories of that event, all exquisitely detailed, calling up the bright pink-and-white decor of the ice cream shop, with its almost piquant cold, dairy smell an abrupt contrast to the torrid American summer beyond the door. I remembered Sheila's enthusiastic delight at the variety of flavours, the way she danced back and forth in front of the glass-fronted counter, giggling with glee.

There must be a word in some language to express the 'a world away' feeling that washed over me as I returned to the present. Arriving at the cafe, Jessie muttered something about not wanting ice cream, which she was either saying to be awkward or as code for how overwhelmed she felt. The only parking was a tight spot that required holding up traffic in both directions as I inched myself backwards into the space. The cafe was dim and dingy, half a dozen Formica tables and metal chairs and the heavy smell of a chip fryer whose oil wanted changing. The only ice cream was soft serve from an ageing Mr Whippy machine. The choice was vanilla, vanilla with chocolate swirls or vanilla with raspberry swirls.

'I don't want one,' Jessie said.

'You like these. Remember? On bowling nights, Enir always stops for them and you rave about them. And you'll get a Flake. You love Flake.'

'I want to go back. I don't want to see the skylarks. I don't feel well.'

'Remember what we practised last week when we did role playing? Now we'll get to use it!' I said brightly. 'You can just roll down the window and go blaaaa!'

Jessie was not amused.

I bought two cones, a vanilla for myself and one with chocolate swirls and a Flake for Jessie. Carrying both to the car, I waited until she got in before handing her hers. Then I handed her mine as well. 'Would you hold it, please, while I get us out of this silly parking space and onto the road.'

'I don't want one.'

'That's okay. They're the smallest size. If you don't want it, you don't have to eat it. I can eat them both.' I took my cone.

'Greedy!' she replied.

I took the back road, which got us out of the urban area faster, although the road itself was smaller and thereby slower.

'This cone is melting,' Jessie said of the chocolate swirl one still in her hand.

'Lick the drips off, would you?' I said. 'I'm not ready for it yet.'

Tentatively, Jessie raised the cone to her mouth. 'I'll just make it tidy here,' she said and licked around the edge.

'I love Mr Whippy ice cream, don't you?' I said.

'Not the plain vanilla. It's too vanilla-y. But I like the colour-ful swirly ones. And the Flake!' She sucked the ice cream off the chocolate stick of Flake. 'Can I have this?'

'You can have it all, if you want.'

'Thanks!' she said brightly, as if she'd never registered that it was bought for her in the first place.

We drove in silence as Jessie ate her ice cream. She appeared to be enjoying it, although she went about it in a rather eccen-tric way, using the stick of Flake like a spoon to scoop the ice cream from the cone. I held my tongue regarding what a mess it was making.

The narrow country lane began to climb upwards from the sea plain. We passed through a small village.

'Llanbedr,' Jessie said, reading the sign. 'That's Saint Peter in English. 'Llanfair means Saint Mary.'

'Llan means parish.'

'I wish you wouldn't be like this,' she said. 'Always correct-ing me. Because you do. You always say "That's wrong" and

"That's wrong" and "That's wrong". Being around you is like being around a teacher. It makes you boring.'

I didn't think this was true, but there didn't seem much benefit in contradicting her, so I said, 'I'm sorry it feels that way to you.'

'You know what else I wish you didn't do?'

'What's that?'

'Always telling me what I feel. That's a very boring trait of yours. I get fed up of it.'

'I see.'

'You were doing that in the cafe when I said I didn't want ice cream. You were trying to make it about my problems and it wasn't. I just didn't want ice cream. But you made me have it anyway.'

'I'm sorry,' I said.

We drove a few moments in silence.

'I'm not mad at you or anything,' Jessie added. 'I'm just saying.'

'It's okay. You were right. I did think you wanted ice cream and I'm sorry I went ahead and bought it for you when you didn't. But these things happen.'

We fell into silence again.

I'd anticipated overexcitement from Jessie, perhaps some effort to control the situation, perhaps a bit of anger and act- ing out, because these were all typical ways she coped with anxiety, but she seemed subdued, depressed almost.

I didn't want to push her too far out of her comfort zone with what was meant to be a fun time, so I asked, '*Do* you want to do this today? Because when we were getting ice cream, I went ahead and bought you ice cream even though you said you didn't want it. At the time you also said that you wanted to go home, but I didn't listen to that either and went ahead and drove us out here. Would you prefer to go home?'

Jessie didn't answer. Instead, she swivelled in her seat and grabbed a box of tissues that had been sitting on the back seat. She took one and began to wipe her sticky fingers.

'I know we planned this, but plans can be changed. There are always other times. I'm happy to carry on, but if you'd prefer not to go to the moor today, I'm also good with that. You can choose.'

'I'm fed up of choosing stuff.'

I had stayed to the small roads all the way, but now we were deep into the countryside, and the shortest way was a single-track lane that traversed the top of the hill. We were only about five miles from coming out onto the moor.

'Maybe I'm having bad memories,' Jessie said quietly. 'Did you think of that? That maybe this reminds me of bad things.'

'Does it?' I asked.

She shrugged.

'If that's what's happening, I'm glad you told me. What sort of bad memories are they?'

Jessie shook her head.

When I came to the next lay-by that allowed me to get the car fully off the track, I pulled in and turned the engine off. Jessie looked over in alarm.

'Everything's okay. I'm not angry or upset or anything. It's just that I want to be able to listen to you properly, so I'm thinking that perhaps it's best to stop for a moment.'

Jessie started to cry.

'The journey seems to have made you sad, and the further we go, the sadder you get.'

'I'm not crying,' she said, 'not actually.' She mopped her cheeks furiously.

'It's all right to cry.'

'I'm *not* crying. It's just that it does makes me sad. Going to the moor is making me start to think about Joseph.'

'Last week you told me that you hadn't been on the moors before, but I remember long ago that you told me Joseph brought you up here.'

Jessie nodded, and then the serious crying started. I leaned across the gear stick to put my arms around her.

Several moments passed with Jessie in tears, heavy, hard sobbing quite unlike anything I'd seen from her before. She was willing to be comforted, clinging to me, grasping tightly, her fingernails pressing through the material of my shirt.

As I held her, my heart was sinking. Here it comes, the real story of what happened between Jessie and Joseph. First Gemma, now Joseph. The truth was coming out, and I was heartbroken at the thought that Joseph too had abused her.

Slowly the tears passed. Jessie straightened herself in the seat, took another handful of tissues and wiped her face.

'Can you tell me what really happened with Joseph?' I asked.

'Joseph used to come on picnics up here. Every single

Sunday. Him and his wife and his boys. His boys got special walking boots and everything, and they would pack a picnic to eat, and even if it was raining, they would come to the moor to go walking. Because he said it was good for them. It's good for you to be out in nature. To get fresh air and exercise, even when it's raining. Joseph always talked about it. He came in every Monday and told us what they did on the moor.'

I sat quietly.

'I wanted to go with him. I asked politely. I asked him and asked him to take me too, but he wouldn't.' She dissolved into tears again. 'He said it was just for his family.'

I put an arm around her shoulders again. 'Coming to the moor made you think of this?'

Jessie nodded. 'He said they went on the moor every Sunday because it was a holy place and he felt close to God. He said he went *every* Sunday, and I wanted to go. Just once.'

'You wanted to go very badly.'

She nodded through her tears. 'I wanted Joseph to be my dad. I wanted him to adopt me.'

'I see.'

'He said he would,' she said.

'Joseph told you he would adopt you?' I asked.

Jessie didn't answer immediately. She fiddled with a mangled tissue before reaching for a clean one. Then she shrugged. 'I'm not sure. I *think* he said it.'

'Or maybe it was a wish?' I asked.

'His wife is called Marina and she has long black hair and when she puts her arms around you, she smells good. And she laughs. And she plays football for fun in their garden. I want her to be my mum so bad. I said I'd be good. I said I'd do anything Joseph wanted. I just wanted them to take me with them. But Joseph wouldn't ever let me come. Even once. Even when I did everything he said.'

'Which was what?' I asked. 'What did he ask you to do?'

'Keep my room tidy. Not get in trouble. Help pick up in the TV room. And I *did* it. I did everything he asked. But he still wouldn't let me come. He took his two little boys and his wife to the moor *every* Sunday. And then he came in and told me about it, even though I didn't get to go.'

'So, what I'm hearing is that you really liked Joseph and Marina, and you wanted to be part of their family, but Joseph said no. Is that right?'

Jessie nodded, her mouth grimacing with tears.

'Joseph didn't invite you along on their picnics. Instead, he came back and told you about what a good time he had, and that made you feel unhappy with him. Is that what happened?'

Jessie snuffled and nodded.

'I can understand how that made you feel left out,' I said.

She started to cry again. 'They don't have a girl. They've only got boys. But my family's got too many girls. So it would be perfect. But he wouldn't do it. He wouldn't take me on even one picnic.'

'You felt very disappointed.'

She nodded.

Silence then.

The interior of the car had grown warm, so I rolled down

305

the window on my side. A breeze brought the complex scents of springtime into the car.

'I didn't mean to say those things,' Jessie said softly.

'What things are those?' I asked.

'That Joseph touched my pussy. I just got so cross with him.'

'Joseph didn't touch you?'

'He kept saying to me, "I can't take you." I just wanted to go once. Just one time. Just once out with him and Marina on a picnic. He didn't even care how I felt, and it made me so cross. So I just said . . .'

There was a long pause.

'I didn't know it would mean I'd never get to see him again. I never, never, never meant that to happen. I just wish I could take it back, and things would be like they were before.'

chapter twenty-nine

There's a place where the lane rises to a cattle grid. On either side, there are aged, rotting gate posts supporting a rickety run of fencing unique to that part of Wales. Made with thin slabs of waste slate, scavenged from the tailings of local slate mines, these are strung together with heavy wire to make more of a wall than a fence. Between the small rise of the land and the slate fence, you don't actually see the moor until you pass over the cattle grid. Then there it is, vast, open and treeless.

Her emotion spent, Jessie was growing lighter-hearted. She sat up in her seat to get a good look. 'Wow, it's bigger than I thought it would be,' she said. 'So where are the skylarks?'

I explained that we wouldn't be able to hear them inside the car. I intended to drive another mile or so to where I could pull the car off the road. We'd get out there and walk for a little ways and the skylarks would fly up around us.

Joseph was still on Jessie's mind because, as I parked the car, she asked, 'Is this a picnic spot? Do you think this is where Joseph and Marina go?'

'I don't know. There aren't any picnic areas out here because the government wants to keep it natural and unspoilt.'

Jessie sat up alertly. 'Probably. Probably this is where they went to, because, see? There's a sign for a public footpath. They liked to walk. Joseph told me. So they could have been here too.'

I pulled the car over and turned off the engine. 'We'll walk along that footpath too, but for the moment just roll down your window,' I said. 'The car will have frightened the skylarks, but if we sit quietly, they will start to sing again.'

It was a perfect day for doing this: clear, but not too hot, no breeze. The moor was alive with birds and insects. And sheep. It was a common area, which meant local farmers brought their sheep up for the summer and turned them out to forage. All were the local native breed, Welsh Mountain, a small, wily sheep. Their shaggy winter coats had not yet been clipped, so they looked a bit bedraggled. A mother-child pair strolled very near the car as we sat, and I noticed Jessie's muscles tensing.

'They won't hurt you. They'll panic and run the moment you open the car door.'

'I wasn't scared. Stop thinking you can read my mind.'

'I'm not "reading your mind". I was just saying.'

'I'm not scared of sheep. I'm not scared of anything,' she replied testily.

I put a finger to my lips to remind her we needed to be quiet to hear the skylarks.

There it was. The first skylark rose up and began its long, liquid song. Then another and another.

Jessie listened, entranced.

I'd pulled the car onto a flat area of hardcore to the left of the lane and the birds we were hearing were further out to our right over the open moorland. They were all far distant, which gave us a good view of their amazing flight behaviour, shooting up high into the air before plummeting back down, but it wasn't easy to see them well, even with the binoculars. Then, unexpectedly, one popped out of the grass very close to my side of the car and landed on the tarmac just ahead of us.

'There!' I cried. 'Look there. One's on the road.'

Jessie craned her neck. 'Where?'

'*There*. In front. To the right. What good luck. It's not easy to see them up close. Here. Use these. You'll get a better look.' I handed her the binoculars.

I suspect it had a nest nearby and was worried about the car being so close, so it was hoping to draw our attention away, because it fluttered back and forth nervously in front of us.

Jessie studied it through the field glasses. 'That's not a skylark,' she said firmly. 'That's just a sparrow.'

'No, it's a skylark. If we keep watching, it may fly up and sing.'

'No, it's not.'

'Yes, it is.'

'*That's* a skylark? For real?'

'Yes. We're lucky to get such a good look, because they can be quite difficult to see when they're flying.'

Jessie lowered the field glasses slowly, her brow furrowed. 'Their feathers are so plain.'

'That's so they can hide in the heath. They nest on the ground, so their colouring helps them stay safe from predators.'

'They don't look like I thought they would. They look like nothing.'

'But they have a beautiful song.'

We then got out of the car to do a little walking. Jessie didn't have the right footwear, despite having been told about it ahead of time, but we walked anyway. I showed her heather and bilberry plants. The latter still had remnants of their red lantern-shaped flowers, and I pulled one apart, showing Jessie how they would form into sharp little berries later in the summer. I told her how my friend and I came to pick them then to make pies.

A little further over, the ground grew wet. I pointed out the bog asphodel that would soon brighten the dark, soggy places with stalks of yellow starry flowers. We searched carefully for sundew, the small, carnivorous relative of the Venus flytrap. This plant fascinated Jessie with its sticky little red tentacles.

Then it was time to go back. We were running quite late, as the stop we had made in the lay-by to talk had added considerably to our journey time, and then we spent much more time walking on the moor than I'd intended. Jessie had come alive in the magical surroundings, laughing and chatting animatedly, pointing out the skylarks we startled up, learning the difference between their song and that of the meadow pipits who also fluttered up from the heather, so I hadn't wanted to hurry us. Nonetheless, time moved on, so I had to call an end to our fun. We headed back to the car.

'Do you think this is what Joseph and his family do when they come up here?' Jessie asked, running her hands through the heather as we walked back to the car.

'You have Joseph on your mind a lot today, don't you?' I said.

She nodded. 'So, do you think? That he comes up here to go for walks and listen to the skylarks? Because I think I might feel God up here. I think this is the place. Do you think this is where he comes?' Jessie asked.

'I don't know, kiddo.'

'I think so.'

A small silence came, embroidered with birdsong.

'I miss Joseph so much,' Jessie said wistfully. 'He was always nice to me.'

On the drive back, Jessie once again fell into contemplative silence. It didn't have the troubled ambience of our journey out, but my sense was that once again she had moved from the simple quietness that comes from being tired after a day out to something darker and more complex.

'What part of visiting the moor did you like best?' I asked.

'When we walked.' She lay her head against the car window and stared languidly ahead. 'I wish I could walk somewhere like that every day. I wish I could live somewhere like that. You're lucky you do. Your little girl is lucky.'

'What was most enjoyable about the walk?'

'All of it. The plants. Learning the plant names. Seeing the little flowers on that bush, because they were like little round globes and you could pop them with your fingernail. And the sundew plants. Some people think plants are boring, but I don't. I like plants. Mostly because they don't talk.'

'Yes, that's a good thing about plants.'

The silence flowed back in around us.

As always seems to be the case, the return journey felt faster. We came down out of the hills and onto the main road quite quickly, and would be back at the group home within twenty minutes, if the traffic wasn't bad.

'You didn't ask me about what part of visiting the moor I hated,' Jessie said.

'So, what was that?'

'The skylarks.'

'How come?'

'Because they were ugly. They looked like nothing better than sparrows, and sparrows are everywhere. Sparrows make a horrible noise. And a horrible mess. They poo all over the concrete where we go out to play.'

'I don't think we can blame the skylarks for the mess sparrows make,' I said.

'No. But I wish I hadn't seen them. I wish they'd stayed in my imagination,' Jessie said. 'The thing I hated most this afternoon was that they didn't.'

After dropping Jessie off, I phoned Meleri to ask if she'd meet me before I went home, because I wanted to discuss what

Jessie had said about Joseph. It was an awkward time of day to meet up, being early evening, as both of us had the demands of our families weighing on us, but equally because convenient places to meet were not easily found at that hour. It was too late for coffee shops and too early for the pubs. As a consequence, we had to settle for meeting at a rather dismal roadside cafe. Nursing a cup of tea so strong it was opaque and sharing a plate of toasted teacakes with Meleri, I went over the outing to the moors.

This was the first time Jessie had said outright that she had lied about Joseph, but, as with everything Jessie said, our challenge now was to determine whether *this* was a lie. Was she telling the truth now and had lied about Joseph's abusing her? Or was she lying now, and had originally told the truth about being abused? It was very easy to feel as if we'd never get out of this particular house of mirrors.

That said, I'd sensed a sea change in Jessie since the disclosure about Gemma. While our sessions were still filled with weird and fantastical conversation, I noticed there was less bald-faced lying. Jessie was also engaging in less antagonistic one-to-one behaviour with me, the kind where she spent all her energy trying to control me and what I did in the session. I discussed this at some length with Meleri that evening, because the two of us hadn't had an opportunity to talk much together over the previous few weeks.

Because I'd noticed these changes, my inclination was to believe what Jessie had told me on the moors about her relationship with Joseph and why she'd said what she did.

Most of the kids I'd worked with were pathetically open about wanting to return to their families, however abusive and dysfunctional they might be, and they were quick to jump on any possibility that that might happen. Jessie, however, had always played the issue of leaving care very close to her chest. In part, I think she was protecting herself. The fewer people who knew the things she desired most, the fewer people who could use them to hurt her. However, I also think that she simply wasn't that well bonded with her family. She just didn't want to go home all that much. Indeed, some of her acting out may have come from worry that she'd be made to go back. Because of this sense of disconnection, it would have been easy for Jessie to idealize Joseph's family and build up fantasies about becoming part of it. She had an obsessive aspect to her personality that I could imagine developing into infatuation. She also had a vindictive side. The behaviour that had brought her into care – her fire-setting – had been about vengeance rather than fascination with fire. Destructive lies designed to get others in trouble were simply a different manifestation of that.

Meleri agreed when I said this. She told me that Dr Hughes, the psychologist working with the police on this case, had come to much the same conclusion. Dr Hughes had interviewed Jessie on several occasions, trying to get a complete account of the abuse from her, and the most notable aspect in her opinion was Jessie's variety of accusations. While Jessie always provided detailed narratives of abuse, they were of different abusive incidents. Dr Hughes had not managed to get Jessie to recount any event multiple times. She would say, 'Tell me about the time Joseph touched you in the shower,' and often as not, Jessie would give a detailed version of something completely new. The summaries were thorough enough that Dr Hughes hadn't been able to categorically say Jessie was lying, but she became aware of this pattern early on and it had raised her suspicions.

As I listened to Meleri telling me all this, in the back of my mind was how much I wished I'd known that the police were sceptical for so long, and that their inability to pin Jessie down was the engine behind the long, drawn-out time frame rather than the investigation into Joseph. I understood, of course, why they hadn't been able to share their perspective, but I would have felt so much better knowing that we all had suspicions. And yet again, I felt so incredibly bad for Joseph. He too would not have known that, despite all the questioning, all the disruption to his life, the police had suspected Jessie was lying.

I couldn't quite break free of these thoughts once they began, the idea that a good man's life had been turned on its head for no good reason, that one little girl could do so much damage in a moment's spite, and the irony of it was that even she hadn't meant what had happened to happen.

There was more news from Meleri. A residential programme for children with mental health problems was being piloted at a special school in Liverpool and it seemed to be giving good results. The approach was more holistic than traditionally found, with an emphasis on teaching self-regulation. Meleri said the programme was showing particular promise with bright, imaginative kids in middle childhood, and when she heard of it she immediately thought of Jessie.

Until recently, the goal had been to return Jessie to her own home with support, but since the disclosure about Gemma this had changed. The Child Protection team thought the best course of action now was to place Jessie into a long-term foster home, but because her behaviour continued to be so challenging, it had to be a therapeutic foster home and there were still no spaces. Consequently, Meleri said they were now considering sending her to the programme in Liverpool.

I was excited to hear this. Jessie was a clever, resourceful girl with genuine potential, but she had been stuck in limbo so long. I knew a residential programme like this wouldn't be a panacea, because Jessie would still be in the system at an age when it was unlikely she would get out before adulthood, but I was heartened to hear that she'd have this new chance to learn more appropriate behaviour.

chapter thirty

The next week when I arrived for our Tuesday session, Jessie was in the quiet room. She'd had a terrible day, starting off early in the morning before school when one of the staff had told her that the hem was coming down on her school uniform skirt and she would have to change into trousers. This provoked a vicious tantrum which went on, according to Lin, for nearly ninety minutes, meaning Jessie missed the school bus. Consequently, she had to be taken in later, which she hated. At school she got into trouble over the lunch hour in what may have been a bullying incident. One of the other children teased her, but her out-of-proportion response meant the school staff punished her as well. Then, on the bus ride home, she'd exploded again over something someone said, so she was back in the quiet room to cool off.

I put my stuff in our usual room and then went to join Jessie. Her eyes puffy from crying, she was sitting cross-legged on the floor in a back corner of the small room. I came over and sat down on the floor too. 'It sounds like you're having a very difficult day,' I said.

'Leave me alone.'

'I'm sorry things have been tough.'

Jessie put her hands over her ears for a moment to block me out, and then slowly she lowered them. She hung her head. Several moments of silence followed. Finally she asked in a soft voice, 'Did you bring Puppy with you?'

'No, I'm sorry. I didn't bring the puppets today.'

'I almost forget what Puppy looks like, I haven't seen him in so long.'

'Puppy's just the same Puppy. And he's safe and sound with the other puppets at my house.'

'Did you bring that ruler thing?' she asked. 'Where you can measure how much you like or hate things? I want to do that.'

'It's in my satchel. When your time is up, we can go in our usual room, and then you can use it, if you wish.'

'What about the draughts board? Do you have that with you?'

I was surprised when she mentioned the game, as she had never wanted to play it in all the time we had been together. Lifting my hands up to indicate that I'd brought nothing but myself into the quiet room, I said, 'It's in the satchel too.'

'You have *nothing* with you?' Then she added in a dejected tone, 'Everything we used to do together is gone.'

I resisted the urge to point out that most of it was less than twenty metres away in the other room. Instead, I said, 'It sounds like you're missing things.'

She nodded.

'Is this to do with what Mrs Thomas told you? Because I

understand she said you might be going to a special place in Liverpool.'

Jessie started to cry. 'And you know what I can't do now? Draw skylarks. That's *your* fault.'

This response befuddled me for a moment. My sense was that Jessie's misbehaviour and her yearning for familiar activities was related to the news of change, and I thought we were headed towards talking about that. Now suddenly she was upset with me about skylarks. 'I'm not sure I'm following you,' I said.

'Because you took me out there!' she said with genuine anger in her voice. 'They're ugly birds! *Ugly*.'

She sounded so fierce I half expected her to strike out at me.

'I was never drawing skylarks at all, and you knew that. You were making fun of me all along, because I thought they were beautiful.'

'Jess, I was never making fun of you.'

'Now I know they are not. They're *ugly*.'

'I can hear you're upset. You enjoyed drawing brightly coloured skylarks, but now you feel like what you saw on the moor isn't the same bird.'

'What I feel like is that they're *ugly*. Don't you hear me? *Ugly*. Like I'm ugly.'

'You feel the skylarks are ugly because they weren't what you expected. You feel you're ugly.'

'*You* made that happen. You made me go with you. You're the one who wrecked everything.'

'Everything seems ugly to you right now and you feel it's my fault.'

She didn't respond.

'I'm sorry it feels that way,' I replied. 'I'm sorry everything seems ugly.'

Silence flowed in around us. Jessie had used up the tissue I'd given her and I didn't have another. Raising her arm, she dried her tears with the sleeve of her school uniform.

'*And* you didn't bring Puppy,' she muttered accusingly. 'You know how much I need Puppy.'

'I'm sorry he's not here to help you feel better.'

Jessie nodded. 'He's the only thing in the world that makes me feel better. And you didn't bring him,' she said accusingly.

Again, silence. I listened into it, hearing the muted noises of after-school activity beyond the door, hearing my heart beating surprisingly loudly in my ears.

I looked over at Jessie. 'It would be nice if things could always be familiar, staying the way we know them. Because it doesn't feel very much like that's happening, does it? First the skylarks aren't like they're supposed to be. Then you get the news about the Liverpool programme. And now Puppy didn't come to the session. It feels like nothing's the same.'

'Yes,' Jessie said in a very small voice.

'It's hard when things change, isn't it? Change makes everything feel out of control.'

Jessie nodded.

'Change is scary,' I said.

Jessie nodded again. 'But you could have brought Puppy,' she said, her voice petulant. 'It's your fault you didn't do that.'

'I'll bring Puppy next week.'

'But what if there isn't a "next week"? What if I get sent away to Liverpool before then and I never get to see Puppy again?'

'Does it feel like you're being sent away?' I asked.

'Yes.'

'Are you worried you've done something wrong? Are you worried they don't want you?'

She started to cry again.

'Because those things aren't true at all. Mrs Thomas chose the programme in Liverpool because she thinks you're a clever, imaginative girl who can turn things around for herself, and that's what this programme is. It's a special programme for kids who have hope.'

'That's stupid,' she muttered.

'Maybe it feels stupid, but it's still true.'

'I don't want to go to Liverpool. I'm Welsh. I want to stay in Wales.'

'You will be able to come back.'

'I don't want to *leave*.'

'Leaving things we know is hard, isn't it?'

'I don't want to leave you and Puppy,' she said, growing tearful again. 'I don't even want to leave the stupid, ugly skylarks. Because I practically *am* a skylark myself. Because I'm ugly too. Because I'm ginger. Everybody makes fun of my red hair.'

'Maybe you could take Puppy with you,' I suggested.

Jessie looked over at me. 'How do you mean?'

'I was just thinking. Perhaps I could give Puppy to you. He could go with you to Liverpool and be your friend.'

Jessie's eyes lit up with interest. 'Would you really give him to me?'

'Yes, I'd be happy to do that.'

'Yes!' she said enthusiastically and grinned.

And so it was. As slowly as everything had gone over the past year with the accusations regarding Joseph, with the difficulties of placing Jessie in an appropriate setting, suddenly we went into fast forward. The move to the programme in Liverpool had been in the works much longer than I knew about; Meleri hadn't seen the point in raising my hopes any more than Jessie's until it was likely to happen, so neither of us had been privy to it. The team had already decided to send Jessie regardless of how the matter with Joseph was resolved, as, if there had been abuse and there would be a trial, she was still close enough to reach for video testimony. They felt that however things played out, it would be good to get her out of the district for a while and provide a clean start. As a consequence, she and I went from being told of the possibility of this move to its actually happening within the space of ten days. I found it hard myself to think that within a fortnight of that strangely timeless afternoon on the moors, Jessie would be gone.

I came over the last evening she was at Glan Morfa, which was a Sunday. The group home was holding a going-away party for her, nothing so big it would create too much excitement and thus court misbehaviour, but big enough to make her feel special.

Enir had made a cake with buttercream icing and such a thick layer of sprinkles across the top that I suspect she used the whole jar. This was just the way Jessie liked it. Eating the cake out of her hand, drawing her lips back to reveal sprinkles smeared across her teeth, Jessie laughed uproariously. She didn't really want to talk to me. She wanted to flit back and forth in front of everyone, showing off her cake-eating skills, getting another piece, showing off again.

Wisely, besides the cake, the only other special feature of the party was that everyone got to watch a film instead of doing their usual Sunday-night-preparing-for-Monday-morning tasks. The film was Jessie's choice and she chose *The Lion King*.

I didn't intend to stay for this, so I called Jessie over when I was ready to go home. 'I have something here for you.'

Her eyes were dancing. 'You mean some*one*.'

I couldn't decide if I should wrap him up like a present or not, but time then got the better of me, so Puppy arrived ingloriously in a supermarket carrier bag. I handed the bag to Jessie.

'I can't believe this,' she said. 'I can't believe you're giving Puppy to me. I don't think I can open the bag. Because maybe he's not in there. I can't believe he's in there, for real.'

From the expression in her eyes, I suspected she was

voicing a genuine fear, disguised as anticipation, so I reached down and pulled the bag open myself.

'Ahhhh!' she squealed. 'It's Puppy! For real! For me!' She took him out and pressed him against her cheek. 'Pupppppppeeee!'

Enir came over to admire him, as did several of the other children. Jessie soon had her hand inside the puppet, manoeuvring his mouth, barking delightedly, biting the arms of the children near her.

That was it, really. Jessie didn't come back to me. She danced happily around the room with Puppy, chattering, making him chatter for her. The TV came on. Jessie got to hold the remote. Puppy, still on her other hand, got to press the buttons.

'I need to go now,' I said from the doorway.

'Bye,' she called from across the room and waved at me.

'Have a good time in Liverpool,' I said. 'Send me a postcard sometime.'

Jessie had Puppy turned to face her. They looked each other in the eye and she gave him a kiss on the nose. Then her gaze went above him to watch the film. She never looked back at me again.

epilogue

After fifteen months of investigation, all charges were dropped against Joseph. No evidence was found to support sexual misconduct or any other form of abuse with any of the children in his charge. Joseph and his family left the area soon after and I didn't see him again.

Jessie remained in the residential programme in Liverpool for three years, after which she transferred to another programme. She did not return to Wales. For the first year or so I sent postcards, but I never heard back from her. As so often happens, the postcards got fewer and fewer, and I lost touch.

Almost ten years passed, and then one day, in a package of fan mail sent to me by my American publisher, I found a large, hard cardboard photo envelope. I opened it and inside was a publicity photo of a tall, long-legged, very beautiful young woman. She was wearing the most astonishing cabaret outfit with a massive gold headdress. 'Lido de Paris' was printed at the bottom.

On the back was a short note in felt-tip pen. 'This is my family. I've been a professional dancer for two years now. I've gone all over the world, dancing. Even Japan. I thought you'd like to know. Love, Jessie.'

Enter the World of Torey Hayden

ONE CHILD

"Hayden is a fine storyteller, recounting the
touching bonds that form among children and
between Hayden and her students."
Washington Post

Six-year-old Sheila never spoke, she never cried, and her eyes
were filled with hate. Abandoned on a highway by her mother,
abused by her alcoholic father, Sheila was placed in a class for
the hopelessly retarded after she committed an atrocious act of
violence against another child.

Everyone says Sheila was lost forever—everyone except
teacher Torey Hayden.

Torey fought to reach Sheila, to bring the accused child back
from her secret nightmare, because beneath the autistic rage
Torey saw in Sheila the spark of genius. And together they em-
barked on a wondrous journey—a journey gleaming with a child's
joy at discovering a world filled with love and a journey sustained
by a young teacher's inspiring bravery and devotion.

"Page after page proves again the power
of love and the resiliency of life."
Los Angeles Times

SOMEBODY ELSE'S KIDS

"A heartwarming book full of tenderness."
Library Journal

A small seven-year-old boy who couldn't speak except to repeat weather forecasts and other people's words. . . . A beautiful little girl of seven who had been brain damaged by terrible parental beatings and was so ashamed because she couldn't learn to read. . . . A violently angry ten-year-old who had seen his stepmother murder his father and had been sent from one foster home to another. . . . A shy twelve-year-old from a Catholic school which put her out when she became pregnant. . . .

They were four problem children, put in Torey Hayden's class because no one else knew what to do with them. Together, with the help of a remarkable teacher who cared too much to ever give up, they became almost a family, able to give each other love and understanding they had found nowhere else.

"Hayden is a fine storyteller."
Washington Post

MURPHY'S BOY

When Torey Hayden first met fifteen-year-old Kevin he was barricaded under a table, desperately afraid of everything around him. He had not spoken in eight years. Torey Hayden refused to call any child a hopeless case, but to help Kevin they needed a miracle.

When at last she penetrated Kevin's silence, she discovered a violent past and a dreadful secret that a cold bureaucracy had simply filed away and forgotten. It would take all of Torey Hayden's devotion to rescue this "lost case." But with a gentle, patient love Torey Hayden made that miracle happen.

JUST ANOTHER KID

"Another fine account by Hayden. . . . An invaluable
model for parents of emotionally dysfunctioning
children and for educators of all stripes."
Kirkus Reviews

Torey Hayden faced six emotionally troubled kids no other
teacher could handle—three recent arrivals from battle-torn
Northern Ireland, badly traumatized by the horrors of war; eleven-
year-old Dirkie, who knew of life inside an institution; excitable
Mariana, aggressive and sexually precocious at the age of eight;
and seven-year-old Leslie, perhaps the most hopeless of all, un-
responsive and unable to speak.

But Torey's most daunting challenge turns out to be Leslie's
mother, Ladbrooke, a stunning young doctor who soon discovers
that she needs Torey's love and help just as much as the children.
As Torey's aide in the classroom Ladbrooke reveals her dark and
troubled life, and Torey must try and rescue the beautiful and
sophisticated parent who had become just another kid.

"*Just Another Kid* is a beautiful illustration of nurturing
concern, not only for a few emotionally disturbed
children, but for one woman facing a personal battle."
South Bend Tribune

GHOST GIRL

"A testament to the powers of
caring and commitment."
Publishers Weekly

Jadie never spoke. She never laughed, or cried, or uttered any
sound. Despite efforts to reach her, Jadie remained locked in her
own troubled world—until one remarkable teacher persuaded
her to break her self-imposed silence. Nothing in all of Torey
Hayden's experience could have prepared her for the shock of
what Jadie told her—a story too horrendous for Torey's professional colleagues to acknowledge. Yet a little girl was living a
nightmare, and Torey Hayden responded in the only way she
knew how—with courage, compassion, and dedication—demonstrating once again the tremendous power of love and the resilience of the human spirit.

"An amazing story."
Washington Post

THE TIGER'S CHILD

"A deeply moving sequel . . . resonates with drama."
Library Journal

Whatever became of Sheila? When special education teacher Torey Hayden wrote her first book, *One Child*, almost two decades ago, she created an international bestseller. Her intensely moving true story of Sheila, a silent, profoundly disturbed little six-year-old girl touched millions. From every corner of the world came letters from readers wanting to know more about the troubled child who had come into Torey Hayden's class as a "hopeless case" and emerged as the very symbol of eternal hope within the human spirit.

Now, for all those who have never forgotten this endearing child and her remarkable relationship with her teacher, here is the surprising story of Sheila, the young woman.

"The characters will haunt you."
Indianapolis News

BEAUTIFUL CHILD

Torey Hayden touches readers with her compelling stories of the special-needs children she has taught and helped. In this wonderful, moving, new book, she introduces Venus, a seven-year-old girl who refuses to speak. Determined to never give up on a child, Torey vows to break through to Venus.

Throughout the school year, Torey utilizes every technique to connect with this wounded young girl. *Beautiful Child* chronicles this amazing teacher's efforts and tells the story of the rest of her small class—other troubled children with their own unique problems. Told with compassion, sensitivity, and humor, this wonderful story will inspire everyone who reads it.

TWILIGHT CHILDREN

Nine-year-old Cassandra—kidnapped by her father and found starving, dirty, and picking through garbage cans—is a child prone to long silences and erratic, violent behavior.

Charming, charismatic four-year-old Drake will speak only in private to his mother, while his tough, unbending grandfather's demands for an immediate cure threaten to cause irreparable harm.

And though she had never worked with adults, Hayden agrees to help fearful and silent eighty-two-year-old massive stroke victim Gerda, discovering in the process that a treatment's successes could prove nearly as heartbreaking as its limitations.